We Who Are Dark

Tommie Shelby

We Who Are Dark

The Philosophical Foundations
of Black Solidarity

The Belknap Press of
Harvard University Press
Cambridge, Massachusetts
London, England

First Harvard University Press paperback edition, 2007

Library of Congress Cataloging-in-Publication Data

Shelby, Tommie, 1967–
We who are dark : the philosophical foundations of
Black solidarity / Tommie Shelby.
p.   cm.
Includes bibliographical references and index.
Contents: Two conceptions of Black nationalism—Class, poverty, and
shame—Black power nationalism—Black solidarity after Black power—Race,
culture, and politics—Social identity and group solidarity.
ISBN-13 978-0-674-01936-2 (cloth: alk. paper)
ISBN-10 0-674-01936-9 (cloth: alk. paper)
ISBN-13 978-0-674-02571-4 (pbk.)
ISBN-10 0-674-02571-7 (pbk.)
1. African Americans—Politics and government.   2. African Americans—
Race identity.   3. African Americans—Social conditions—1975–
4. Black nationalism—United States.   5. Black power—United States.
6. Ethnicity—Political aspects—United States.   7. Racism—Political
aspects—United States.   8. United States—Race relations—Political aspects.
I. Title.

E185.615.S475   2005
305.896′073—dc22   2005045329

To Mattie Brock and in loving memory of Vernell Shelby

Contents

Preface

Can black political solidarity lead to a more just society and world? If so, what form must it take to produce this result? These are the questions that drive this book. Historically, political unity among black Americans has contributed much to the cause of social justice. It was essential to the abolition of chattel slavery. It was instrumental in bringing down Jim Crow segregation. It played a crucial role in the establishment of constitutional and legislative guarantees of equal civil rights for all citizens. But now, in what has come to be dubbed the "post–civil rights era," does black political solidarity have any purpose to serve? Many people, including a growing number of blacks, would answer with a resounding no. But my answer is yes, and in this book I offer my reasoning. I believe that black political unity still has an important role to play in making our society, and perhaps our world, a more just one, though the role it should play today differs from what many in the history of black political thought have envisioned. *We Who Are Dark* is a philosophical rumination on the current significance of black political solidarity.

I first began to think systematically and critically about the meaning of black solidarity as an undergraduate at Florida A&M University (FAMU), a historically black university in Tallahassee.

Although I had previously attended de facto racially segregated public schools (in Jacksonville, Florida, and in Los Angeles), FAMU was the first school I attended that regarded the education of black youth for leadership as part of its official mission. Looking back on that time, I can see that several events and chance encounters had a big impact on my intellectual development and outlook on black politics.

Like many in the student body, I initially majored in business administration. It was at one of the biweekly forums organized by the School of Business and Industry, during which one or another high-ranking executive from the corporate world would speak, that I first heard "Lift Every Voice and Sing." Or at least, that day in the fall of 1986 was the first time I remember hearing the song, despite the fact that I grew up in James Weldon Johnson's hometown. Listening to the words then, sung by my fellow students and faculty, stirred my pride in blackness and my sense of unity with other African Americans, past and present. I suspect that every person in the hall felt a similar connectedness—both to one another and to our ancestors who had fought so hard to make equal citizenship a reality for those of us singing the "Black National Anthem." But how many of us had thought deeply about what solidarity requires of us? I certainly hadn't. As business students at a black college, were we to carry out the project of black capitalism in the spirit of Booker T. Washington or embrace the teachings of Marcus Garvey? Were we to continue the protest tradition of W. E. B. Du Bois and the NAACP, or should we take the more revolutionary approach of the African Blood Brotherhood or the Black Panthers? Were we to build and maintain black institutions like the one we were attending? What part, if any, of the legacy of the civil rights movement or Black Power should we carry forward? What part, if any, ought we leave behind? I didn't have any answers to these questions and, frankly, didn't spend much time looking for them. Yet I was convinced that African Americans should possess a strong black identity and should maintain their bonds of solidarity. I figured that the precise content of that identity and unity could be worked out later.

Two years later, after a range of courses in the humanities and social sciences, a brief period as a religion major, and much soul-searching, I opted for perhaps the most impractical of all majors for a first-generation college student—philosophy. The discipline challenged me intellectually, forcing me to rethink long-held beliefs. Moreover, my study of the history of political philosophy taught me to think critically and theoretically about politics. As a FAMU philosophy major, I was fortunate to have David Felder as a teacher and mentor. Without his unfailing encouragement and guidance, I probably would not have found my vocation and certainly would not have had the courage to pursue an academic career. I am eternally grateful for having met this kind and generous man.

In the spring of my junior year, I met another philosopher who would have an enormous impact on my intellectual development. Kwame Anthony Appiah, sponsored by the Woodrow Wilson Foundation, had come to FAMU to encourage promising black students to consider academic careers. In addition to our various one-on-one conversations, Appiah gave two public lectures—at the time he was developing his influential critique of the idea of racial identity—that forced me to rethink my uncritical belief in black solidarity. My encounter with, and subsequent study of, Appiah's ideas led me to two conclusions. First, I became convinced that the concept of race, as commonly understood, was a problematic foundation for African American identity and black political solidarity. Second, I came to see how philosophy could be used to rethink the normative basis of black self-understanding and group unity. Both lessons are reflected in this book. Since our first meeting, Anthony has become a mentor, colleague, and friend. Though he disagrees with a number of the theses I argue for in this book, he has, in more ways than I can recount here, made its appearance possible. For this, and for much else, I thank him. And to those who don't think black role models affect the aspirations and self-confidence of black youth, think again!

I have also had the good fortune to learn from my colleagues in the Department of African and African American Studies at Harvard. I cannot imagine a better context within which to write such a book. I am grateful to all of my colleagues, both those still at Harvard and those who have left. In particular, I'd like to thank Larry Bobo, Kim DaCosta, Michael Dawson, Jennifer Hochschild, Susan O'Donovan, Naomi Pabst, Gwendolyn DuBois Shaw, Werner Sollors, and Bill Wilson. Cornel West, a pioneer in African American philosophy, has been a source of encouragement, wise counsel, and inspiration. Special thanks are also owed to Henry Louis Gates Jr. He pushed me to turn what I had initially imagined would be two or three articles on a theme into a book-length argument. And I'm glad he did, because now I have someone to blame its flaws on! Seriously, I'm indebted to Skip not only for encouraging me to write the book, but for his confidence in my readiness to undertake the project. Without both, I doubt that it would have come to fruition.

Many thanks also go to my fellow members of the Philosophy and Race reading group in Cambridge, Massachusetts—Larry Blum, Jorge Garcia, Sally Haslanger, Lionel McPherson, Ifeanyi Menkiti, and Ajume Wingo; our lively discussions have greatly sharpened the arguments in this book. I owe a special debt to Lionel, with whom I have written on some of these ideas elsewhere.

I've been inspired by Bernard Boxill; his writings on the history of African American political philosophy, especially his pathbreaking *Blacks and Social Justice,* have served as a model for me, and his personal encouragement has sustained me in moments of self-doubt. I also thank Linda Alcoff, Howard McGary, Charles Mills, and Laurence Thomas for their longtime feedback and support. I'm grateful to Martha Biondi for her frequent admonitions to study more African American history and for lending her expertise even when I'd failed to heed her advice. I've been debating with Bob Gooding-Williams and John Pittman about questions of race, identity, and solidarity over the last few years—and loving every minute—and each has provided rich insights and thought-provoking criticisms. Tim Scanlon and Sylvia Berryman graciously agreed to comment on several chapters of the penultimate draft, making invaluable suggestions for improvement. Derrick Darby has been my philosophical interlocutor and closest friend, really a brother, for over fifteen years. There are few arguments in this book that we have not discussed or he has not scrutinized—which is not, of course, to say that he accepts them all. Jessie, my cherished partner and wife, in addition to providing unfailing love and support, read every line and used her keen editor's eye to make my prose considerably leaner and more readable.

Countless other friends, students, and colleagues have commented on drafts of chapters or discussed these issues with me at length; they include Lawrie Balfour, Sascha Beutler, Eddie Glaude, Peter Gordon, Michael Hanchard, Dan Farrell, Bill Lawson, Ron Mallon, Lucius Outlaw, Diana Raffman, Marques Redd, Kathleen Schmidt, Sarah Loper Sengupta, and Brandon Terry. The anonymous reviewers of the manuscript also offered useful advice and constructive criticism. Dave Brighouse and Ryan White provided invaluable research assistance. Lindsay Waters of Harvard University Press has been a wonderful editor, and his enthusiasm for the project has been a great source of motivation. Wendy Nelson, an excellent manuscript editor, was a model of professionalism and efficiency.

Portions of the book were or will be published elsewhere. I am happy to acknowledge permission to reprint material from "Foundations of Black Solidarity: Collective Identity or Common Oppression?" *Ethics* 112 (January 2002), copyright 2002 University of Chicago; "Two Conceptions of Black Nationalism: Martin Delany on the Meaning of Black Political Solidarity," *Political Theory* 31

(October 2003), copyright Sage Publications; and "Race, Culture, and Black Self-Determination," in *Pragmatism, Nation, and Race: Community in the Age of Empire,* ed. Eduardo Mendieta and Chad Kautzer (Bloomington: Indiana University Press, forthcoming). I would also like to acknowledge generous support from the Ford Foundation, which financed a sabbatical at a crucial moment in the writing process.

I have benefited greatly from feedback I received from audiences at the American Philosophical Association, the American Political Science Association, Baruch College, College of the Holy Cross, the Collegium for African American Research, Du Bois Scholars Institute, Harvard University, Howard University, Northwestern University, St. Anselm College, Stanford University, the Society for Phenomenology and Existential Philosophy, the Society for the Study of Africana Philosophy, SUNY Stony Brook, UCLA, and Yale University.

Finally, I have dedicated this book to my grandmother and in memory of my mother. They raised me under unenviable circumstances and sacrificed much to give me the opportunity to grow and become the person I wanted to be.

What do we want? What is the thing we are after? As it was phrased last night it had a certain truth: We want to be Americans, full-fledged Americans, with all the rights of other American citizens. But is that all? Do we want simply to be Americans? Once in a while through all of us there flashes some clairvoyance, some clear idea, of what America really is. We who are dark can see America in a way that white Americans cannot. And seeing our country thus, are we satisfied with its present goals and ideals?

—W. E. B. Du Bois, "Criteria of Negro Art" (1926)

Lift ev'ry voice and sing,
Till earth and heaven ring,
Ring with the harmonies of Liberty;
Let our rejoicing rise
High as the list'ning skies,
Let it resound loud as the rolling sea.
Sing a song full of the faith that the dark past has taught us,
Sing a song full of the hope that the present has brought us;
Facing the rising sun of our new day begun,
Let us march on till victory is won.

—James Weldon Johnson, "Lift Every Voice and Sing" (1900),
widely regarded as the "Black National Anthem"

Introduction

Political Philosophy and the Black Experience

Black leaders have frequently urged African Americans to become a more unified political force to achieve the full freedom and equality that American ideals promise, and many blacks continue to believe that such solidarity is essential. But what does black solidarity entail? Traditionally, this sense of solidarity has a dual basis, one positive and the other negative. The shared racial identity and cultural heritage of African Americans provide a foundation for black unity, and those in the ethnoracial community of African descent often seek to preserve and celebrate the group's cultural distinctiveness through group loyalty, communal intercourse, ritual, and collective self-organization. On the negative side, the black experience of unjust treatment and discrimination has helped create strong bonds of identification. A common history of oppression and vulnerability to racism has engendered a need for political solidarity and group self-reliance, if only as a matter of self-defense in a non-ideal world. Among blacks, this dual foundation for black unity—positive collective identity and shared oppression—is often taken for granted, treated as a matter of common sense. Yet, given mounting criticism and changes in the sociohistorical context, there is a pressing need to rethink these foundations of African American solidarity and perhaps even to reevaluate the very idea of black political unity.

In recent years, the concept of "race" has come under attack from a number of academic quarters, including the biological sciences, the social sciences, philosophy, history, legal studies, literary theory, and cultural studies. The problem is not simply that the notion has no analytical or explanatory value in helping us understand human variety—a claim that, while not universally accepted, is now widely endorsed by a diverse set of scholars and scientists. Nor is the trouble merely that the idea of race continues to be used to justify or conceal various forms of racism—a view that is also widely held, if not quite taken seriously enough. The criticism that seems to threaten the very idea of black solidarity, attacking it at its roots, involves the much more controversial claim that "race" is not a sound basis for social identities, cultural affiliations, membership in associations, public policy, or political movements. Some argue that racial identities and the forms of solidarity that they (allegedly) sustain are irrational, incoherent, rooted in illusions, or morally problematic. Others contend that in light of increasing interracial antagonism and the need for multiracial cooperation, any form of racial particularism is invidious and needlessly divisive. Still others maintain that race-based solidarity is incompatible with widely cherished ideals such as racial integration, the affirmation of a shared American identity, and a color-blind society.

We should add to these concerns the well-known criticisms of "identity politics": namely, that such identity-based programs suffer from dangerous forms of essentialism and groupthink; that they distract from more pressing or important concerns, such as poverty, rising socioeconomic inequality, human rights violations, and the negative consequences of globalization; and that they are inconsistent with the liberal democratic values of individual autonomy, tolerance, and open public dialogue across lines of group difference. These criticisms have seemed to some to have particular force against political movements organized around the familiar ethno-racial identity of "blackness."

Despite criticisms of the idea of race, some political philosophers remain convinced that it has a positive role to play in politics. They insist not only that this notion is necessary for social-scientific analysis, social critique, and the enforcement of civil rights laws, but that blacks must hold on to their racial identity as a basis for political solidarity, cultural identity, and group self-realization. Thus, these philosophical treatments focus on how to conceptualize "race" and "racial identity" so that these are not vulnerable to attacks against their empirical adequacy, analytical cogency, moral legitimacy, or political significance. But few of these analyses draw out, in an extended and theoretical way, the politico-philosophical implications of retaining or rejecting "race." In this book I take up that task through a critical examination of the normative and conceptual ground of black political culture. I aim to reflect on and ultimately to assess the value of racial solidarity as a basis for current political practice among African Americans.

These aims fit within a research agenda that extends beyond the abstract concerns of philosophy. A number of theorists have sought to reconceive black politics, to modernize, as it were, the objectives and strategies of black freedom struggles for the post–civil rights era.[1] My book contributes to this collective project by providing a reconstruction and defense of the underlying principles of black solidarity. This defense is forthrightly anti-essentialist. I seek to identify a basis for black political unity that does not deny, downplay, or disparage individual or group differentiation within the black population. I insist that there are many, perhaps incommensurable, ways to be black, none more "natural" than the others. Yet I also defend a conception of black solidarity that is not only, or even primarily, concerned with questions of identity, but that urges a joint commitment to defeating racism, to eliminating unjust racial inequalities, and to improving the material life prospects of those racialized as "black," especially the most disadvantaged.

I will argue that it is possible to dispense with the idea of race as a biological essence and to agree with the critics of identity politics about many of its dangers and limitations, while nevertheless continuing to embrace a form of blackness as an emancipatory tool. I will show that a theoretically coherent and practically feasible black political solidarity can and should be sustained. The key to creating and maintaining this bond is to highlight and distinguish between the various forms of unfair social disadvantage that African Americans face. This approach shifts the focus away from questions of social identity as such and toward the various dimensions of racial injustice. This would be a form of political solidarity that would subordinate questions of who blacks are as a people to questions about the ways in which they have been and continue to be unfairly treated. Moreover, it would be a black politics that would concern itself with what blacks themselves, as a racialized subordinate group in America, might do to eliminate or lessen this burden, although the burden should not be theirs alone to remove. I will advance this oppression-centered conception of black solidarity through a critical engagement with the history of black political thought, focusing explicitly, though not exclusively, on many of its more nationalist strains.

Black Nationalism and Its Critics

For better or worse, black political solidarity has come to be associated with black nationalism. For many, the very idea of black nationalism conjures up scary and unflattering images of the Black Power movement and of controversial spokespersons for the Nation of Islam, SNCC, the Black Panther Party, US, and other influential black nationalist organizations of the 1960s and early 1970s. This association leads many people, including some blacks, to be suspicious of calls for black political unity. In fact, at least since the mid-nineteenth century, many have been hostile toward, dismissive of, or frightened by black nationalism.

Conservatives who believe that the fight for racial justice has already been won naturally reject black nationalism. They see calls for black political solidarity as symptomatic of a pathological "victim's mentality" and generally urge African Americans to stop complaining about their situation and instead to take advantage of the many opportunities that America offers. As they see it, the color line is not a serious problem in the twenty-first century. Indeed, some conservatives insist that the roots of black America's problems lie in the self-defeating attitudes and dysfunctional behavior of blacks themselves. Yet there are conservative forms of black nationalism. These typically eschew political programs aimed at structural transformation, opting instead for group self-help strategies that emphasize the need for in-group racial responsibility. Conservative black nationalists do not deny the continuing significance of racism. On the contrary, they often regard racism as a permanent feature of social life in America. They believe that it is futile to struggle to end racial injustice in the United States and that African Americans should form self-reliant black communities without making further demands on the state for racial reform.

I reject both forms of conservatism.[2] I reject the first because I hold that racism still negatively affects the life prospects of African Americans in the United States and therefore racial justice has not yet been achieved. I reject the second because I believe that antiblack racism is not incorrigible and that blacks can work together to help effect meaningful social change. Thus, my argument is mainly directed to progressives. Yet I mean "progressive" to be understood broadly: namely, any political orientation which maintains that there are basic social injustices in our society that should, and can, be corrected by organized collective action or state policy but which denies that these reforms are a matter of returning to

some allegedly better form of social organization that existed in the
past. The point of focusing on progressive black politics rather than
on its conservative counterpart is that the former, though not the
latter, typically holds that our society still faces serious problems of
racial injustice and that correcting them requires concerted action
on the part of concerned citizens *and* their government. My argument proceeds on the assumption, no doubt controversial, that this
progressive view on race is correct.

Liberals often portray black nationalists as divisive, fanatical,
dangerous, unprincipled, racist, delusional, and even mad. Liberal
political philosophy is moreover often thought to be antithetical to
nationalism in all its forms—from its basic social ontology to its
fundamental principles.[3] Indeed, many liberals find the label *nationalist,* like the label *Marxist,* enough to regard a thinker or ideology so labeled as politically dangerous, morally corrupt, and intellectually bankrupt. Accordingly, there has been little incisive critical
engagement with the black nationalist tradition by liberal political
philosophers.[4]

However, there is a strand of black nationalism that is compatible with the core values of liberalism—values such as equal citizenship for all persons; respect for individual autonomy; democratic constitutional government under the rule of law; the basic
right to freedom of conscience, expression, and association; tolerance for different conceptions of the good; equal opportunity in education and employment; and a guaranteed minimum standard of
living. This form of black nationalism has a role to play in helping
to realize these liberal ideals. Liberals should not dismiss or fear the
black nationalist tradition, for there are indispensable insights to be
gained from a sympathetic yet critical engagement with black nationalist theory. But if black nationalism is to be sustained in the
post–civil rights era, some of the ideas commonly associated with
the tradition will have to be rethought. In this way I conceive of a
viable form of black nationalism as one that is compatible with

what John Rawls calls political liberalism (as opposed to comprehensive liberalism).[5] This rethinking of black nationalism will force
us to reconsider elements of the intellectual legacy of the Black
Power movement, as this radicalization of the black freedom struggle is often mistakenly viewed as making a sharp break with liberal
political philosophy.

Marxists, on the other hand, have long been engaged with the
black nationalist tradition. Some have thought that black nationalism is a reactionary ideology that the racially oppressed sometimes
resort to when they become politically disillusioned. Some have insisted that the principal spokespersons for the ideology are dema-
gogues who for their own economic gain and self-aggrandizement
exploit the desperation of the black masses. Marxists often contend
that the black middle class accepts nationalist notions and pro-
motes them among the lower classes because this advances their
narrow petit-bourgeois interests and legitimates their hegemony
over the black working class and the black poor. Some even argue
that black cultural nationalism allows the black elite to imagine
(though with considerable self-deception) that they are both spiritually connected to the black working class and poor and deeply
concerned with their interests, when in fact, so it is claimed, they
are anxious about the tenuousness of their own social position and
eager to exert authority over a lower-status group as compensation
for their lack of full acceptance by white elites.

But not all Marxists have been so intensely critical of black nationalism. In fact, some self-described Marxists also think of themselves as black nationalists. These black radicals or, as some prefer
to be called, "Black Marxists" have sought to synthesize the two traditions, taking the best from each to define a new approach to issues of race and class. The struggle for Black Marxists has been to
get orthodox Marxists to take the black experience seriously; to appreciate the importance of ethnic and national identity to politics;
to not reduce racism to class conflict or false consciousness; to view

the black struggle for freedom as on equal footing with the class struggle against capital; to acknowledge that white workers often benefit materially, and not just psychologically, from antiblack racism; to accept that there can be no interracial working-class unity until there is racial justice; and to recognize the legitimacy of the demand for black self-determination.

The treatment of black solidarity in this book, while seeking to build constructively on insights from both the black nationalist and Marxist traditions, is not intended as a defense of Black Marxist theory. Yet, as will become clear, I am sympathetic to black radicalism, and the defense of black solidarity that I make is, in many ways, compatible with it. In particular, I show that a proper focus on class differentiation within the black population and on the nature of racist ideology (understood in the Marxist sense) compels us to rethink many basic assumptions underlying black nationalist conceptions of political solidarity. I also argue for a moderate form of skepticism toward both middle-class nationalist pretensions and black elite claims to legitimate leadership.

Some feminists have been critical of the patriarchy that they see as, perhaps necessarily, bound up with nationalist projects. Black feminists in particular have viewed the insistence on "self-respect" that is so characteristic of black nationalism as a thinly veiled attempt on the part of some black men to secure for themselves the full privileges of patriarchal authority, as a way of asserting a specifically masculinist conception of blackness. Moreover, several feminists have argued that the logic of black nationalism—its dominant tropes, romantic narratives, basic theoretical categories, messianic themes, and "manly" heroes—cannot fully accommodate the concerns of women and often forces them into subordinate or "supporting" roles within black political struggles. This book assumes as a basic premise that no viable and principled black political solidarity can exist if black women and black men do not treat each other as equals. This means, at a minimum, that black women must be an essential part of the leadership of such movements, that black men and women should share power and decision making within political organizations, and that the particular concerns of black women ought to be taken just as seriously as those of black men. Thus, I want to show that the nationalist tradition, while historically dominated by men and male interests, is compatible with a more progressive approach to questions of gender.

Rethinking Black Nationalism

This book takes a philosophical approach to black nationalism, viewing it specifically as a distinctive political philosophy. It draws on the ideas and values of black nationalism as represented by the best writings in the tradition. I am not concerned with the alleged institutional embodiment of these ideas and values in particular self-described black nationalist organizations. As with other, better-known political philosophies (such as conservatism, liberalism, and Marxism), not every self-described black nationalist or would-be black nationalist organization is faithful to the tradition's best ideals. I also distinguish the core ideas, concepts, and principles of black nationalism from the motives and personalities of the theorists who best articulate these notions. These theorists are only human and thus possess many all-too-familiar weaknesses and flaws—jealousy, self-hatred, arrogance, greed, vanity, and pettiness. These traits and tendencies are not my concern. Thus I do not speculate about how they might have affected the ideas of the nationalists I consider. My interest is in the political philosophies of these thinkers, paying careful attention to the soundness of the arguments they put forward to defend their ideas, and to their relevance today.

I will focus on the work of certain canonical figures in the history of African American political philosophy, as they have defined the tradition we have inherited. Through a charitable reading and sympathetic critique of their well-known doctrines, and building upon their lasting insights, I describe a form of black solidarity that is still defensible. This reconstructed form of group solidarity must, however, distance itself from certain familiar tendencies in the black nationalist tradition. In particular, I will argue that it is necessary to reject three influential but fundamentally flawed doctrines.

First, I discuss and critically evaluate "classical black nationalism." According to this view, black solidarity and self-realization must be rooted in a shared African or Pan-African ethnoracial identity, which black Americans must reclaim and develop. This group consciousness, which some have termed "Afrocentric" or "Afrikan," is held to be a necessary and proper foundation for a transnational and self-determining black community. I contend that many nationalists vacillate between, and sometimes confuse, classical nationalism and what I call "pragmatic nationalism"—the view that black solidarity is merely a contingent strategy for creating greater freedom and social equality for blacks, a pragmatic yet principled approach to achieving racial justice. On a variety of grounds, I urge the rejection of classical black nationalism. Yet I defend a version of pragmatic nationalism as an alternative.

Second, I offer an extended critique of the Black Power conception of group solidarity. According to this conception, black people should form an independent and autonomous community, with significant collective control over its sociopolitical, economic, and cultural life. I show that this view has not adequately come to terms with the changing social conditions of blacks in the post–civil rights era; it relies on the ill-founded idea of a homogeneous black population; it underestimates the sociopolitical significance of class and status stratification within the black population; and it fails to appreciate and truly respect differences within the group—for instance, along the lines of gender, sexuality, national origin, multiraciality, generation, region, religion, cultural affiliation, and political ideology. I examine the ideal of "collective control" through a critical discussion of two variants—community nationalism and cultural nationalism—both of which continue to have adherents.

Third, I argue against the familiar claim that it is necessary and politically useful for blacks to develop a positive shared identity—to collectively define a group-affirming conception of blackness. According to this doctrine, a collective identity is essential for an effective solidarity whose aim is liberation from racial oppression; thus, blacks who are committed to emancipatory group solidarity must embrace and preserve their distinctive black identity. I argue that a collective identity is not a necessary condition for cultivating effective bonds among African Americans, and in fact that attempting to forge one would be self-defeating. I contend that we should separate the need for an emancipatory black solidarity from the demand for a common black identity. The former continues to be a valuable resource in the struggle against racism and racial inequality. But the latter is a legacy of black nationalist thought that African Americans do better to abandon.

I should emphasize, however, that this analysis of black nationalist ideas is not wholly negative. On the contrary, my goal is to arrive at a philosophy of black solidarity rooted in the unfinished project of achieving racial justice. I continue to believe that such solidarity is both possible and defensible, and that some of the resources needed to provide such a defense are to be found in the black nationalist tradition. In this way, the treatment of black nationalism in this book is not a wholesale rejection of this philosophy but a revisionist interpretation of it.

Solidarity and Oppression

As an alternative to conceptions of black solidarity that emphasize a shared identity among blacks (whether racial, ethnic, national, or cultural), I defend a conception of solidarity based strictly on the shared experience of racial oppression and a joint commitment to resist it. The practicality and scope of black solidarity depends on a diagnosis of the complex forces that constitute black oppression and on the extent to which blacks suffer specifically because of antiblack racism, past and present. Thus, I seek to articulate a conception of black oppression that can serve as a basis for unity and cooperation among blacks living in the United States. This account highlights the continuing social and psychological effects of racist ideology in America, a mystifying form of social consciousness that has served to create and sustain the socioeconomic disadvantage and political marginalization of blacks.

The normative questions that I take up in this study are approached largely from the standpoint of what John Rawls calls *nonideal* political theory.[6] The primary goal is not so much to describe the political principles that black Americans should embrace in a fully just political order, but rather to consider how blacks should relate politically to the United States, a country still plagued by racial discrimination, unjust economic disparities, and unequal opportunities. These and other forms of social injustice disproportionately affect African Americans, a racially stigmatized minority group with relatively little political power. In order to consolidate what power they do have and to marshal this for social reform, blacks have traditionally embraced black solidarity. Thus, my defense of the normative underpinnings of this political solidarity should not be understood as an account of a racial (or post-racial) utopia. Nor am I offering a black theory of justice. Instead, my concern is to explain and defend the role of black political unity in bringing about a just society.

I should also make clear that this pragmatic black solidarity is not meant to be a comprehensive political program—that is, one that fully defines the political outlook of African Americans. Nor is it meant to address every form of social disadvantage that blacks experience or that significantly affects them. Its focus is racial oppression and its consequences, as virtually all blacks are vulnerable to being victimized or disadvantaged by antiblack racism and thus can identify with one another on that basis. Nevertheless, this type of solidarity does take seriously the multiple forms of social oppression that different blacks face and are struggling to overcome—such as sexism, economic disadvantage, homophobia, cultural intolerance, and political marginalization—even as it recognizes that blackness is an inadequate foundation to fully address them. This conception of black solidarity conceives of black political unity as narrow in scope, not because blacks should limit their political activity to matters of racial justice—which would be a tragic mistake—but because this is as much as African Americans can reasonably expect from black unity in the post–civil rights era. Other forms of group solidarity, coalition building, and new strategies and tactics will be necessary to fully pursue social justice, in all its forms, in America and beyond.

African American Philosophy: Theorizing between Disciplines

This book seeks to increase the dialogue between philosophy and African American studies. Specifically, I apply the traditional analytical and critical tools of philosophy to central problems within black political thought. This kind of work, which has come to be called African American philosophy, takes seriously both the Western philosophical tradition and the African American experience, while always emphasizing that these are not mutually exclusive.[7]

Within the broader discipline of philosophy as practiced in the United States, African American philosophy is still largely marginalized. Many philosophers regard it as not real philosophy at all. And when it is considered philosophical, it is given the label *applied philosophy,* a term often used derisively to denote work that is considered "soft" or only marginally philosophical. Indeed, apart from debates about affirmative action, African American issues are rarely given sustained and explicit philosophical treatment in mainstream venues (such as leading journals, college courses, and departmental colloquia). My purpose in noting this is not primarily to speculate about why this is so—though I will do a bit of this in a moment. Nor is it to protest the lack of inclusiveness and diversity in our discipline, though such protest would surely be justified.[8] Rather, I want to make a few related points that I hope will help the reader navigate this text, which for some may lead to unfamiliar territory.

First, philosophers often speak and write as if they were viewing the world from a purely "human" point of view, abstracting away from historical contingencies and the peculiarities of different cultural traditions. This feature of philosophical reflection has much to do with the fact that philosophers so often concern themselves with intellectual problems that have (or at least appear to have) a timeless or universal quality, those that are vexing to almost all who consider them—such as, what does it mean for a proposition to be true, what are the basic constituents of reality, how do we know what we know, and what are the limits of reason in thought and action? Still, the highly abstract and often ahistorical character of philosophy leads some, especially some women and nonwhites, to be suspicious of the enterprise. This suspicion springs in part from the fact that the discipline is practiced in such a way that the experiences and perspectives that are taken seriously and productively engaged with are mainly—and until quite recently almost exclusively—those of white men. The situation is made worse by the fact that philosophers so often deny that their views and the questions they pose reflect a particular set of interests or a contingent set of social circumstances, a denial that many women and nonwhites view as disingenuous. The claim that Western academic philosophy is irredeemably white or patriarchal is, I believe, false, but to adequately rebut this charge, the experiences and perspectives of a wider range of people must be brought into the great discussion.

If the subfield of African American philosophy is to flourish, it is also important that philosophers overcome their aversion to historical particularity.[9] The subject matter of philosophy is usually taken to be "the human condition," with a focus on general and (near) universal features of human existence. Because questions of racial identity and racism are historically contingent features of human life, emerging only in the modern era and then only in certain parts of the globe, they are sometimes viewed as outside the purview of philosophy and better suited to sociology, political science, or psychology. When these questions are taken up by philosophers, they are often simply subsumed under more general categories—individual vice, multiculturalism, or social justice—without a close look at the peculiar features of the relevant phenomena. I contend, though, that the questions of race that directly bear on the lives of African Americans require a more historically informed approach than is typical in philosophy.

However, it is generally agreed that philosophizing is often aided by focused attention on historically specific examples. (Think of how systematic reflection on the practice of modern science has aided us in answering or better understanding more general problems in epistemology and metaphysics.) Thus, this is one way (though not the only way) that the black experience can provide philosophical insight. We can think through philosophical questions—such as the limits of state coercion, the requirements of social justice, the distinction between reality and mere appearance, the meaning of love and happiness, and the significance of life and death—by considering them in relation to the lives and experiences of black people or, better yet, by listening attentively, critically, but open-mindedly to black people themselves as they philosophize about these questions against the background of their history, practical concerns, and long-standing aspirations.

I want to emphasize that the current reception of African American philosophy within the academic profession of philosophy should not lead the uninitiated to conclude that philosophy, as a mode of inquiry and a set of vexing questions, does not possess the methodological resources to enlighten us about important dimensions of the black experience. It is not just that philosophy has the unrealized potential to shed light on puzzling features of black life. Some philosophers have already demonstrated the usefulness and relevance of philosophical methods for understanding core themes in African American studies. Yet their work, with a few notable exceptions, is frequently ignored.[10]

Drawing parallels with the development of feminist philosophy, Charles Mills has usefully distinguished three necessary steps to bring issues of race and the black experience closer to the center of philosophical concern.[11] First, there is the discovery, analysis, and critique of the racism of the major figures in the philosophical canon (such as Hume, Locke, Kant, and Hegel).[12] This is meant to be a general challenge to the Eurocentric bias of academic philosophy and its implicit assumptions about the universality of the white experience. Second, there is the effort to rediscover oppositional writings by members of racially subordinate groups (for example, Frederick Douglass, Anna Julia Cooper, and W. E. B. Du Bois).[13] Within African American philosophy, the primary goal here is not so much to vindicate "the race" but to show that there is a rich philosophical tradition of resistance that can be developed and built upon. Third, there is the effort to reconceptualize the sociopolitical order so as to make explicit what would be necessary to bring blacks and other subordinate racialized groups into the body politic on terms of equality, reciprocity, and mutual respect. Within African American philosophy, all three tasks are well under way. In this book I seek to advance the second and third of these tasks: to draw out and build on the insights of several black thinkers in order to develop a conception of black political solidarity that has contemporary import.

The field of African American studies comprises a community of scholars carrying out disciplinary, multidisciplinary, and interdisciplinary research on the history, social condition, political struggles, intellectual achievements, artistic accomplishments, and cultural life of blacks in America and beyond. Within the field, scholars engage in many different modes of inquiry and employ diverse methodologies, producing an enormous array of results, which vary in scope, focus, and degree of disciplinary specialization. Despite the breadth of its subject matter and the methodological pluralism that rightly reigns in the field at large, African American studies has yet to fully embrace philosophy as integral to its enterprise.

Because African American studies emerged in the context of severe racial oppression and was eventually brought to predominantly white college campuses through militant Black Power activism, it is not surprising that establishing philosophy as an important subfield has not been a priority. The rarified and generally esoteric character of academic philosophy can seem far removed from the pressing practical matters that concern most black Americans and the scholars who study them. Indeed, W. E. B. Du Bois, one of the founders of our field and the original source for many of the ideas that I develop and defend in this work, would appear to have taken just such a position on the significance of philosophy for African American scholarship. Despite his expressed love for philosophy and after having majored in the subject while an undergraduate at Harvard, Du Bois chose instead historical sociology as his scholarly vocation: "I revelled in the keen analysis of William James, Josiah Royce and young George Santayana. But it was James with his pragmatism and Albert Bushnell Hart with his research method, that turned me back from the lovely but sterile land of philosophic speculation, to the social sciences as the field for gathering and interpreting that body of fact which would apply to my program for the Negro."[14]

Perhaps Du Bois was right, not merely about his own intellectual calling, but more importantly about the relative value of philosophy to those seeking black liberation. It hardly needs to be said that blacks will not be made free and equal citizens by philosophical speculation. Nor is the study of philosophy even necessary for blacks to achieve their emancipatory aims. Indeed, Marx was probably correct when he suggested that intellectuals, especially philosophers, have a tendency to overestimate the significance of their ideas for the course of history. Nevertheless, to the extent that philosophical inquiry can provide insight into the history, social life, and thought of black peoples, it must have a place within our evolving field. No study of African Americans can be complete without attending to the philosophical ideas of their greatest minds. And insofar as the field concerns itself with the political realm, it must surely include consideration of African American political philosophy.

Work on black political thought is of course productively carried out within other disciplines in the humanities and the social sciences, and some of this work can be quite similar to philosophical inquiry. But there are important differences, and to the extent that I am addressing a multidisciplinary audience, as I hope to do, I want to outline these distinctions here. For instance, intellectual historians working in the area tend to focus on the development and spread of influential ideas, the biographical background of significant thinkers and prominent spokespersons, the reconstruction of neglected traditions, the sociohistorical context within which certain ideas emerged and were shaped, and the ideologies of social movements. Some social scientists have collected and analyzed survey data on black political thought over various stretches of time, demonstrating trends and significant shifts in black public opinion. This historical and social-scientific work is largely empirically driven and typically (though not always) aims at value-neutrality. Thus, those working in such areas do not generally take a position on the soundness of these doctrines or the coherence of these ideas. Nor do they seek to question the validity of the arguments that are offered in support of them. Nor, finally, do they attempt to develop or build upon the political theories and ideas that they investigate. Literary scholars do engage in the critical evaluation of the work of important black political thinkers, but their treatments tend to focus on rhetorical technique, narrative form, dominant tropes, thematic affinities, and aesthetic value; or they are primarily concerned with constructing or legitimating a venerable black intellectual tradition.

In contrast, philosophical analyses of black political thought focus squarely on the details and nuances of the arguments put forward by black thinkers and on subtle doctrinal differences between like-minded figures. Such analyses strenuously avoid treating these ideas and arguments as mere rationalizations for class or group interests. They do not reduce them to the effects of sociohistorical causes or structuring discourses. Nor do they consider them only in relation to their legitimating or counterhegemonic social functions. Rather than treating ideas and the reasons or evidence offered in defense of them as mere social or psychological phenomena to be empirically investigated and perhaps explained, philosophers engage with them *qua* ideas and reasons. The political ideas of black thinkers are not seen as mere instruments to advance some agenda in a strategic context but are viewed as political positions about matters of principle and strategy that are worthy of consideration and critical engagement for their own sake. African American philosophy is therefore openly evaluative in its aims, seeking to submit these ideas and arguments to philosophical scrutiny in an effort to gain insight into and clarity about important contemporary social issues facing black Americans. In this way, African American philosophy is not value-neutral, and its practitioners openly advocate for substantive moral and political positions, often building upon the very ideas and theories advanced by the thinkers they sharply critique.

Still, my book is not a manifesto. Nor do I specify a political agenda that activists can readily put into action. I aim to articulate and defend the basic moral and political principles that should undergird contemporary African American political unity. My focus on philosophical foundations is not a search for fundamental premises that are self-evident or beyond criticism and revision (as if there could be such), but a self-conscious, critical engagement with basic conceptual and normative questions, the answers to which are too often merely assumed rather than closely examined and argued for. In my view, black solidarity—that seemingly involuntary readiness of most blacks to act individually and collectively to protect black people from harm and injustice—is an invaluable moral and political resource. This study seeks to make this implicit understanding explicit and, in the process, both to evaluate this component of black thinking, revising and supplementing it where necessary, and to defend it against its detractors.

But African American philosophy does not typically make public policy recommendations. Although engaged with social realities and historical events, its mode of inquiry still tends to be relatively abstract and somewhat tentative in its conclusions, often asking more questions than it answers. It operates at the level of general principles rather than offering concrete proposals for social change. The intellectual culture of the United States has a strong bias against speculative inquiry, and thus philosophical work of the kind I engage in here may frustrate some readers, especially those interested in ideas largely for their immediate practical application to concrete problems. Political philosophy in particular can appear as worthless pontification or superfluous splitting of hairs. Moreover, given that African American philosophy scrutinizes and defends basic normative ideals, it might seem to be hopelessly utopian, as engaged in painting a picture of an ideal world in which none of us will ever live. Because of this, some who are eager to get on with the important work of changing the world and not merely interpreting it become impatient with philosophical reflection—often concluding that, at best, it is irrelevant to practical matters or, at worst, it is a meaningless form of recreation engaged in by a self-important cadre of the intellectual elite. This study hopes to vindicate African American philosophy of the charge of practical irrelevance by using philosophical techniques to analyze current social problems that African Americans face.

The Structure of the Book

Chapter 1 foreshadows my core themes and conclusions by offering a new interpretation of the political philosophy of Martin R. Delany, a mid-nineteenth-century radical abolitionist and one of the founders of black nationalism. Competing strands in Delany's social thought—"classical" nationalism and "pragmatic" nationalism—offer two different foundations for black political solidarity. I argue that the pragmatic variant is the more cogent of the two, and the one that can still serve usefully as a theoretical schema through which African Americans can understand and carry out important political projects.

Chapter 2 takes up the challenge that class differentiation among black Americans poses for their solidarity, a subject Du Bois grappled with throughout his life. Focusing on his account of the relationship between black ideals, political solidarity, self-help strategies, and elite leadership, I argue that Du Bois, while never fully rebutting the charge of elitism often made against him, puts forward a conception of black solidarity that fuses moral principle, racial identification, and self-interest into a motivational basis for collective action across class differences. This account does not eliminate the threat of class-based fragmentation within the greater black population, but it does show that, despite growing class differentiation and social cleavages, black American political cooperation on terms of fairness and equal respect is still possible. It also helps us to better understand the significance of black pride and militancy for black politics.

In Chapter 3 I examine the conception of black solidarity that was initially urged by Malcolm X and then later developed by Black Power advocates during the late 1960s and early 1970s. Despite several critical flaws, this thinking still shapes the political orientation of many African Americans today. I criticize the Black Power conception of black solidarity, focusing specifically on its commitment to black institutional autonomy, its social analysis of the black condition in terms of white supremacy, its treatment of the black population as a cohesive kinship unit that is capable of speaking with one voice, and its tendency to exclude, marginalize, and sometimes alienate needed nonblack allies.

In light of the problems with Black Power but retaining its key insights, in Chapter 4 I offer an alternative conception of black political solidarity. I argue that black unity must operate across multiracial political organizations; it must recognize that the sources of black disadvantage cannot all be reduced to racism; and it should acknowledge the need for a decentralized network of black advocacy. This conception identifies the basic aims, political principles, and proper scope of black politics. It also suggests a way to conceive of the relationship between the demands of racial justice and the ideal of racial equality.

In Chapter 5 I critically discuss black cultural nationalism (or cultural pluralism). I argue against including the goal of cultural autonomy among the basic aims of black political solidarity, and I suggest that the so-called politics of difference is not an appropriate model for contemporary black politics. I first provide a general characterization of the ideal of black cultural self-determination in the form of eight tenets, ranging from the claim that there is a distinct black culture to the thesis that blacks are, and should be regarded as, the foremost interpreters of the meaning and worth of their cultural ways. I then highlight the conceptual and normative errors that are frequently committed by those who defend this conception of cultural politics.

Once again using Du Bois as a point of departure, in Chapter 6 I offer an extended discussion of the relationship between social identity and political solidarity. Relying on the analytical groundwork developed in previous chapters, I distinguish thin conceptions of blackness, which view black identity as a vague social marker imposed from outside, from thick conceptions, which view the marker as signifying something "deeper," perhaps even something that blacks can autonomously and positively embrace as a component of their self-conception. I show that a shared thick black identity, whether "racial," ethnic, cultural, or national, is not needed for political solidarity and that, in fact, the attempts to develop such an identity are counterproductive to blacks' emancipatory aims.

In the conclusion I elaborate the pragmatic nationalist conception of political solidarity. I draw out the implications of the foregoing argument by integrating its various strands. In particular, I offer an interpretation of the ideal of black self-determination that demonstrates the coherence of the pragmatic nationalist outlook and its relationship to the broader nationalist tradition in African American political thought. This interpretation highlights a significant but often unnoticed connection between the value of individual autonomy and the emancipatory aims of black unity, revealing important common ground between political liberalism and black nationalism, which many scholars have overlooked.

1

Two Conceptions of Black Nationalism

Black nationalism is usually treated by the mass media as
a sensational but peripheral phenomenon of no more than
passing interest. Actually, nationalism is imbedded in the social fabric of black America, and this must be understood if
the problems of the black liberation movement are to be fully
appreciated.
—Robert L. Allen, *Black Awakening in Capitalist America* (1969)

Black nationalism is one of the oldest and most enduring traditions
in American political thought.[1] Black nationalists advocate such
things as black self-determination, racial solidarity and group self-
reliance, various forms of voluntary racial separation, pride in the
historic achievements of persons of African descent, a concerted effort to overcome racial self-hate and to instill black self-love, militant collective resistance to white supremacy, the development and
preservation of a distinctive black cultural identity, and the recognition of Africa as the true homeland of those who are racially
black. Many of these ideas have seemed to some to be at odds with
the goal of advancing a nonessentialist, progressive black politics,
for they appear to reify that dubious category "race," to assume the
existence of a transhistorical and organic "black essence," or to im-

ply the desirability of an authentic and unitary black plural sub-ject—"the black community."

Some political theorists, such as K. Anthony Appiah, Adolph Reed Jr., and Paul Gilroy, have challenged the currency of these ra-cialist ideas by attempting to dismantle and discredit black nation-alism altogether through a radical critique of what they take to be its various conceptual, empirical, political, and moral flaws.[2] Yet if the point of such critiques is to shift black political culture in a more progressive direction, this strategy is unlikely to be effective. Strains of black nationalism have become, for all practical pur-poses, a constitutive component of the self-understanding of a sub-stantial segment of the African American population. These strains run so deep that an uncompromising and comprehensive attack on them will surely be met with hostility or suspicion, if it is taken seriously at all. If we are to avoid alienating potential allies and thereby further fragmenting and weakening the collective fight for social justice, then whenever possible we should opt for a more constructive form of critique, one that highlights the weaknesses within the black nationalist orientation while drawing out and building upon its valuable elements.[3] The transformation of black political consciousness—or the political consciousness of any group, for that matter—is more likely to come about if the new vi-sion can be comprehended as an extension of, rather than a radical rupture with, traditional beliefs of the group. Despite its shortcom-ings, we should not discard the heritage of black nationalism in our efforts to rethink the foundations of black politics.

Delany's Two Nationalisms

Black nationalist theorists suggest a number of foundations for po-litical solidarity—typically organized around some particular, and always contested, conception of "blackness." Many of these ways of conceptualizing the normative foundations and political signifi-cance of black unity are, to be sure, either unsound or impractical for contemporary black American politics. But in the work of an early and influential black nationalist theoretician, we find a conception of black solidarity that is still viable.

The militant abolitionist Martin Robison Delany (1812–1885) was born free in Charles Town, in what is now West Virginia. He was an activist, a physician, a novelist, a journalist, an African explorer, and a politician; and, more importantly for our purposes, he is widely regarded as the "father" of black nationalist theory.[4] The parental designation is quite appropriate, for not only is practically every core tenet of black nationalist thought prefigured in his writings but, like Marcus Garvey and Malcolm X after him, Delany was a central spokesperson, charismatic leader, and principal architect of a movement for blacks to establish a separate nation-state.

In 1852 Delany published the first extended defense of African American emigration from the United States, urging free and fugitive blacks to collectively form an independent republic that would enable them to live under conditions of equality and liberty. This influential work, *The Condition, Elevation, Emigration, and Destiny of the Colored People of the United States,* was written in the wake of the draconian Fugitive Slave Law (a component of the notorious 1850 Compromise), which enabled slaveholders to pursue runaway slaves even in non-slaveholding territories and which, in effect, also made free blacks (even more) vulnerable to being enslaved, as they would have no reliable legal recourse should a slaveholder falsely claim them as fugitive property.[5] This white supremacist tactic caused a budding mass movement for black emigration to grow and be energized.

In *The Condition,* Delany famously described blacks in the United States as an oppressed "nation within a nation."[6] These subjugated internal nations are, he claimed, unjustly deprived of equal treatment by the ruling classes, subjected to naked and brutal exploitation, and often restricted to the most devalued positions within the society in which they live and work. Moreover, in order to legitimate its dominant status, the ruling elite regards these subordinate nations as inherently inferior and thereby incapable of self-government.

It is clear why Delany regarded blacks in the States as a severely oppressed people, perhaps even a stigmatized caste. Yet it is less obvious, and even somewhat puzzling, why he would choose to characterize them as a "nation." If we were to use Will Kymlicka's well-known criteria for a "national minority"—a previously self-governing, territorially concentrated, institutionally complete, culturally cohesive group that has been incorporated (forcibly or otherwise) into a larger state but that maintains its cultural distinctiveness and independence from the majority culture—then it is not at all clear that black Americans in Delany's time (much less now) should be described as an internal "nation."[7] Given the forced migration to the New World brought about by the transatlantic slave trade, the vast majority of blacks in America are not properly described as immigrants or descendants of immigrants either. Moving beyond the pithy and influential slogan, then, I want to clarify Delany's conception of black nationality and his program for nation building by discussing two doctrines advanced in his writings:

Strong black nationalism: The political program of black solidarity and voluntary separation under conditions of equality and self-determination is a worthwhile end in itself, a constitutive and enduring component of the collective self-realization of blacks as a people.

Weak black nationalism: The political program of black solidarity and group self-organization functions as a means to create greater freedom and social equality for blacks.

The two doctrines are not incompatible, because one might justify black political solidarity as both a means and an end. Indeed, many black nationalists hold exactly this two-pronged view. But it is important to see that the two positions, if taken separately, would have quite different practical implications.

Strong black nationalism treats the establishment of an independent black republic or a separate self-determining community as an intrinsic goal of black liberation struggles. It advocates the development of a national identity, group self-reliance, and separatism, not only because it could help bring about racial justice, but also because it is the political destiny of African Americans and perhaps all persons of black African descent. E. U. Essien-Udom usefully summarizes the strong nationalist position (though without labeling it as such) as "the belief of a group that it possesses, or ought to possess, a country; that it shares, or ought to share, a common heritage of language, culture, and religion; and that its heritage, way of life, and ethnic identity are distinct from those of other groups. Nationalists believe that they ought to rule themselves and shape their own destinies, and that they should therefore be in control of their social, economic, and political institutions."[8] Weak nationalism, on the other hand, urges black solidarity and concerted action as a political strategy to lift or resist oppression. This could of course mean forming a self-governing black nation-state or a separate self-determining community within a multinational state. Yet it could also mean working to create a racially integrated society or even a "postracial" polity, a political order where "race" has no social or political meaning.

We might call the strong nationalist position *classical nationalism*.[9] And let us call anyone who justifies black political solidarity on the grounds that it serves as a means for bringing about social justice a *pragmatic nationalist*. The solidaristic commitment of pragmatic nationalism is based on a desire to live in a just society, a society that need not be, nor even contain, a self-determining black community. Notice that the program of black emigration from the United States is consistent with both forms of nationalism. On the classical view, emigration to build a black republic would be desir-

able in itself—that is, besides fulfilling the desire to escape the suffering caused by injustice; whereas pragmatic emigrationism would
treat it as a mere means to fight or avoid oppression, a strategy that
could be discarded if another one appeared more promising.[10]

Wilson J. Moses usefully distinguishes the "classical" age of black
nationalism (1850–1925) from its "modern" period (1925–present).[11] The classical era begins roughly around the 1850 Compromise and ends with the imprisonment of Marcus Garvey. We can
view the modern period (though Moses does not conceptualize it
as such) as roughly marking the decline of Garveyism through the
rise of the Nation of Islam and the Black Power movement in the
post–World War II period to its various contemporary manifestations in the post–civil rights era, such as Afrocentricity and hip-hop
nationalism. My distinction between classical and pragmatic nationalism, as a way to distinguish two related doctrines, is meant to
cut across this historical periodization, and unlike Moses I consider
a nationalist position "classical" even if its call for group self-determination falls short of a call for statehood.[12]

Given these distinctions, my primary contention is that Delany
vacillated between (and perhaps even confused) classical nationalism and pragmatic nationalism, and that this tendency can be
found throughout the black nationalist tradition. Although I will
here focus my discussion on Delany's nationalism(s), my general
hypothesis is this: Classical nationalism is often merely a defensive
and rhetorical posture that is taken up so that its proponents and
the group they take themselves to represent are seen not as merely
reacting to white dominance but as asserting the equal right of African Americans to collective self-determination alongside other
national groups. Pragmatic nationalism, on the other hand, is the
more firmly held position among black nationalists, despite the fact
that they occasionally evince the classical form. In support of this
diagnosis, I will demonstrate that Delany exemplifies this wavering
tendency. My strategy shall be to reconstruct the arguments he of-

fers in favor of each of the two doctrines and then to show that, contrary to standard interpretations and notwithstanding his occasional lapses into classical nationalism, he is most deeply committed to pragmatic black nationalism.

In speaking here of pragmatic nationalism, my use of the term *pragmatic* is not meant to be philosophically loaded. It is to be understood in its everyday sense: namely, concerned with achieving practical results in light of the contingent and changing features of the context. In particular, my defense of pragmatic black nationalism does not presuppose or rely on the philosophical doctrines of American pragmatism (the tradition founded by Charles S. Peirce, William James, and John Dewey). My hope is that the arguments I provide will be compelling to readers regardless of their epistemological or metaphysical views.

The interpretation I defend is a view about the internal tensions and shifts within the development of black nationalist theory. It is not an attempt to *explain* black nationalism as a social movement or social tendency. My interest in black nationalism is primarily as a social philosophy or political theory, and only secondarily as a sociohistorical phenomenon. In this way, my project differs from that of intellectual historians like August Meier, who has proposed that "nationalist tendencies tended to be salient during periods when conditions were becoming worse and white public opinion more hostile, while the integrationist became salient when the blacks' status was improving and white public opinion becoming more tolerant."[13] I suspect that Meier's hypothesis is correct, and my account of the relationship between classical and pragmatic strands in black nationalist theory is, I believe, perfectly compatible with it. But I am attempting to understand the conceptual and normative basis of black nationalism and the ways in which nationalist ideas get developed and shaped within the *thinking* of its principal exponents, not with the social shifts between nationalist and integrationist movements within the larger black population, though the two are no doubt related.

Before proceeding to that account, let me briefly address the following concern. Among scholars and laypersons, the question of how to define black nationalism is a hotly contested issue.[14] This should not surprise us. Black nationalism is an old political tradition, and like all such traditions (such as liberalism or Marxism), the content of its core tenets is debated among partisans and sharply critiqued by opponents. Over time, the content and boundaries of the tradition get blurred as revisions are made in response to theoretical developments, criticism, and changing circumstances. The shifting character of political philosophies should not be regarded as a flaw, because such revision can sometimes be a sign that partisans have learned from past errors; and recognition of fallibility and openness to change can help keep a philosophy from becoming mere dogma. Yet this dynamism in political traditions makes consensus about their main characteristics nearly impossible.

For the philosopher, the core elements of the black nationalist tradition, like all intellectual traditions, must be reconstructed retrospectively.[15] We look to our nearest contemporary exponents of the doctrine and ask whom they consider to be their most important intellectual forebears. We then look to those designated persons to see whom they refer to as forebears, and so on. We also look to "founding texts," the ones studied by all who claim affinity with the tradition. We include works by figures who everyone agrees are a part of the tradition—such as Delany, Garvey, and Malcolm X. We then trace the intertextual dialogue between these figures and their critics. These sources give us something approaching a canon, which we use as a basis for interpreting the most important features of the tradition. But even if we agree on what belongs in the canon, any interpretation of it will be theory-laden and disputed.[16] There simply cannot be an innocent philosophical interpretation of black nationalism. My interpretation is no exception. Whether it is, in the end, the most compelling is of course up to the reader to decide. But we should not pretend that there is some neutral definition to which all can readily agree.

In keeping with the approach just described, I maintain that when the idiom of black nationhood is deployed (a) to mark the distinctiveness of a black people, (b) to identify the shared interests of its members and thereby the "general will" of this imagined community, and (c) to create or sustain the bonds of political solidarity needed to carry out the group's will, the label *black nationalism* is appropriate, even if the political goal is not the creation of a separate self-determining corporate unit. The mark of black nationalism is, in a phrase, the politicization of black peoplehood. Blacks will have become fully post-nationalist in their political outlook when they no longer deem it necessary or beneficial to regard their peoplehood as a basis for political action.

Some may complain that pragmatic nationalism, as here defined, is not, strictly speaking, a form of "nationalism" at all, for this form of politics is not committed to a claim of territorial sovereignty or collective self-government, as many, perhaps most, nationalisms are.[17] Exactly what the *general* features of nationalism are is an interesting sociological or historical question, one where comparative analysis is entirely appropriate. But this is not my question. I am offering a philosophical reconstruction of the black nationalist tradition *from the inside,* from the standpoint of persons who identify with the tradition, from a hermeneutic point of view. As Eddie Glaude has convincingly shown, the meaning of the language of "nation" in early nineteenth-century black political thought (when black nationalism first crystallized) was intensely contested, as it still is today, with several prominent black leaders advocating what I am here calling a pragmatic conception of "black nationhood."[18] Delany, a widely acknowledged progenitor of black nationalist theory, was among those struggling to define a conception of black nationality that could be used for emancipatory purposes, and his nationalism, as I will demonstrate, sometimes fell short of a demand for black sovereignty.

Political and Moral Ideals

One method for understanding the theoretical motivation of Delany's black nationalism is to examine the moral and political values he defended or assumed in the course of developing his nationalist program. Three core principles undergird his political philosophy: social equality, democratic citizenship, and self-government.

Like other liberal thinkers, Delany believed that, as a matter of social justice, all members of society should be accorded *equal respect* within the basic political and economic institutions of social life; and that all citizens should possess the same basic rights and duties.[19] But he also maintained that blacks would not have true social equality with whites until blacks (more or less) matched them in cultural and economic achievement. This commitment to substantive, rather than merely formal, equality is necessary because accomplishment engenders both self-respect and the respect of others.[20] Thus, only with proportionate black and white attainment in the central spheres of life can the two races truly live together on terms of mutual respect.

Delany also believed that blacks must have *democratic citizenship* within their home country. The rights of a citizen should include not only the equal protection of the laws but also the right to enjoy positions of honor and public trust. Citizenship, then, is a matter of not merely having the right to vote for members of the dominant group but also, on possession of the requisite abilities and skills, having a fair opportunity to occupy positions of authority within the country in which one permanently resides.[21]

Closely related to the principle of democratic citizenship is the right of *self-government.* Delany maintained that true political freedom requires that each adult citizen forms an indispensable part of the sovereign authority of the republic: "A people, to be free, must necessarily be *their own rulers;* that is, *each individual* must, in himself, embody the *essential ingredient*—so to speak—of the *sovereign principle* which composes the *true basis* of his liberty. This principle, when not exercised by himself, may, at his pleasure, be delegated to another—his true representative."[22] Delany argued that self-government is necessary for self-defense, because one cannot be secure in one's life, welfare, property, or liberty without an equal and effective say in matters of public concern.

In addition to these familiar liberal egalitarian principles, Delany valued and sought to encourage the moral virtue, if one might call it that, of *manhood.* Despite the unfortunate term, manhood, as Delany understood it, is a quality of character that is not peculiar to men, as many women also value and fully embody it. No doubt, Delany was not using the term *manhood* in a purely gender-neutral way; and I am not at all suggesting that he did not have many traditional patriarchal attitudes (such as a belief in a conventional domestic sexual division of labor and the "practical" education of women to equip them for child rearing). However, some commentators have tended to exaggerate the degree of Delany's sexism. Paul Gilroy, for example, goes so far as to call Delany "the progenitor of black Atlantic patriarchy."[23] Not only is this statement anachronistic but it also underplays the progressive elements in Delany's thought with regard to gender. As Robert Levine rightly points out, "Delany wrote of the need for women to take up business enterprises, he encouraged the participation of women (including his wife) at all the emigration conventions he sponsored, and, true to his sense of women as political entities in their own right, he presented the reader of *Blake* [his novel] with actively engaged women revolutionaries."[24] Delany certainly did have patriarchal beliefs and sentiments, as of course did most people at the time.[25] But we should also recognize that, despite these typical but inexcusable sexist prejudices, Delany clearly wanted women to cultivate a "manly" character, though perhaps not to the same extent or in quite the same ways as men. *Vigor* would perhaps have been a more appropriate and less masculinist term to describe the relevant ensemble of traits.

One of the most important of these qualities is autonomous thinking. Delany was particularly dismayed when blacks allowed whites, even those sympathetic to black interests, to think for them; and so he consistently urged blacks to resist white paternalism.[26] He made this point repeatedly with regard to religion, claiming that blacks had unthinkingly accepted their oppressors' interpretation of Christianity, an interpretation that encouraged passivity in the face of subordination and exploitation.[27] Moreover, he found it disgraceful, and a sure sign of degradation, when blacks would slavishly imitate the conduct of their oppressors. Thus, he urged blacks to be creative and imaginative in their individual and collective endeavors. This of course required a degree of self-confidence and faith in one's own abilities, which Delany believed blacks were sorely lacking and must therefore make a concerted effort to cultivate.

This confident and innovative spirit was to be joined with laudable ambition. According to Delany, as soon as they were able to acquire a few conveniences and some leisure, blacks too often became complacent about their second-class status in American society. But he insisted that "manhood" requires a constant, though moderate, striving for superior achievement in every central sphere of life. Courage is also among the traits of a vigorous character, as it engenders the respect of others, even sometimes of one's oppressor. Perhaps more importantly, courage, along with independence of mind, is a sign of self-respect. He especially valued and urged the cultivation of the kind of courage that expresses itself in the fight for freedom and equality under conditions of domination. Closely related to this is the trait of determination: that earnest resolve that does not falter when confronted with adversity.[28]

Finally, vigor involves self-reliance. Delany held that, rather than expecting the burden of racial oppression to be lifted by some other agency, whether at home or abroad, blacks should realize that they must rely on themselves, as individuals and as a collective, in their effort to rise above their low position in U.S. society and within the international community.[29] It is not that he held blacks responsible for their subordinate position. He simply believed that self-respect and prudence suggest that self-help is the surest road, if not to freedom, then at least to a dignified existence.

Delany vividly represented the qualities of a vigorous character through the main hero of his novel, *Blake; or, the Huts of America* (1859), a fictional slave narrative written as a critical response to Harriet Beecher Stowe's depiction of slaves as docile, ignorant, long-suffering, and helpless, in her immensely popular antislavery novel *Uncle Tom's Cabin* (1852).[30] Werner Sollors aptly describes Delany's novel as "an unusually radical book, both in its creation of a black and beautiful protagonist who is an aristocratic hero, revolutionary superman, and slave conspirator and instigator and in a more or less continuous opposition to American national symbolism."[31] The Afro-Cuban Henry Blake, in stark contrast to Stowe's character Uncle Tom, is a highly intelligent, militant, and visionary runaway slave who organizes a general slave insurrection throughout the United States and in Cuba. Blake risks his freedom and life to work for the abolition of slavery in the New World. In an effort to develop an independent mind, he throws off the degrading religion of his oppressors, urging other people of color to do the same. He cleverly and successfully devises schemes to free his family and friends from slavery, and repeatedly outwits those who would return them to bondage. He is defiant in the face of oppression and always self-assured. And he is tireless in his effort to enlighten the oppressed and to motivate them to concerted action for their liberty and uplift. Indeed, with the help of his cousin Placido, Blake manages to infuse vigor into an entire community of would-be revolutionaries in Cuba. Notice how Delany describes a gathering of this group, composed, notably, of both men and women: "There was no empty parade and imitative aping, nor unmeaning pretentions observed in their doings, but all seeming fully to comprehend the importance of the ensemble. They were earnest, firm, and determined; discarding everything which detracted from their object, permitting nothing to interfere. Thus intelligently united, a dangerous material existed in the midst of such an element as Cuba."[32]

There is an important relationship between Delany's three political principles and the qualities of a vigorous character. Delany believed that part of the reason blacks often failed to exhibit the traits of vigor—independence of mind, creativity, self-confidence, ambition, courage, self-respect, determination, and self-reliance—is that they were severely oppressed. In particular, they lacked socioeconomic equality, the rights of democratic citizenship, and political self-determination. This kind of deprivation weakens the character of many (though not all) who suffer under it, and blacks had been acutely debased by their many years in bondage. It is also clear that vigorous persons are the ones most likely to struggle and fight for the realization of these liberal egalitarian principles. Over time, subjugated persons will often become accustomed and resigned to less than full liberty and equality. Delany maintained, therefore, that blacks must find a way, through group self-reliance and solidarity, to reinvigorate themselves, if they are to overcome their oppressed condition and thus to become the "nation" they should be.

Now these political principles and moral values can be given an individualist interpretation or a collectivist one. That is to say, the claims of social equality, democratic citizenship, and self-government can be founded on the rights of individual persons or of peoples; and vigor is a property that can be possessed by individuals or by communities (where the "manliness" of the community is not

reducible to the vigor of its individual members). Delany seems to
have been aware of this distinction but remained somewhat vague
about whether his nationalism should be understood as ultimately
rooted in individual or group claims. For instance, when he defended the principle of self-government, he emphasized that it is a
right of the *individual,* but then he goes on to say in this regard,
"what is true of an individual is true of a family, and that which is
true of a family is also true concerning a whole people."[33] Moreover,
it would seem that Delany's core values are realizable in principle—
though, given the pervasiveness and persistence of racism, perhaps
not in practice—within either a multiracial state or a monoracial
one. And these values can be embraced on universalistic and cosmopolitan grounds and/or endorsed for reasons of ethnoracial partiality and loyalty. As we shall see, Delany offered arguments that
support both an individualist-universalistic reading of his nationalist philosophy and a collectivist-particularistic one.

Classical Nationalism and "Original" Identity

Delany's most forceful defense of classical nationalism is found in
his essay "The Political Destiny of the Colored Race on the American Continent." This was the keynote address to the first National
Emigration Convention (1854), of which Delany was president pro
tem and for which there were delegates, both men and women,
from twelve states and from the Canadas, with, by Delany's count,
nearly sixteen hundred persons in attendance. In his address, which
was adopted as the convention's official report, he argued that
blacks must constitute, in terms of sheer numbers, the "ruling element" of their body politic. The basis of a democratic polity, he
contended, must be a shared national identity, a so-called "original"
identity: "Upon this solid foundation rests the fabric of every substantial political structure in the world, which cannot exist without
it; and so soon as a people or nation lose their original identity, just
so soon must that nation or people become extinct."[34] According to

Delany, this common national identity creates strong bonds of affinity and is also the principal basis upon which a group lays claim to the right of self-government.[35] Indeed, he maintained that without a shared national identity, the people of a republic would lose their common interest and purpose in remaining together, thus creating internal instability that could in turn make them vulnerable to being dominated by a more cohesive national power.[36]

In accordance with this classical nationalist view, what then, for Delany, constitutes the original identity of black Americans? At times he seems committed to what Appiah calls *racialism*—the now defunct view that being of the same "race" is a matter not merely of sharing superficial phenotypic traits, such as skin color or hair type, but of sharing a distinctive "biological essence" that gives rise to both these morphological traits *and* a set of psychological dispositions and natural endowment.[37] Delany claimed that blacks have certain "inherent traits" and "native characteristics" that distinguish them from other races.[38] Among these are civility, peaceableness, and religiosity. Blacks are also naturally gifted at languages, oratory, poetry, music, painting, ethics, metaphysics, theology, and jurisprudence; and they are said to be industrious, talented at agricultural development, adept at the training of horses, and adaptable to almost any climate.[39]

But there are two obvious problems with this "organicist" method of establishing the distinctiveness of the black nation within a nation. First, there are clearly lots of nonblacks who possess these traits and talents; and second, there are plenty of blacks who, we must admit, do not. Delany recognized this. Thus, because he could not argue plausibly that *all* or *only* blacks have these characteristics, in order to demonstrate that blacks have a distinctive and noteworthy national identity, he argued that blacks were the *first* race to display them or that they *best* exemplify them.

His most comprehensive attempt to build a case for black originality and superiority can be found in his relatively obscure and final work, *Principia of Ethnology: The Origin of Races and Color*.[40] In response to influential social Darwinist and polygenetic accounts of the development of racial kinds, where blacks were invariably seen as inferior stock, Delany offers a part-theological and part-biological account of the origin of races. He claimed that God's purpose in creating the varieties of humankind is the development and spread of civilization for his glory, where "civilization" is a matter of advanced intellectual achievements (for instance, in religion, philosophy, art, and science) and practical accomplishments (in agriculture, industry, architecture, political organization, and the like).[41]

Relying on the familiar biblical narratives of Noah's Ark and the Tower of Babel, Delany claimed that, not long after the flood, humankind divided itself into three separate groups, each marked by a different skin color—white, yellow, and black—and each set off to populate a different geographical region (Europe, Asia, and Africa, respectively). Each of the three groups had its own language, which, because of the confusion of tongues, the other two groupings could not understand, causing the individual members of each group to have a special affinity for one another.[42]

Delany insisted that it was the African branch of the human family that was the first to found civilized legal orders. To show this, he tried to demonstrate the greatness and originality of the ancient African civilizations of Egypt and Ethiopia, which he regarded as a unified kingdom.[43] He claimed that these ancient Africans were the first to establish municipal law, the first to establish and propagate the science of letters, and the first to spread intellectual civilization. They invented astronomy, astrology, and geometry; they initiated advanced architecture; they specialized in agricultural development; and they were the first to develop a monotheistic religion with a self-created and benevolent god.

Now of course this outstanding record of original achievement would be irrelevant to Delany's project of forging a founding myth for the black nation in America unless he were able to show that the ancient Ethiopians and Egyptians were racially "black" or "Negroes." His evidence was mainly ancient paintings with representations of persons of high social standing who possess paradigmatic "black" phenotypic features—dark skin color, woolly hair, flat nose, and full lips. He also claimed that because the sphinx has the "head of a Negro woman on the body of a lion or lioness," we have indisputable evidence that the original inhabitants of Egypt were Negroes. In order to link modern blacks to their ancient African heritage, Delany invoked racialism and divine providence. He claimed that the Ethiopians led the march of civilization because of the "inherent faculties" of the African race, and that God created this race specifically for the purpose of civilizing all of humankind.[44]

We now have a better idea of what Delany means by the "original" identity of the black nation within a nation. Black Americans are the descendants of a great and ancient African people. The greatness of this African civilization is to be explained, at least in part, by the "native characteristics" of the original African race. And according to Delany, modern blacks in the African diaspora, even those of "mixed blood," still possess the natural abilities and tendencies of their original identity.[45]

But now we must ask, in light of their original identity, what sort of "nation" should modern blacks strive to be? Delany argued that if blacks are to become the self-determining nation they should be, then their original homeland, Africa, must be regenerated. And the members of the African race, or some subset thereof, must themselves carry out this project of African redemption and restoration.[46]

Delany outlined the program for African regeneration in his "Official Report of the Niger Valley Exploring Party" (1860), a document that also chronicles his travels in Africa and his discussions with African leaders about possible African American settlements.[47] The Executive Board of Commissioners at the National Emigration

Convention in Chatham, Canada West, authorized this topographic and diplomatic exploration of Africa in 1858. In his report Delany defended the view that if Africa is to be the nation it should be, it must have a "national" character and the effective right of self-government; and its level of civilization must be comparable to that of other great nations in the world—morally, religiously, socially, politically, and economically. But, he maintained, this essential development will not occur unless a "new element" is introduced into the African context, an agency that already possesses the requisite attainments of modern civilization.[48] This new element should possess the "natural" traits and inclinations of the African race and must share with it the special sympathies characteristic of racial kinship. This regenerative agency, as will come as no surprise, can only be some segment of the most enlightened and vigorous of those of African descent in America. Delany wanted a carefully selected African American vanguard to establish social and industrial settlements in Africa, with the purpose of instituting the pursuits of modern civilized life.

Delany contended that three fundamental principles are the basis of a great nationality.[49] The nation must (1) control a geographical territory, (2) be sufficiently populated, and (3) have an immense staple production as a solid source of wealth. Africa, with its vast native population and potential for agricultural development, would thus be a natural site for the establishment of a black nation-state. It is this vision of a free, economically self-reliant, self-governing, and vigorous Pan-African nation that Delany hoped would be realized through the efforts of African Americans: "Our policy must be—and I hazard nothing in promulgating it; nay, without this design and feeling, there would be a great deficiency of self-respect, pride of race, and love of country, and we might never expect to challenge the respect of nations—*Africa for the African race, and black men to rule them.* By black men I mean, men of African descent who claim an identity with the race."[50]

Yet this classical nationalist philosophy is not the only one Delany can be found defending. He just as often, and in fact more persuasively, made the case for a pragmatic nationalist vision, one with quite different practical implications. I now turn to that account.

Pragmatic Nationalism and Racial Domination

Recall Delany's claim that blacks must be the "ruling element" in any body politic of which they are a part. Now, on the principles of classical nationalism, the justification for this stance is that original identity must be the basis of any national republic, for such a collective identity is allegedly needed to create lasting common interests and to ensure unity of purpose. But sometimes Delany argued that blacks must be the ruling element in their country merely for purposes of self-defense against antiblack prejudice and political marginalization. Here, he urged black solidarity, group self-reliance, and mass emigration as a way to achieve social equality, democratic citizenship, self-government, and "manhood" for those oppressed on account of their "blackness." This pragmatic nationalist strategy does not, however, require blacks to retain or regain their "original" identity, because the basis of black unity is not their glorious national past or their so-called native characteristics but their mutual recognition of their common vulnerability to white domination and their collective resolve to overcome it. In the remainder of this section, I will sketch the arguments Delany offered in favor of this vision of black political solidarity.

I begin with the question of the relevance of black identity for pragmatic nationalism. That is, what, on the pragmatic account, is the distinctive nature of this oppressed subnation, and what kind of nation should it strive to be? We know that black nationality cannot be a matter of blacks sharing a distinct culture, because, according to Delany, black Americans, for better or worse, have been stripped of their African cultural heritage and consequently have merged with the dominant culture of the United States—in religion, language, values, habits, and customs.[51] Moreover, he did not advise blacks to return to the "original" cultural ways of their African ancestors or any of their African contemporaries. That seems to leave us, as it did with classical nationalism, with "race" as a basis for modern black nationality. To explore this possibility further, let's return to Delany's remarks about the nature of races.

In his *Principia of Ethnology*, Delany stressed his view that all humans, of whatever race, have common ancestors—Adam and Eve, and then later Noah and his wife. Moreover, the separation of Noah's offspring into three distinct groups did not give to each resulting population any special attributes except a common language, and, on Delany's account, linguistic peculiarities just *happened* to correspond to differences in skin color. He insisted, furthermore, that God did not change the physical constitution of the three groups; thus, any biological differences that existed between them would have been the result of normal physiological processes. Indeed, it is quite telling that, despite his overt use of racialist language, the entirety of his discussion of the biological peculiarities of the different races concerns the explanation of differences in skin color. But even here Delany maintained that different shades of skin were merely the result of different concentrations of pigment, or what he sometimes called "rouge." Noah's sons were supposedly born with different degrees of pigmentation—Shem the same as Noah, Ham a little more, Japheth a little less. According to Delany, God did not need to effect a miracle to create these color differences, for, as we know, parents of similar complexion, eye color, or hair type often produce offspring who differ from them with respect to these phenotypic traits: "The Divine Creator had but *one plan;* so in the human races, running through all the *various shades of complexion*, there is but *one color*, modified and intensified from negative to the extremest positive, as seen from the purest white, in *all intermediate colors,* to the purest black. *This is the solution of the problem which reveals to us the great mystery of the races of man.*"[52]

Because languages no longer—if they ever did—correspond to complexional hue, skin color turns out to be the only distinguishing characteristic by which the "original races" could be reliably identified over time. Indeed, given global migration patterns, these color differences themselves would likely fade in the absence of a norm of complexional endogamy. Thus, it seems that Delany *should* have said, though he sometimes did not, that race is only skin-deep. This "thin" account of racial identity is consistent with other things Delany said about race. For instance, he claimed that blacks and whites share a common inner life, despite their different exterior physical traits: "So is it with the whole class of colored people in the United States. Their feelings, tastes, predilections, wants, demands, and sympathies, are identical, and homogeneous with those of all other Americans."[53]

Moreover, though Delany presents a detailed account of the origin of color differences between the "original" continental populations, he provided no argument or evidence for the existence of a racial essence that causally explains both skin color and inherent behavioral dispositions. On the contrary, he sometimes emphasized that Africa's natural environment and physical peculiarities were especially conducive to the rapid development of human faculties, which could explain why, on Delany's own account, the African race was the first to establish civilization.[54] Indeed, advocating a racialist argument about innate black characteristics would be incompatible with his vision of spreading the positive values of African civilization throughout the world.[55] How could he expect other races to properly emulate the black race if the intellectual and practical achievements of the latter were the result of a natural endowment that other racial groups did not share?

Furthermore, Delany was not particularly disturbed by so-called miscegenation. He did not suggest that interracial reproduction compromises or retards the "black essence." Nor did he view "race-mixing" as a practice that has negative biological consequences, either for the "mixed-bloods" or for the so-called pure races.[56] *Blake* portrays many multiracial persons as heroic and as leaders; and in *The Condition,* Delany lists with pride the many accomplishments of blacks with varying degrees of black ancestry. Indeed, his wife, Catherine Richards Delany, was biracial, daughter of a black father and white mother.[57]

Some would argue that Delany must have been a committed racialist, because he spoke with such pride about the achievements of "pure" blacks.[58] Against this objection, I maintain that his praise for "unmixed blackness" was just a rebuttal to whites who charged that whenever blacks do achieve anything of note, this success is due to their possession of some "white blood."[59] Also in this regard, he maintained that the subordinate status of mixed-race persons depends, both logically and causally, on the stigma attached to "pure" blackness.[60] This point is driven home dramatically in *Blake,* where in the context of a secret meeting among slaves and their free colored allies, arranged for purposes of discussing a general slave insurrection in Cuba, a woman objects to the emphasis being placed on obtaining equality for those of African descent with "unmixed blood." A biracial hero of the novel, Placido,[61] offers the following reply:

The whites assert the natural inferiority of the African as a race: upon this they premise their objections, not only to the blacks, but all who have any affinity with them. You see this position taken by the high Court of America [in the *Dred Scott* decision], which declares that persons having African blood in their veins have no rights that white men are bound to respect. Now how are the mixed bloods ever to rise? The thing is plain; it requires no explanation. The instant that an equality of the blacks with the whites is admitted, we being the descendants of the two, must be acknowledged the equals of both. Is not this clear?[62]

Thus, Delany's commitment to racialism was, at most, half-hearted, invoked merely to lend credence to his claims of black national distinctiveness and to link modern blacks to their symbolic ancient progenitors. But this romantic racialism is wholly unpersuasive, and, in any case, he made no serious attempt to defend it. Yet, as Delany was certainly aware, a merely skin-deep conception of race is a rather superficial basis for black identity, hardly an inspiring foundation for black national consciousness and a new independent republic. So, again, what is the significance of black identity for black politics? Ultimately, for Delany, the political importance of black identity had to do with the peculiar character of racial subjection as a form of oppression.

According to Delany, the ruling class of America wanted a subservient class to do its drudgery, a group too powerless to successfully resist being enslaved.[63] Such a group would be even more easily exploited if they were to share some distinguishing physical mark, because the dominant group would then have a basis for differential sympathy, preferring those who lack the mark to those who have it. And this exploitative relationship would be firmly secured and buttressed if the dominant group were able to successfully spread an ideology of inherent inferiority based on the saliency of this mark, for this would reduce the sympathy of powerful outsiders who might intervene on behalf of the oppressed. Thus, after the genocide of indigenous peoples in the attempt to make them slaves and to strip them of their land, Africans were selected for this servile role. Delany contended that Africans were not initially chosen because whites hated African peoples or those with dark skin, or because blacks were regarded as inferior in some way. Rather, they were selected for purely pragmatic reasons: to increase com-

mercial profit and leisure time for a nascent, slaveholding elite. It is
in this way that dark skin and other paradigmatic "black"
phenotypic traits came to have immense social significance. Such
somatic characteristics became a physical sign of degradation, a
symbol of inferior social status.

Delany maintained that once this implicit association of dark
skin with low status had been established, there was virtually nothing blacks could do (short of extensive race-mixing or passing for
white) to elevate themselves to social equality.[64] Advancing an argument made famous by Alexis de Tocqueville, Delany insisted that
even the abolition of slavery would not end black oppression or racial antagonism, because the stigma of forced servitude would have
become attached to their easily observable "distinguishing mark."[65]
Thus, the skin color of blacks would remind whites, and also blacks,
of their former slave status, causing many whites to have contempt
for blacks and some blacks to have self-contempt.

Delany initially thought that this association of skin color with
forced servitude might be broken if blacks were to rise to positions
of honor and status within the United States. For this reason, he
implored blacks to avoid taking on menial labor and service roles,
an injunction that some commentators have wrongly reduced to a
form of conservative elitism.[66] However, Delany was not critical of
blacks who were forced to take such positions out of material necessity; he simply insisted that no self-respecting person would do
so, as some did, just to buy ostentatious clothes and modern conveniences. Indeed, he argued that when an *individual* performs the
role of servant, this is not necessarily degrading at all, but when a
disproportionate number from a recognizable social group do, they
inevitably come to be viewed as a "naturally" subservient people.[67]

Yet Delany became convinced that blacks could not erase the
stigma attached to their color while remaining in the United States
and thus urged them to emigrate elsewhere. He mounted a powerful case, on purely pragmatic nationalist grounds, in support of this

radical conclusion. The Fugitive Slave Law of 1850 effectively denied equal citizenship to even "free" blacks, a denial that was later solidified and made explicit in the *Dred Scott* decision (1857).[68] He maintained that whites could not be rationally or morally persuaded out of their prejudice because they had a material stake in black subordination and too little sympathy for what they considered a degraded race.[69] Blacks, even if well organized, could not compel whites to treat them as equals, because whites greatly outnumbered them and had significantly more power.[70] Blacks could not achieve economic parity with whites while living among them, since whites all but monopolized land, capital, and political power.[71] Living under such oppressive conditions also fosters servility and resignation among the oppressed.[72] Thus, if blacks were to remain in the United States, they not only would be sacrificing their right to equal respect, democratic citizenship, and self-government, but also would be foregoing the cultivation and expression of a vigorous character, which no group can do and retain its dignity. And even if blacks were to gain *legal* equality with whites in the States, the antiblack attitudes of whites, along with their overwhelming power and sheer numbers, would make it quite difficult, if not impossible, for blacks to fully exercise their civil rights.[73]

Delany concluded, therefore, that blacks had to leave the United States. Notice, though, that emigration was thought to be necessary, not because Africa is the "fatherland" to which blacks must return to reclaim and develop their original identity, but because blacks needed to go where they could realize the principles of equality, democratic citizenship, and self-government and cultivate the traits of a vigorous character. In fact, Delany did not even advocate mass black emigration to Africa. Rather, he urged the vast majority of blacks to remain in the New World. He stated repeatedly that the Western Hemisphere was the "home" of blacks, and that they were fully entitled to remain there.[74] And in response to William Lloyd Garrison's critique of his racial separatism, Delany said, "I would as willingly live among white men as black, if I had an *equal possession and enjoyment* of privileges," but, he explains, "I have no hopes in this country—no confidence in the American people—with a *few* excellent exceptions."[75] His principled position, then, was that blacks should live wherever they do not infringe upon the rights of others; self-government and citizenship on terms of social equality is possible; and a vigorous character can be developed and freely expressed.[76] Thus, he suggested, somewhat surprisingly perhaps, that blacks emigrate from the United States to Central and South America, for these locations had all the resources needed for building a democratic and free nation.[77]

Delany strongly encouraged blacks to cultivate solidarity with American Indians and Latin American peoples. This suggests that his primary concern was with undermining or avoiding white domination, not with creating an exclusive black national polity. He believed that there was no legally sanctioned race prejudice in Latin America, except in Brazil; and that the peoples of those countries were ready and eager to receive U.S. blacks. Delany was particularly concerned to combat U.S. and European imperialism, and thus he urged all "colored" peoples to work together in an effort to defend themselves against white domination. He even hoped blacks and other people of color would eventually create a United States of South America.[78]

It is important to see that this new self-reliant and sovereign people could not be held together by their common racial identity, as they would be a racially heterogeneous and hybrid population. Nor would this be a country committed to black cultural nationalism, as some have suggested.[79] Instead, Delany advocated cultural syncretism among the new population, strongly urged blacks to become bilingual by learning Spanish, and evinced firm support for religious tolerance and nonsectarianism.[80] This would not, therefore, be a nation built on the edifice of "original identity." Rather, "practical necessity"—self-preservation and common defense—

would be the social bonding agent among this newly emerging, anti-imperialist, "colored" people.[81] Most importantly, this multiracial "nation" would be committed to social equality, democratic citizenship for all, self-government, and the cultivation of a vigorous citizenry.[82]

Still, the following challenge is appropriate: If Delany was really a pragmatic black nationalist, what then are we to make of his project of regenerating Africa? That is, how can this seemingly romantic program be understood without relying on classical nationalist principles? Actually, Delany viewed this project as primarily a strategy to combat domination, one that had the admittedly ambitious goal of undermining white supremacist ideology, the African slave trade, and Euro-American imperialism. Here he provided an argument that is analogous to the one he offered in defense of the emphasis on the achievements of so-called pure blacks. He suggested that if Africa remained underdeveloped and associated with slavery, this would contribute to the stigma attached to all black peoples, wherever they happened to live. In addition to their dark color, the fact that blacks are of African descent would be a "sign" of their degradation so long as Africa is viewed as a place where primitive, savage, and dependent peoples reside. Thus, he believed Africa's redemption and modernization must be a part of any general effort to bring about racial equality and true freedom for those of African descent.[83]

But again, in advocating the development of Africa, Delany did not suggest that all or even most African Americans should settle there, but only a select few. He also insisted that the fact that black Americans will not relocate to Africa is no more a sign of disrespect for their original homeland than is the fact that many whites consider America their home a sign of disrespect for their European origins.[84] Moreover, Delany did not recommend a nostalgic return to African ways of old. Rather, he suggested that Africans retain what is good in contemporary Africa and try to improve upon it, that they incorporate what is valuable in the civilizations of other races, and that they reject whatever is inimical to modern progress, regardless of its national roots.[85]

It is often claimed that Delany either was inconsistent or changed his mind about Africa as the ultimate destination for black Americans.[86] But though he regarded it as perfectly permissible for any black to emigrate who desired to do so, Delany never advocated a general return of African Americans to Africa but just the return of a select number of the "enlightened freedmen" from the United States in the hope that they might help in the regeneration of their ancestral homeland. This position is not inconsistent with holding that the vast majority of American blacks should relocate to Latin America or wherever they might best flourish. In a supplement to the "Constitution of the African Civilization Society" (1861), which was written by Delany, this view was made quite clear: "The Society is not designed to encourage general emigration, but will aid only such persons as may be practically qualified and suited to promote the development of Christianity, morality, education, mechanical arts, agriculture, commerce, and general improvement; who must always be carefully selected and well recommended, that the progress of civilization may not be obstructed."[87]

Delany did not, however, view the regeneration of Africa as simply a means to improve the condition of blacks living in the New World. This is clear from the fact that he implored all civilized nations, not just black ones, to help in Africa's modernization.[88] This prescription, which he claimed was a "duty," could hardly have been expected to motivate nonblacks to action if it were merely based on racial loyalty or the need to improve the position of blacks in the diaspora. Instead, it must have been premised on common humanity, social justice, and perhaps mutual economic advantage. Hence, the program for Africa's redemption was, for Delany, a cause worthy of universal endorsement quite apart from its advantages for black Americans.

Toward a Post-Ethnoracial Republic

I have urged that we read Delany as a pragmatic nationalist who sometimes misleadingly expressed himself as if he were a committed classical one. The primary justification for this somewhat nonstandard interpretation is that it makes the best sense of his various seemingly inconsistent statements. Yet perhaps the clearest evidence in support of the claim that Delany was really a pragmatic nationalist is that after the Civil War he ceased to advocate mass black emigration and instead worked for "a union of the two races" in the United States, especially in the South.[89] If we read him as a pragmatic nationalist, then this change is perfectly consistent with his fundamental political and moral principles. Black political solidarity and group separatism were never ends in themselves but merely strategies for realizing his most cherished values—social equality, democratic citizenship, self-government, and "manhood." These goals seemed to him more achievable within the United States after the war, as of course they did to most blacks at the time. Indeed, during the early years of Reconstruction, his optimism was surely warranted—though in retrospect it clearly was not.[90] In less than a decade, slavery was abolished by constitutional amendment (1865), blacks born in the United States were declared citizens and constitutionally guaranteed equal protection under the law (1868), and black men were granted the franchise (1870). During Reconstruction, many blacks held public office, even as high as the U.S. Senate. Delany himself became the first black commissioned field officer in the U.S. Army, served as an administrator for the Freedmen's Bureau, and later ran, though unsuccessfully, for lieutenant governor of South Carolina. Under these improving conditions for blacks, it is not surprising that he would have abandoned his program for black emigration.

Indeed, Delany came to take up what some might consider rather conservative and possibly even elitist political positions.[91]

For example, instead of pushing for the confiscation of former slaveholders' land for redistribution to freedmen, he advocated a "triple alliance" of northern capital, southern planters' land, and black labor, a profit-sharing scheme that would have left the means of production largely in white hands and would have greatly favored the interests of capitalists over workers.[92] He lectured on the virtues of temperance, marriage, and hard work. And he pledged his support for the Democrats over the Republicans in the 1876 national and state elections, a decision that many blacks at the time considered a tragic betrayal. However, although he abandoned a radical approach to black politics, we should not conclude that Delany had thereby rejected pragmatic nationalism, because it was quite clear to him that much work remained to be done in the cause for racial equality and that, in the meantime, blacks still needed the self-protection provided by their political solidarity: "When my race were in bondage I did not hesitate in using my judgment in aiding to free them. Now that they are free I shall not hesitate in using that judgment in aiding to preserve that freedom and promote their happiness. What I did and desired for my race, I desire and would do if duty required for any other race. The exercise of all their rights, unimpaired and unobstructed, is that desire."[93]

Yet Delany's political thought not only is intrinsically interesting and neglected by students of political philosophy, but also can help us better appreciate the need to rethink the foundations of contemporary black solidarity. Indeed, an examination of his thought might even aid us in developing a more suitable black nationalist philosophy for the post-segregation era. Within much of current black political thinking there is still a tendency to vacillate between, and at times to conflate, classical and pragmatic forms of black nationalism. This is understandable. No subordinate group wants to think of itself as merely reacting to or naively accepting the dictates and ideology of the dominant group. Instead, it quite naturally wants to express self-directed agency, to forge its own path, against the grain if necessary.

Ironically, as Frederick Douglass observed, classical black nationalism, rather than exposing the more dangerous elements in the nationalist ideologies of the United States and Europe, further buttresses them by reproducing them in a black-inflected form.[94] Yet, true vigor should go beyond this uncritical and superficial emulation. As Delany urged, a vigorous character should dispose one to be courageous, determined, and creative in pursuit of the highest ideals. This may require rethinking and even discarding many of the beliefs, values, and practices that have been inherited from previous generations of blacks and the broader society and world. Such a reflexive stance is surely a sign of independent thinking and self-respect. Moreover, this creative reevaluation ought not be limited to the expression of individuality but should also extend to the political realm, at least where matters of social justice are at stake. Thus, while pragmatic nationalism inevitably draws on Western nationalist ideas, it should do so with a critical eye and an improvisational spirit, joined with a healthy suspicion of politicized ethnoracial identities and a steadfast commitment to justice for all.

Adapting a distinction from Tocqueville, I urge that we abandon the "spontaneous solidarity" that is characteristic of classical forms of nationalism in favor of the reflective solidarity of a well-considered pragmatic nationalism. Tocqueville thought of spontaneous nationalist sentiment as a form of "instinctive patriotism," which he described this way:

There is a patriotism which mainly springs from the disinterested, undefinable, and unpondered feeling that ties a man's heart to the place where he was born. This instinctive love is mingled with a taste for old habits, respect for ancestors, and memories of the past; those who feel it love their country as

one loves one's father's house. They love the peace they enjoy
there; they are attached to the quiet habits they have formed;
they are attached to the memories it recalls; and they even
find a certain attraction in living there in obedience. This
same patriotism is often also exalted by religious zeal, and
then it works wonders. It is itself a sort of religion; it does not
reason, but believes, feels, and acts.[95]

Perhaps Delany was drawn to the undeniable magic of instinctive patriotism, hoping to exploit it for purposes of motivating
blacks to collective action. Perhaps, too, this romantic racial patriotism was useful in helping to bring down the regime of slavery and,
later, Jim Crow. Yet I contend that African Americans no longer
need to, nor should they, depend on charismatic leadership and
demagogic emotional appeals to move them to action, and that
their basic political principles can and ought to be embraced with
transparency and on the basis of rationally motivated consensus.
An enlightened pragmatic nationalism that eschews the classical
form is, perhaps, less inspiring, altruistic, and passionate. But it is a
more appropriate outlook for a people engaged in protracted struggle for freedom and equality in the United States today. Accordingly, rather than continue the ambivalent attachment to classical
nationalism—with its emphasis on inherent racial characteristics,
primordial ethnic origins, cultural purity and distinctiveness, an
ancient "homeland," and territorial sovereignty—blacks should
abandon this misleading discourse altogether, notwithstanding its
obvious evocative and symbolic resonance.

Contrary to what some critics have supposed, forsaking this ideology would not necessarily mean giving up black solidarity. Indeed, what holds blacks together as a unified people with shared
political interests is the fact of their racial subordination and their
collective resolve to triumph over it. The "racial" blackness of
blacks, then, while in one sense only skin-deep—constituted as it is

by relatively superficial phenotypic traits—has tremendous social importance, as these somatic traits carry the stigma of subordinate social standing. Yet blacks need not cherish or valorize this peculiar ascribed identity in order to see that it makes them all vulnerable to various forms of mistreatment. Building on this recognition and their shared goal to break down all unnecessary barriers to social equality, this culturally diverse, intergenerational, and geographically dispersed community can firmly and consistently embrace pragmatic black nationalism. This philosophy would treat black solidarity as a strategy for bringing about substantive racial equality and, in the meantime, as a means of collective self-defense against racial oppression. Pragmatic nationalism is therefore in principle compatible with interracial cooperation. Indeed, it is perfectly consistent with the goal of bringing about a world where "racial" identities—hegemonic or oppositional—are no longer thought useful or appealing, even to those who have historically been most disadvantaged by racism. It should be viewed as just one among a number of possibly effective programs for ending, or at least surviving, racial injustice.

What Pragmatic Nationalism Is Not

I want to briefly contrast my vision for a progressive black politics with two similar accounts—Black Atlantic cultural politics and strategic essentialism. Gilroy has also recently examined Delany's nationalism, and my analysis is, in some ways at least, quite compatible with his and owes much to his creative engagement with Delany's philosophy.[96] Yet my approach differs in its basic aims, theoretical focus, and argumentative strategy. Gilroy is primarily concerned with critiquing ethnocentric and nationalist conceptions of black cultural production and replacing them with a conception of "Black Atlantic" modes of cultural expression, which are transnational, dynamic, and thoroughly hybrid. He is against a "narrow" focus on national cultural politics in our increasingly global world, where migration and ethnoracial intermixing are commonplace. For him, Delany functions largely as a metaphor for the rootlessness and syncretic character of all diasporic black cultures. He therefore uses Delany's life and thought to illustrate the alleged ambivalence of diasporic blacks toward the West, their would-be "new home," and toward Africa, their original "homeland."

By contrast, the thin conception of blackness that I defend as the proper basis for black solidarity and to which I think Delany was ultimately committed is not a mode of *cultural* blackness at all, at least not if we are talking about *expressive* culture—such as art, language, style, social custom, ritual, or religion—as opposed to *political* culture, the values and practices that are directly concerned with the legitimate use of social power, especially state power. Delany's "ambivalence" did not concern "ethnic roots" but the seemingly ever-changing prospects for realizing black equality, freedom, civil rights, and "manly" virtue in this or that geographical locale. Although the context and details of Delany's life give us insight into his social philosophy, my primary concern is with the contours and plausibility of his *thought,* taking care to avoid the all too common tendency to flatten out the thinking of black writers by reducing their ideas to their sociohistorical context or class position. While Gilroy is largely concerned to show how nationalist thinking negatively affects black cultural production, I am primarily concerned with how such thinking (negatively and positively) affects black political solidarity, especially as this relates to an antiracist progressive agenda. And ultimately I am interested, as I think Delany was, in so-called narrow American politics, even as I recognize its interconnections with geopolitics. For although the political significance of the modern nation-state may be dramatically changing in this era of intensive globalization, I am cautious about rashly concluding that internal contestation over the organization and actions of nation-states is no longer politically important to social justice. Nor do I think that black collective activism directed toward the

U.S. government on behalf of its black citizens necessarily demonstrates a lack of concern for others who are racially or otherwise oppressed.

Note also that pragmatic black nationalism, as a public philosophy for the black liberation struggle, is not a form of "strategic essentialism," at least not in the sense in which the latter is usually understood—that is, within a post-structuralist theoretical framework.[97] For one thing, pragmatic black nationalism is not skeptical about our ability to understand empirically the structure and dynamics of modern racism. Nor is it hesitant to embrace certain moral principles as universally applicable. Indeed, it presupposes that such understanding of, and principled ethical opposition to, the current racial order is absolutely necessary for the very coherence of the outlook. Pragmatic black nationalism openly rejects racial and ethnic "essences" and has no need to deploy them, strategically or otherwise, in order to carry out its emancipatory aims. It does not require idealizing fictions about race, nationality, or primordial origins, but simply recognition that antiblack racism unjustly circumscribes the freedom and opportunities of millions in the United States and around the globe. Pragmatic black political consciousness, while certainly self-consciously strategic and aimed at transforming the oppressive conditions that make it necessary, does not ultimately seek the destruction of all black identities, just those that are stigmatizing, rigid, and reactionary. In this way it is not "necessarily self-alienating." But at the same time, pragmatic black solidarity does not require those who are racialized as black to embrace blackness, of any ethnoracial genre, as a valued or necessary component of the "self" at all.

2

Class, Poverty, and Shame

Perhaps no one has thought longer and more systematically about the philosophical foundations of black political solidarity than W. E. B. Du Bois, one of the principal architects of the modern civil rights paradigm for black political action and a co-founder of America's oldest civil rights organization, the National Association for the Advancement of Colored People (NAACP). Since his death, blacks have formally secured equal citizenship rights through federal statutes that outlaw racial discrimination in education, voting, employment, housing, lending, and public accommodations. The federal government has also instituted programs designed to improve the socioeconomic condition of black citizens (such as affirmative action and minority set-aside programs), helping to create a relatively large black middle class.

However, significant racial inequality remains—for example, in average household income, wealth, home ownership, employment opportunities, and access to quality health care. Racial discrimination within the housing and employment markets is still entirely too commonplace. Popular support for civil rights laws appears to be weakening, and the institutional mechanisms for the enforcement of these laws are often underfunded and inadequately administered. De facto racial segregation in urban settings continues, with grave consequences for employment and educational opportunity for those living in inner-city communities. Racial profiling and police brutality are still menacing forces, especially for African American youth, and the mass incarceration of young black men and women has reached crisis proportions. Thus, despite their undeniable progress in some arenas, African Americans are still seeking to realize fully the freedom, equality, and prosperity that American ideals promise.

Many now contend that the model of black politics that Du Bois advocated is no longer adequate for addressing the problems that blacks face and therefore that it has become necessary to reassess the tradition of public protest and racial solidarity for the contemporary context. Such reexamination, we must admit, is certainly needed. Yet even after careful scrutiny, we would find that there is much to be learned from the paradigm of political engagement that Du Bois articulated several decades ago, lessons that are pertinent to the post–civil rights era.

In particular, we can benefit from a reconsideration of Du Bois's analysis of the challenge that class differences among African Americans pose for progressive black politics. But in order to properly appreciate his approach to this long-standing race/class conundrum, we need to understand how he conceptualized black political solidarity. I begin by outlining Du Bois's most basic political ideals. I then offer a general conception of group solidarity, and using this framework, I explain Du Bois's account of the requirements of a specifically "black" solidarity. Next I briefly recount his changing views on the role of elites in advancing black interests, focusing on the qualifications and responsibilities of black leaders. With this background, I then take up two vexing problems of class and consider Du Bois's solutions.

Du Boisian Ideals

Throughout his long life, Du Bois devoted most of his intellectual and political energies to solving the so-called Negro problem in America. Indeed, his best-known work is a complex and stirring meditation on this old and still contentious issue. *The Souls of Black Folk* (1903) describes, explains, and dramatizes how slavery, segregation, and racism had combined to create a stigmatized and underdeveloped caste in America.[1] According to Du Bois, white domination engendered a social group in America that suffered from severe self-alienation. Despite the abolition of slavery and the Reconstruction Amendments, blacks were still incapable of developing an independent collective identity and were limited to viewing themselves through the eyes of their white oppressors. The truncated and inauthentic consciousness that they did possess was suffused with feelings of inferiority and self-doubt, internalized through racist propaganda, material deprivation, and violent repression. Even worse, whites refused to accept blacks as fellow citizens, thus denying them a common American national identity. One of Du Bois's most fundamental political aims, then, was to end racism and caste distinctions, to erase the "color line" that serves to subordinate and humiliate those of darker hue, especially those of African descent. He also sought to explain how the black divided self—part American and part African—could be properly integrated into a "better and truer self" but without the loss of either, a goal he believed blacks were both explicitly and implicitly striving to attain.[2]

The "veil," his famous metaphor for the vicissitudes of racial oppression, created other obstacles to black group advancement. Du Bois believed that blacks must embrace and aggressively pursue independent collective development, but that a history of black subjugation had retarded their best efforts. In particular, the efforts of more educationally advantaged blacks to attain their "two warring ideals"—attempting both to be unqualified Americans and to foster independent black development—have had the unintended consequence of slowing the progress of black people toward modernization. It would seem that the pursuit of these seemingly incompatible ideals in a context of severe racial oppression was often self-defeating, producing the misleading appearance that black ability is limited and inferior, perhaps inherently. Many black elites who take up both ideals therefore become discouraged and disillusioned, and some, having lost faith in black ability, fail to have the appropriate pride in their people. But despite these obstacles and pitfalls, Du Bois insisted that blacks must both seek to acquire full and equal American citizenship, with all the rights and responsibilities that this entails, and work together to foster independent black development in the spheres of education, morals, culture, politics, and economics.

To accomplish this double task, he believed, blacks must have equal educational opportunity according to ability and ambition.[3] That is, those with similar endowment and motivation should have equal prospects for educational attainment, regardless of their race. Such education must not be limited to industrial and vocational training, but must also include, crucially, a liberal arts education in a college or university. Quality higher education in the arts and sciences, Du Bois maintained, is needed to combat widespread black ignorance of the world and life, to produce a qualified crop of teachers for black youth, and to provide the black intelligentsia with the tools necessary for analyzing the condition of their people. But more than this, such education allows time for critical self-examination, such self-scrutiny being an essential starting point for the development of true self-consciousness and the basis for overcoming black self-estrangement.

The key to self-realization, according to Du Bois, is self-determination in accordance with a distinctive ideal. He believed that this ideal is implicit in the very nature of black people, a component of their spiritual being, which blacks need only discover through study and critical introspection: "He [the educated Negro] began to have a dim feeling that, to attain his place in the world, he must be himself, and not another."[4] Thus, when the educated black person begins to "see" (in that revelatory sense of the word), he sees "himself"; and consequently the implicit injunction he discovers is that "he must be himself." Du Bois here exhibits a commitment to so-called positive liberty, a conception of freedom in which self-realization necessarily involves authenticity or a reaffirmation of one's "true" or "higher" self. For black Americans, this means developing and articulating their distinctive message, one both cultural and political.

Du Bois advocated a moderate form of black cultural nationalism, or what some have called "cultural pluralism."[5] In "The Conservation of Races" (1897) Du Bois maintained that each great race has its own distinctive message to give to civilization. But the black race had not yet given its full message to the world. The distinctive ideals of each race must be realized, not by individuals acting alone, but by the development of these race groups *qua* races: "If in America it is to be proven for the first time in the modern world that not only Negroes are capable of evolving individual men like Toussaint, the Saviour, but are a *nation* stored with wonderful possibilities of culture, then their destiny is not a servile imitation of Anglo-Saxon culture, but a stalwart originality which shall unswervingly follow Negro ideals."[6] The maintenance of black cultural distinctiveness in the United States, he insisted, is not incompatible with a multiracial polity. Racial conflict is inevitable where group differences are reflected in territory, laws, language, religion, and economic prosperity. But where there is substantial agreement in these, there is no reason why different "racial ideals" should not be able to develop and flourish in the same country. This position is reiterated in *The Souls of Black Folk,* where he suggests that blacks have a deep desire to "merge" their double selves: "In this merging he [the Negro] wishes neither of the older selves to be lost. He would not Africanize America, for America has too much to teach the world and Africa. He would not bleach his Negro soul in a flood of white Americanism, for he knows that Negro blood has a message for the world. He simply wishes to make it possible for a man to be both a Negro and an American, without being cursed and spit upon by his fellows, without having the doors of Opportunity closed roughly in his face."[7]

Later in life, despite his turn toward Marxism, Du Bois continued to advocate cultural nationalist ideals. In "The Talented Tenth: Memorial Address" (1948), after favorably comparing African Americans to the peoples of several countries—Czechoslovakia, Saudi Arabia, Ethiopia, Portugal, and others—he says to the Negro in America: "A *nation* of such size, such history, such accomplishment, should be able to look forward to something more than complete effacement and utter absorption in another and foreign entity. It should have legitimate dreams of continuity, unity, and immortality."[8] Indeed, in this essay, he invoked, as he had done before in "The Conservation of Races," a specifically cultural conception of race: "This group was not simply a physical entity: a black people, or a people descended from black folk. It was, what all races really are, a cultural group."[9]

Du Bois's political vision for the American Republic was one in which all citizens participate in collective self-governance through the exercise of equal voting rights.[10] He argued that it is not possible for blacks to advance economically without political rights and equal civic status, for these legal protections are needed to defend their possession of property and to ensure their access to employment. Moreover—and this is reminiscent of Delany's emphasis on "manly" virtue—self-respect is incompatible with silent submission to racism and civic inferiority. Living under such oppressive conditions without protesting against them would damage the character of black people in the long run, depriving them of much-needed moral vigor. Du Bois maintained furthermore that equal citizenship should not require cultural assimilation. Hence, both equal civic status and black cultural preservation are needed if blacks are to progress while maintaining their self-respect.

Du Bois also believed that economic development must be a component of any black politics. However, his views on economic justice shifted throughout his life, from merely advocating equal economic opportunity within a market society, to demanding a liberal capitalist welfare state, to urging state control over production and distribution in the interest of the common good, and finally to embracing economic democracy within a classless society in accordance with the Communist ideal.[11] Despite these changes in his economic philosophy, he consistently rejected laissez-faire ideology, crass materialism, and conspicuous consumption. He also urged blacks to eschew the single-minded pursuit of profit and wealth and instead to take creative measures to meet their material needs—for example, by forming consumer cooperatives.

Du Bois claimed that with shifts in historical circumstances, black ideals have appropriately changed—from abolishing slavery, then to acquiring political power through universal suffrage, next to gaining education commensurate with ability and ambition, and finally to establishing equal economic opportunity and ending poverty. Taken singly, none of these ideals is sufficient. Blacks need all of these if they are to achieve self-realization. The key to this, he maintained, is to unify these ideals into one coherent political philosophy. Moreover, blacks must carry out this program through racial solidarity and group self-determination. Ultimately, however, the goal is "human brotherhood" and a common civic identity in the United States. Thus Du Bois held that his racial solidarity politics is compatible with the best ideals of the American Republic. It does not advocate interracial conflict or contempt for other races. On the contrary, he claimed that black solidarity would one day make it possible for the members of all races, living together in one society, to complement each other rather than be antagonists. In fact, blacks had already made contributions to this end by providing America with many of its most distinctive cultural elements—its music, folklore, and spiritual expression.

Du Bois saw black political solidarity, then, as a temporary though possibly long-term strategy for realizing a multiracial American polity that embodies democratic ideals and cultural pluralism. Thus, I would suggest that we think of Du Bois as a classical nationalist about culture—as an advocate of black cultural integrity as an end in itself—but as a pragmatic nationalist about politics. According to Du Bois, the resolution of the "Negro problem" is necessary if the underlying political principles of the United States are to be more than mere rhetoric. The "spiritual strivings" of black folk include an incredible though inescapable burden on the descendants of black slaves, as it is their responsibility to lead the way in this unfinished collective project, not only in the name of the black race but also in the name of America and humanity. Du Bois, articulating his vision in the idiom of the prophetic tradition, viewed the world-historical mission of African Americans to be the perfecting of the ideals of America democracy.[12] Only by carrying out this task could they reconcile and unify their dual strivings and thus attain true self-consciousness.

Norms of Group Solidarity

To enhance our appreciation of the strengths and weaknesses of Du Bois's vision, I want to offer a general conception of group solidarity, to identify just what kind of "unity" is at issue. This analytical specification is not meant to depart from common sense; I take these characteristics to be intuitive, familiar, and relatively uncontroversial. Although I have drawn on empirical work in social psychology to construct my account, my aim is not to *explain* group solidarity as a sociopsychological phenomenon.[13] Rather, I want to offer a philosophical reconstruction of the norms that constitute it.

Solidarity is certainly a type of feeling or sentiment. Yet it is a feeling that entails normative constraints. It is because I feel solidarity with group X that I *ought* to do this or that for or on behalf of fellow members of group X. I believe there are five core normative requirements that are jointly sufficient for a robust form of solidarity. By "robust" I mean a solidarity that is strong enough to move people to collective action, not just mutual sympathy born of recognition of commonality or a mere sense of group belonging.

Identification with the group. One of the most salient characteristics of group solidarity is the tendency of group members to identify, both subjectively and publicly, with each other or with the group as a whole. Because of what they have (or believe themselves to have) in common, members regard themselves as sharing a special bond. In virtue of this bond, fellow members are treated as if they were an extension of the self, so that one feels pride when a member of the group does something praiseworthy or shame when a fellow member does something embarrassing, almost as if one had done the deed oneself. It is mutual identification that accounts for, or rather constitutes, that familiar sense of "we-ness" that is so characteristic of solidarity groups. Mutual identification can have a variety of bases. It can, for example, be based on a shared ethnic or cultural heritage (whether real or imagined). But its basis may also be the fact that group members believe themselves to share a similar plight or some significant, perhaps life-shaping, experience. Such commonality often engenders mutual empathetic understanding.

Special concern. The relevant kind of mutual understanding is not, however, merely a matter of sympathy, which may be nothing more than an involuntary reaction to the plight of others, an emotional state that need not include a disposition to come to the aid of those with whom one sympathizes. Rather, solidarity requires special concern, in particular a disposition to assist and comfort those with whom one identifies. Yet this concern is not a matter of fulfilling one's impartial moral duty to help anyone in need but is the expression of particularistic identification. This special concern is a form of partiality, in that it is limited to those within the group. But it is not necessarily incompatible with a sense of moral duty to those outside the group. As Jorge Garcia points out, I may feel closer to the members of my group than I do to those outside it without feeling hatred or callousness toward the latter. I may give the members of my group more than they have a moral claim to get from me and more than I offer others, while nevertheless giving these others everything to which they are morally entitled and perhaps even more.[14] Thus, others get fully what is owed to them morally, but those in the solidarity group receive more than what morality strictly requires.

Shared values or goals. Members of a solidarity group also share a set of values or goals, and each knows, or at least confidently believes, that fellow group members are committed to these. The values or goals might take the form of more or less vague ideals, specific policies, practical principles, broad social programs, political ideologies, or utopian social visions. Such common values and goals often (at least partially) define the group, constituting a central component of its distinctive self-conception.

Loyalty. One of the most important yet controversial components of solidarity is group loyalty. This entails faithfulness to the group's values, principles, and ideals, and a willingness to exert extra effort to help members of the group and to advance the group's interests. Moreover, group loyalty is always at least somewhat exclusionary and is often defined in opposition to some other group(s). In other words, it involves an "Us" and a "Them"—an *in-group* and an *out-group*. Members of a solidarity group show loyalty to in-group members as opposed to those of the relevant out-group, whose interests, goals, or values may differ from or conflict with those of the in-group. Though it does require that one be willing to resist threats to one's group created by its enemies, the partiality that loyalty engenders need not be adversarial. Peaceful coexistence, even coalition, between different solidarity groups is often possible.

Mutual trust. Group solidarity also requires that members trust one another to some significant degree, for mutual trust is the foundation of meaningful cooperation and collective action. Because loyalty can make one vulnerable to exploitation, it is necessary that this trust be well founded, so that group members have some measure of security. Each must have reason to believe that the others will not let him down, betray the values of the group, or free ride on the sacrifices of his fellows. Mutual trust enables members to act collectively to achieve group goals, especially when the obstacles to be overcome are daunting and success is uncertain.

Many different types of groups may exhibit solidarity. Among the most familiar are families, nations, workers, ethnic groups, religious organizations, political parties, police officers, street gangs, military personnel, and organized crime syndicates. Rather than illustrate the components of solidarity by focusing on one of these quite complicated (and, with some, quite problematic) forms of solidarity, a simpler and more suitably paradigmatic case is the solidarity that is sometimes displayed between members of a sport team. Players on, say, a basketball team often identify with each other. They think in terms of "we" instead of "I." When the team wins a game, all rejoice in victory, and when it loses, everyone suffers "the agony of defeat," no matter how much or how little each may have contributed to the win or loss. The members of a sport team that has solidarity will show special concern toward one another, so that when a member has been injured or is not doing well otherwise, other members will offer comfort and support, even when this has no direct bearing on the team's collective goals. Such sport teams will, however, also be jointly committed to a set of values or goals. For example, they may be committed to fair play and sportsmanship, a particular style of play, or a win-at-all-costs philosophy. Team solidarity also requires that each be loyal to the group's values and to teammates. Members of the team will work hard during practice sessions, stick to the game plan, put aside individual goals that would conflict with the good of the team, expend as much effort as is necessary for the team to win, and so on—giving the clichéd "110 percent." Finally, players must trust one another, especially if they are to be successful. Each must feel confident that teammates will perform their designated roles on the team; and each must know that if he or she makes an honest mistake that costs the team a game, teammates will offer words of encouragement rather than berate and blame him or her. Such trust is often built by mutual displays of individual loyalty to the team or by repeatedly struggling together against formidable opponents.

To summarize: Robust group solidarity exists whenever a set of individuals identify with each other as members of a group, show special concern toward one another, are jointly committed to certain values or goals, are loyal to the group and its ideals, and trust each other. Thus, black solidarity would be robust if blacks, as a group, were to exhibit each of these five characteristics.

Solidarity and Self-Help

To avoid misunderstanding, it is necessary to distinguish the idea of black solidarity from the philosophy of racial self-help. We might say that the five normative features of robust solidarity constitute the *form* of black solidarity. These features must all be present for robust black unity to exist, which is not to say that the degree of its robustness, its relative strength, cannot vary. The *content* of black solidarity is defined by the specific values or goals that blacks embrace as members of a solidarity group. Exactly which values or goals blacks jointly commit themselves to, and thus the precise content of black solidarity, will vary with the historical conditions and sociopolitical context.

The philosophy of self-help, on the other hand, is one way of giving content to black solidarity. Segments of the black population have advocated this philosophy at various points in American history, including the present. Interestingly, self-help does not belong exclusively to any particular political ideology. Conservatives, liberals, radical democrats, and classical nationalists have defended it. Du Bois's political rival Booker T. Washington (1856–1915) is perhaps the most influential exponent of racial self-help in the history of black political thought. Washington's program for black uplift included four main components.

First, he advocated agricultural and industrial education as preparation for entering the workforce and undertaking entrepreneurial enterprises.[15] He argued that such education would create self-reliant individuals. Economic independence was paramount for Washington, as the foundation of many things that are valuable in life. He thought higher education in the liberal arts should be subordinated to training in a useful trade or profession, and often criticized blacks who went out of their way to learn ancient Greek or philosophy but lived in utter poverty and degraded conditions.

Second, he emphasized the importance of moral virtue. Among the virtues to be cultivated were a sense of dignity in labor and an appreciation for hard work. Washington believed that many blacks wrongly depreciate and avoid manual labor because of its association with slavery or servitude. But he insisted that there is no shame in working with one's hands. The problem with slavery was not that it involved work of this kind but that it entailed coerced labor for the benefit of whites—race-based exploitation. Intense manual labor builds character and cultivates useful skills, preparing the ground for economic independence. Washington also emphasized the importance of the virtues of cleanliness, grooming, and being well dressed. Discipline in one's appearance, he thought, engenders and reflects a sense of dignity, which elicits respect from others. Moral development, for Washington, also includes cultivating the virtues of patience and generosity. It involves a willingness to make sacrifices in the short term for greater gains in the future. Perhaps most importantly, it requires that individuals cultivate a sense of personal responsibility. That is, each black person should take primary responsibility for her or his condition rather than blaming others. While acknowledging the impact of slavery and racial discrimination on the condition of blacks, Washington thought that blacks should not view themselves as victims; nor should they encourage others to look upon them as such. Instead, blacks should individually and collectively work to raise themselves up out of their degraded condition without demanding compensation for past wrongs.

The third component of Washington's self-help philosophy is institution building and racial self-organization. In particular, he encouraged blacks to develop profitable businesses that would cater to the needs of black people. He supported the idea of black newspapers and educational institutions, like his Tuskegee Institute, which was a model of institution building for purposes of racial uplift. The Institute emphasized agricultural and industrial education; and it cultivated in its students the petit bourgeois virtues of hard work, thrift, self-sacrifice, efficiency, cleanliness, and patience. Tuskegee was Washington's social philosophy put into practice. In his view, this collective project of institution building and race-based organizing was a way of making forced segregation work in favor of black interests instead of seeing it as solely a limitation and an intolerable constraint.

Finally, Washington emphasized economic advancement rather than political agitation and protest. Indeed, the other components of his philosophy—vocational training, moral development, and group self-organization—served as steps toward the goal of economic advancement, which, according to Washington, is the true road to independence and freedom. Washington advocated land ownership and the accumulation of capital, and he encouraged blacks to save and invest rather than spend money on entertainment and luxury goods. His economic approach to racial uplift eschewed direct political agitation for civil rights, which he believed would be futile and self-defeating under such oppressive conditions. Direct political action would be effective only with the creation of a dignified and worthy race, one that whites could respect for its achievements under difficult circumstances and for its economic power. Indeed, Washington believed that whites would be willing to help in this project of economic advancement, at least insofar as it also advanced their own material interests. As he said, "harmony will come in proportion as the black man gets something that the white man wants, whether it be of brains or of material."[16] Though whites in general were disposed to resist black demands for social equality and civil rights, Washington maintained that they could be counted on to support many of the economic goals of blacks, for these material objectives often converged with their own. The best way to enlist the help of whites, Washington insisted, is not to demand that they do so on grounds of justice but to appeal to their interests. As he says to a white audience in his famous "Atlanta Exposition Address" (1895): "Nearly sixteen millions of hands will aid you in pulling the load upward, or they will pull, against you, the load downward. We shall constitute one third and more of the ignorance and crime of the South, or one third its intelligence and progress; we shall contribute one third to the business and industrial prosperity of the South, or we shall prove a veritable body of death, stagnating, depressing, retarding every effort to advance the body politic."[17] Washington packaged his self-help philosophy with a conciliatory approach to the white South and a tendency to publicly blame blacks for their low position in society—a tactic that earned him severe criticism and, perhaps unjustifiedly, led to his being labeled an "Uncle Tom."

Marcus Garvey (1887–1940), another fierce opponent of Du Bois, also advocated black self-help. His version of racial uplift ideology was, by his own admission, deeply indebted to Washington's, though Garvey also emphasized the importance of militant black pride, advocacy of black emigration, and a plan for blacks to work together for the redemption of Africa through the creation of a wealthy nation-state in their original "fatherland." In this way, Garvey joined his self-help philosophy with the familiar doctrines of classical black nationalism.[18]

Like Washington, Garvey championed capitalism as the road to black liberation, and he believed that the development of black businesses on a global scale would ultimately lead whites to respect blacks and to deal with them on equal terms. This black capitalism was to be founded on racial loyalty and group self-reliance, where African-descended peoples were to invest in and patronize black business enterprises. Garvey, like Washington, was skeptical about the effectiveness of public protest for getting whites to grant blacks equal rights and thus thought that blacks should work together for their collective uplift without relying on concessions from white citizens or the U.S. government. But unlike Washington, Garvey maintained that whites would never come around to accepting blacks as their equals unless forced to do by the superior economic and military power of blacks. Such racial peace as was possible could not be attained as long as the races lived together under the same government.

Garvey appealed directly to working-class blacks (both blue-collar and low-status white-collar) rather than to college-educated blacks, black professionals, or the black intelligentsia. He regarded the black elite as little more than a self-serving group of individuals who were too closely aligned with white interests. He believed that this privileged group, particularly those of mixed-race ancestry, could not be trusted to lead blacks out of their degraded condition, for they benefited from white supremacy and lacked sufficient pride in their African heritage.

Though Du Bois had fundamental political disagreements with both Washington and Garvey, he also accepted some elements of racial self-help. The similarities and differences between these three preeminent black leaders are important and sometimes subtle. A brief comparison can help us see that there is more than one way to specify the political content of black solidarity.[19]

Like Washington and Garvey, Du Bois contended that the ideals of black folk could not be realized unless African Americans work together through self-organization and group self-reliance. He did not, however, envisage a separate black nation-state for African Americans; instead he urged blacks to insist on their right to equal American citizenship. Though he strongly encouraged blacks to organize independently for their general uplift, he did not favor a self-segregated black community as an end in itself. He is thus rightly called a committed racial integrationist, though not, as we have seen, a cultural assimilationist.

For Du Bois, as for Garvey, black solidarity requires racial identification, group pride, and the preservation of a distinctive ethno-cultural identity.[20] As with any form of group solidarity, it also requires loyalty to the group and its ideals, especially when either is seriously threatened. Blacks must also build independent and self-governing black institutions and organizations, as both Washington and Garvey maintained. This is a matter of group self-reliance, which is necessary for self-respect and to protect against the racial animus and moral complacency of the dominant group. Yet Du Bois insisted that although solidarity is needed for group development and self-defense, blacks will not flourish unless nonblacks, especially whites, encourage and support black efforts, not simply by accepting the principle of racial equality, but through concrete measures that would actually realize this principle. Indeed, Du Bois claimed that Washington's primary flaw as a leader was his failure to emphasize this point.[21] In Du Bois's view, Washington's philosophy tended to encourage whites, both northern and southern, to place the burden of solving the Negro problem on the backs of blacks themselves, as whites sit on the sidelines criticizing and mocking blacks' attempts to improve their condition. In contrast, Du Bois argued that the burden belongs to the nation as a whole, and all must do their share to lift it. Thus, though Du Bois did advocate some of the core elements of self-help ideology, he was not a conservative nationalist. He saw no contradiction in, and indeed insisted on the necessity of, calling for both racial self-reliance and state intervention to address black disadvantage.

In opposition to Washington's accommodationism and to Garvey's skepticism regarding moral suasion, Du Bois maintained that black solidarity requires political self-assertion and persistent agitation in support of the group's ideals. Blacks must always keep their ideals in view, never compromising them for short-term advantages. This requires determination, confidence in black ability, and faith in ultimate triumph. It also requires the courage to resist injustice even when faced with formidable opposition:

> The Negro knows perfectly what freedom and equality mean—opportunity to make the best of oneself, unhandicapped by wanton restraint and unreasoning prejudice. For this the most of us propose to strive. We will not, by word or deed, for a moment admit the right of any man to discriminate against us simply on account of race or color. Whenever we submit to humiliation and oppression it is because of superior brute force; and even when bending to the inevitable we bend with unabated protest and declare flatly and unswervingly that any man or section or nation who wantonly shuts the doors of opportunity and self-defense in the faces of the weak is a coward and knave. We refuse to kiss the hands

that smite us, but rather insist on striving by all civilized methods to keep wide educational opportunity, to keep the right to vote, to insist on equal civil rights and to gain every right and privilege open to a free American citizen.[22]

The Role of Leadership

Leaders play a central, if not defining, role in Du Bois's conception of black solidarity. Though he discusses the role of black leaders in "The Conservation of Races" and *The Souls of Black Folk*, his most extended treatment of this question is found in his essay "The Talented Tenth" (1903).[23] Some forty-five years later (1948), he revised and restated his position in "The Talented Tenth: Memorial Address." My interpretation of his considered views on black leadership takes account of these works and others, noting shifts in his position where appropriate.

Du Bois identifies three specific responsibilities of black leaders. First, they must publicly oppose those who would deny blacks their rights and call upon the government to ensure fair treatment.[24] They cannot sit idly by while blacks are treated unjustly and deprived of their rights. It is their duty to expose evil and injustice. Such leaders must be the public voice of black protest. They must even be willing to openly criticize would-be black leaders who, whether their intentions be honorable or base, compromise the group's ideals.

Second, it is the duty of black leaders to articulate and defend the group's ideals and to fashion a broad and long-range political vision in accordance with them.[25] Through these efforts they are to influence and shape black public opinion. For example, they should convey to their people that American ideals of democracy should be embraced but that U.S. arrogance, moral decadence, unrestrained consumerism, individualism, and anti-intellectualism should be rejected.[26] This of course requires that black leaders be capable of thinking independently of, and sometimes in opposition to, American national ideology.[27] The artists must create paintings, music, and literature that inspire ordinary black folk to action and that embody and give creative expression to the group's ideals. Du Bois famously maintained that "all Art is propaganda and ever must be," and he insisted that, though artistic production must be free and unconstrained by law, this freedom should never be used to distort or compromise what is true and just.[28]

Third, black leaders must oversee and coordinate black cooperation and collective progress.[29] This principally involves leading the churches, educational institutions, civil rights organizations, and business enterprises of the community. Black leaders must take on the burden of developing and uplifting their people: "Progress in human affairs is more often a pull than a push, surging forward of the exceptional man, and the lifting of his duller brethren slowly and painfully to his vantage-ground."[30] This labor of love will entail educating the youth who have been deprived of a decent liberal arts education. Black leaders must provide role models for children by embodying an important ideal and thereby showing it to be attainable. And they must acquaint the masses of their people with the culture and habits of modern social life.[31] Du Bois insisted that education is not to be confined to schools, but must trickle down, as it were, through family life, to relationships with friends and associates, and to others of one's social class. He argued that black children get the bulk of their education and socialization in their own community, and that the leaders of their people should guide this transmission of knowledge.[32]

But who among the black population should be acknowledged as its rightful leaders? Perhaps the most famous line of the original "Talented Tenth" essay—which is both its first sentence and its final sentence—is this: "The Negro race, like all races, is going to be saved by its exceptional men."[33] Du Bois firmly believed, contrary to Garvey's contention, that an educated elite should lead the black struggle for freedom and equality. Given their responsibilities, these would-be leaders must possess exceptional intellectual ability and moral character.[34] In particular, leadership should come from those who have had a quality liberal arts higher education, not simply vocational training. The purpose of this education is not primarily to cultivate a black bourgeoisie but to develop leaders of intelligence and humanistic understanding, individuals who have broad knowledge of history, culture, and the present social world.

In addition to intelligence and advanced education, leadership requires five essential character traits: Leaders must be willing to sacrifice narrow self-interest in order to promote the interests of the group.[35] They must have integrity—they must be men and women of principle, who are sincere and earnest. These leaders must have courage—they must not allow themselves to be silenced by opposition but must always speak out against injustice, even when perpetrated by blacks themselves, and they must not be afraid to express their beliefs as to what is true and right even when doing so would be unpopular.[36] Those who would lead must be loyal to black people and their ideals—such faithfulness must include a commitment to never compromise their most basic principles even when this might seem to yield immediate concrete gains.[37] Finally, black leaders must show determination—they must believe in the ultimate success of black struggles and have the stamina to see the project through to the end. Du Bois summarizes these character traits in *Dusk of Dawn* (1940), writing: "In addition to mental ability there is demanded an extraordinary moral strength, the strength to endure discrimination and not become discouraged; to face almost universal disparagement and keep one's soul; and to sacrifice for an ideal which the present generation will hardly see fulfilled."[38]

Racial Identification and Class Division

For most of his life, Du Bois either outright denied that there was meaningful class differentiation among black people or downplayed the significance of such intraracial stratification for his proj-

ect of reforming American democracy through black political solidarity. In "The Class Struggle" (1921), for instance, Du Bois
admitted that blacks were separated into a middle class and a working class, but he maintained that they were not separated either
physically or ideologically.[39] Ten years later in "The Negro and
Communism" (1931), he forthrightly rejected the Communist
charge that black petit bourgeois groups dominated and exploited
members of the black working class, and he said in response to this
"fantastic falsehood," as he called it, that "there is no group of leaders on earth who have so largely made common cause with the low-
est of their race as educated American Negroes, and it is their foresight and sacrifice and theirs alone that has saved the American
freedman from annihilation and degradation."[40] In his "Marxism
and the Negro Problem" (1933), Du Bois finally conceded that petit
bourgeois groups were beginning to evolve within black America.[41]
However, he argued that the black petite bourgeoisie was not a significant employer of black labor and the members of this class
themselves suffered from the racism of white capitalists and white
workers. Thus, he insisted, it would be irrational and self-defeating
for the black proletariat to rebel against the black elite. Instead, as a
means of self-defense, black laborers and the black petite bourgeoisie must work together through interclass self-organization to protect themselves from white capitalists and white labor but without
succumbing to full-blown capitalistic exploitation among themselves.

Notwithstanding his unshakeable faith in the emancipatory potential of black solidarity, Du Bois very early on recognized that, because of differences in education, income, occupation, and regional
opportunity, there would inevitably exist a more advantaged group
within the black population whose material interests might diverge
from those of their more disadvantaged racial kin. He also recognized that some members of this black elite would be tempted to
gain their civil rights and inclusion within America at the cost of

their black identity. Even as early as the writing of *The Souls of Black Folk,* Du Bois was acutely aware that some black elites sought to distinguish themselves from the masses of black folk in order to gain acceptance into the mainstream of U.S. society. He described, for instance, how some free blacks during the antebellum period accepted the existence of slavery in the South and simply insisted that they themselves were not slaves and therefore deserved all the rights of a citizen.[42] According to Du Bois, these blacks were prepared to assimilate to the dominant culture and thus to become one with the rest of the nation, and they thought of themselves as "people of color" as distinct from "Negroes." But whites refused to recognize them as such and instead considered all blacks, whether slave or free, "niggers." Hence free blacks were forced to turn to either the emigrationist movement or the abolitionist movement as their only alternatives.

Du Bois took up this issue again during the Depression era in an essay entitled "On Being Ashamed of Oneself: An Essay on Race Pride" (1933).[43] Here he suggested that there have been two extreme tendencies of blacks when it comes to race pride. Some have opposed the idea that they are Negroes and worked to assume a quintessential American identity, shedding all association with "black" modes of expression and behavior. Others saw their blackness as a badge of honor, a sign of their racial superiority, and sought to celebrate blackness in much the same way that white supremacists do whiteness.

The first tendency eschews racial solidarity and group self-organization, maintaining that such collective action only leads to further racial discrimination and degradation. But Du Bois speculated that part of what motivates the assimilationist position among some blacks is that they are ashamed of their blackness—or, more precisely, that they do not want to be identified as black because they have come to believe, or at least suspect, that black folk are largely deserving of the contempt they so often receive. Thus they seek, futilely Du Bois thought, to escape their blackness; and to make matters worse, their attitudes and actions end up, perhaps unwittingly, lending support to the racist view that blacks are not worth associating with.

However, around the time of the New Negro movement of the Harlem Renaissance, Du Bois came to think that a significant evolution had taken place in the attitudes of the black elite, a change of heart in which many former assimilationists discovered that there were black people of whom they could be proud, people of cultural refinement and intellectual achievement and whose company they greatly enjoyed. In this way, black America had rediscovered itself as a vibrant and vigorous community. But the problem with this renaissance noir, according to Du Bois, was that it was class-specific. The proud New Negro was typically a part of a social elite based on education, income, occupational status, and cultural capital. This still left a class of poorly educated, uncultured, and impoverished blacks of which the black elite were ashamed. What was worse, because they did not want to be mistaken as belonging to this lower-status group, or because they were worried that the latter would be widely viewed as *representative* of what blacks had to offer, the black elite tended to avoid social contact with the black poor. Indeed, in *The Souls of Black Folk,* Du Bois expressed this anxiety himself, as when he decries the fact that white elites fail to distinguish accomplished, hardworking, and morally upright blacks from blacks who are incompetent, lazy, or criminal.[44]

What all this suggests, Du Bois maintained, is that the physical characteristics that are associated with the black race—dark skin, kinky hair, full lips, and so on—are *stigmata of degradation.* The stigma of blackness is constituted by the general, though sometimes implicit, assumption that African-descended peoples, especially those who are descendants of slaves, share an inferior social status. It cannot be erased through individual intellectual achievement, cultural refinement, occupational status, or wealth. Therefore, blacks of all classes must make common cause as a matter of collective self-defense and group advancement. Du Bois admitted that such solidarity is quite difficult to cultivate and sustain. For one thing, black elites often resent the fact that despite their achievement and education they are still treated like ordinary black folk and that deserving blacks do not get credit for their accomplishments. They feel "embarrassed," he says, that they are lumped together with a mass of people over whom they have no real control. Nevertheless, Du Bois continued to insist that black elites must embrace racial solidarity. Indeed, as we will see, he urged blacks to radicalize their ideals by aiming at the formation of a new nation in America that is more thoroughly egalitarian and democratic than most whites were at that time inclined to favor.

Du Bois anticipated the objection that the then-current moment, defined as it was by the economic devastation of the Great Depression, called for advocating a post-racial political order, not racial solidarity. In response he described the following "new dilemma" that blacks had to face: Racial discrimination by capitalists and organized labor had made it practically impossible for blacks, even those of obvious ability and training, to advance economically in the rapidly industrializing society of the United States or to be integrated into the new global economic order. In the first quarter of the twentieth century, blacks had advanced mainly through self-organization and black institutions. Despite considerable progress, blacks had made few inroads in industry, the professions, and national political life. Racism was yielding no significant ground, and blacks did not have sufficient power to compel whites to live up to their own professed ideals. The solution? Embrace the horn of racial particularism: "The next step, then, is certainly one on the part of the Negro and it involves group action. It involves the organization of intelligent and earnest people of Negro descent for their preservation and advancement in America, in the West Indies and in Africa; and no sentimental distaste for racial or national unity can be allowed to hold them back from a step which sheer necessity demands."[45]

I will not consider the merits of Du Bois's Depression-era economic strategy or his Pan-Africanism. Instead, I want to focus on his approach to the problem that intraracial class differences pose for black American solidarity, to ask whether this approach is applicable in the post–civil rights context of U.S. race relations. We must first recognize that the black middle class has grown significantly since the major judicial and legislative gains of the civil rights movement. Some blacks are clearly able to advance economically in postindustrial market society, both through their own determined efforts and with the help of preferential treatment. One must now admit that although the stigma of racial inferiority cannot be completely erased by individual action (except perhaps by passing), it can be significantly mitigated—for example, by advanced education. Access to higher education enables a relatively small but nevertheless significant segment of the black population to gain access to a wide range of well-paid professional occupations, the salaries from which they can use to buy their own homes and accumulate other assets. Once attained, elite class status does in the contemporary context lessen the burden of blackness.

Indeed, as William Julius Wilson has argued, such class advancement has weakened the burden of racial stigma to such an extent that so long as federal antidiscrimination statutes are effectively enforced—an important condition that is not always met—the life prospects of black elites are not greatly hampered by the persistence of antiblack racism.[46] Of course, black elites are still subject to discrimination and racial insult, in both the public sphere and the market, a fact that should not be dismissed or minimized. Thus they still have an interest in combating racism, by, for example, making sure civil rights laws are enforced and exposing the covert racism of public officials. But apart from these measures, it is much less clear that their economic interests are tightly bound up with the black working class and the jobless urban poor.

Yet, if Du Bois was correct about how black somatic characteristics function as stigmata of degradation, then to the extent that black social identity is widely and strongly associated with severely disadvantaged blacks, the social status of more privileged blacks is threatened. In dealing with this problem, black elites have at least four options, all of which have been taken up at one time or another by various affluent blacks. First, they could simply do nothing, recognizing that they will be subject to racist contempt and the psychic costs that this entails but consoling themselves with the thought that their life prospects—in terms of income, educational opportunity, and employment—will not be seriously affected by this unfortunate circumstance. Second, despite the fact that many people value and take great pleasure in having a black identity, black elites could attempt to eliminate or deinstitutionalize the social category "black" altogether, perhaps by delegitimizing the concept "race." Third, they might try to rehabilitate blackness by promoting a "positive" public image of black people, perhaps by working to associate the category "black" with the black elite—the new and improved "New Negro." Or, following Du Bois, they can make common cause with more disadvantaged blacks to resist anti-black racism and to broaden the scope of opportunity for all blacks, which would necessarily include addressing the problems of racial inequality and ghetto poverty.

As should be obvious, there is no philosophical solution to this problem. Its resolution will depend, as Du Bois suggested, on whether there is a sufficient segment of the black elite with the requisite compassion, integrity, courage, and determination to fight with more disadvantaged blacks for social reform. If black elites approach the problem of inferior social status solely from the standpoint of their own narrow self-interest, then they will choose whichever option seems most promising and cost-effective under the social conditions at the time. Currently that might be a complacent individualism, attempting to abolish "race" as a publicly recognized social distinction, or claiming the prerogative to define the meaning of being black in America. But if their sense of racial identification is strong and their general commitment to social justice is principled, then, given that they too are racially stigmatized, they will join in solidarity with the most disadvantaged among their people.

Du Bois, while an idealist, was not a utopian thinker, at least not in the bad sense. He did not expect black people to be altruistic toward one another just because they share a similar fate within the racist society of the United States. Nor did he expect African Americans to be moved solely by their sense of justice, for he recognized that, as laudable as this motive is, it is often compromised or abandoned when it conflicts with one's material interests and thus it alone will be insufficient to the task. He therefore maintained that choosing the option of a morally based, racial solidarity not only is the responsibility of the black elite, but also is in their long-term interests. As long as nonblacks regard the condition of the worst-off African Americans as a sign of the inferiority of black people as a whole, the black elite cannot both affirm their black identity and share equal social status with their nonblack elite counterparts.

Hence, Du Bois sought to fuse together moral principle, racial identification, and simple self-interest in order to strengthen black political solidarity. Taken alone, none of these would likely be robust enough to motivate black elites to set aside their narrow interests in order to work for the good of all black people. Yet at those political sites where moral commitment, black identification, and interest converge—and these, I take it, are many—there is a possibility for a meaningful form of black solidarity. To the extent that black solidarity is needed to bring about racial justice in America, this tripartite motivational foundation has become increasingly

necessary in an era where class differentiation and increasing economic polarization among African Americans have produced two
distinct but closely related status groups within the black nation
within a nation. This normative framework, which we owe to
thinkers such as Delany and Du Bois, has implications for black
political unity that I will explore and elaborate in the remaining
chapters.

The Black Elite and Political Leadership

Many progressives recoil at Du Bois's conception of group leadership, which they regard as "elitist."[47] At an extreme, this charge
might imply that Du Bois was committed to a nondemocratic form
of government in which power is largely in the hands of an educated elite. Alternatively, and more plausibly, it might suggest that
within Du Bois's conception of leadership one can find a thinly
veiled contempt for ordinary working people and an arrogant but
unjustified expression of elite superiority, a kind of black noblesse
oblige. Yet another possibility is that Du Bois wrongly held that
black elites by virtue of their education are more "enlightened"
about politics and the social world than their less-educated racial kin.

Given careful consideration of his basic political writings, it
should be clear that the defense Du Bois offered in favor of his view
of leadership does not rest on either of the first two assumptions.
As early as *The Souls of Black Folk,* Du Bois defends democratic
principles: "Honest and earnest criticism from those whose interests are most nearly touched,—criticism of writers by readers, of
government by those governed, of leaders by those led,—this is the
soul of democracy and the safeguard of modern society."[48] He was a
fierce opponent of aristocratic and plutocratic forms of government and, at least by the time he wrote *Darkwater* (1920), was a
consistent defender of the right of all adult citizens—regardless of

gender, race, national origin, class, or education—to vote in elections and to run for public office.[49]

In response to the second charge of elitism, we should note that in the "Memorial Address" Du Bois explicitly denied that the black intelligentsia are inherently superior to less-educated blacks: "They [the Talented Tenth] must first of all recognize the fact that their own place in life is primarily a matter of opportunity, rather than simply desert or ability. That if such opportunity were extended and broadened, a thousand times as many Negroes could join the ranks of the educated and able, instead of sinking into poverty, disease and crime."[50] In *Dusk of Dawn*, he warned the educated elite not to assume a "technocratic right to rule," and he exhorted them not to "despise" the masses of their people but rather to appreciate the socioeconomic causes of their degradation and to sympathize with their undeserved plight.[51] That said, there is little doubt that Du Bois believed, throughout his life, that those who excel in higher education are deserving of special praise and honor, and that their educational achievement partly justifies their positions of leadership within the black community.

Even as early as the original "Talented Tenth" essay, Du Bois recognized that some would criticize his emphasis on the "exceptions" within the race, as this focus might seem to ignore the poverty and powerlessness of many blacks or perhaps even to blame them for their condition. But he argued that the educated black elite did not create this mass of impoverished blacks; instead, they were created by a long history of brutal racial oppression, economic exploitation, political disfranchisement, educational deprivation, and social neglect, all perpetrated by members of the dominant group. However—and here again we hear echoes of Delany—despite these obstacles to black development, some ambitious and hardworking blacks of marked ability, a "saving remnant," have managed to cultivate a vigorous character and to achieve great things. These

exceptional persons show the promise of blacks, demonstrating
to all that blacks are capable of achievement if given the chance.
Their role as racial exemplars partly justifies their right to lead, for
through their example they show that black people can be developed and thus should be given the opportunity to occupy positions
of authority, just like the members of any other race.

He also argued that if blacks of ability were not suitably educated, leaders would nonetheless inevitably emerge within black
communities. Many, if not most, of those leaders would be dema-
gogues, hustlers, dilettantes, or fools. Some would no doubt be influential and charismatic persons, but whether through good intentions or bad they would likely lead the masses away from what is
true and just.[52] Yet this is precisely where the charge of elitism has
some bite. Du Bois seems to have assumed that only those with a
formal college education will have the requisite knowledge, intelligence, and foresight—what we might call "practical wisdom"—
needed for effective leadership, surely a dubious assumption. A
weaker and possibly more acceptable premise would be that those
with such education are more likely, all things being equal, to have
the necessary practical wisdom. This claim is based on the com-
monsense view that knowledge, intelligence, and prudence are
greatly enhanced, both in breadth and in depth, by training in
higher education. Thus, given their desire for wise leadership,
blacks should generally, though not necessarily without exception,
choose their political leaders from among the well educated.[53] Here
a college education is not treated as a necessary qualification for
leadership, but it is viewed as a considerable asset, one that should
be given due weight in the selection of leaders. Du Bois, at least
sometimes, seems to endorse this weaker view, as when he asks rhe-
torically: "Is there not, with such a group [Negroes] and in such a
crisis, infinitely more danger to be apprehended from half-trained
minds and shallow thinking than from over-education and over-re-
finement?"[54]

This weaker assumption about the importance of training in higher education strikes me as entirely reasonable.[55] But some will nevertheless reject it as too restrictive. Critics might insist, for instance, that given the increasing corporate refashioning of higher education, a college education is not a relevant qualification for black leadership, for such education provides no advantage—and may even be a disadvantage—in cultivating the forms of practical wisdom that bear on progressive political leadership. Even more radically, they may argue that black people do not need leaders, whether highly educated or not, for ordinary black folk are quite capable of organizing to emancipate themselves without the direction of would-be spokespersons or moral exemplars. A related but less extreme view is that Du Bois underestimated how much everyday black people actually know about the causes of and remedies for their predicament and that thus he was led to give too much weight to formal education as a qualification for leadership. Or, finally, they could argue that black people need more leaders—perhaps substantially more—than the educated elite can realistically provide. All four objections have merit, and any adequate defense of Du Bois's view of leadership must attend to them. Du Bois, however, did not seriously entertain these criticisms. And defending him against them is beyond the scope of my argument. My primary aim in reconstructing Du Bois's conception of black leadership is not to defend either his austere requirements for leadership or his conception of the role that leaders should play in black politics, but to begin to address the concern that leadership by elites would actually *undermine* pragmatic black nationalism.

Some critics, while perfectly willing to acknowledge the advantages of having college-trained leaders, will still object that there is no reason to believe that educated persons will use their practical wisdom for good rather than ill, for the benefit of their people rather than for their own benefit. This is an important observation, and Du Bois was well aware of it. This is why he insisted that a good character is a necessary qualification for effective leadership. A leader must be intelligent, learned, prudent, *and* morally upright. But now someone might correctly point out that most of those who get a college education these days join the ranks of the new petit bourgeois elite or the so-called new middle class; that is, they become owners of small businesses, managers, professionals, or advanced technicians. They do not generally develop the broad-minded and cosmopolitan sensibility of the intellectual or artist but instead cultivate the narrowly self-interested and materialistic outlook of the typical bourgeois. There is some reason to believe, then, that such persons will not be concerned with the development and uplift of black people when the interests of the group diverge from or conflict with their own private interests. Moreover, there is certainly little reason to believe that most black elites are especially well equipped to think independently of American national ideology, for their economic ambitions are an obvious expression of it.

In his "Memorial Address," Du Bois confessed to having overlooked this problem in his earlier articulation of the Talented Tenth doctrine. He says that he had naively assumed that with education and knowledge, a willingness to sacrifice for the betterment of humanity would automatically follow. He later came to realize, however, that many of the educated elite were in fact selfish, self-indulgent, and primarily concerned with accumulating wealth, leisure, and status for themselves, with little or no regard for the welfare of most black folk. If this group were to assume leadership, then ordinary working-class blacks would likely be exploited, and the dislocated black poor neglected altogether. But in his restatement of the view, he offers a neo-Marxist, or "Black Marxist," solution to this problem.[56] This revision is an even more radical vanguardism than he defended at the turn of the century, for it requires more intensive educational training and greater ideological unity among black leaders, thus further restricting the pool from which reliable black leadership should be selected. On this more radical view, black leaders not only must be intellectually gifted, learned, morally upright, and loyal to the ideals of the race, but must have a thorough understanding of modern economics and be committed to socialist principles of distributive justice.

Du Bois insisted that blacks need leaders who have expert knowledge of modern economics.[57] Such expertise is needed to guide blacks in a rapidly changing global economy, in which the growth of technology is radically altering the structure and dynamics of modern societies and developing countries. One of the revolutionary social changes that Du Bois believed blacks must be concerned with is the rapid growth of scientific knowledge, not only in the natural sciences but in the social and historical sciences as well. Thus he claimed it is necessary for educated persons to continually keep abreast of the current state of knowledge, augmenting what they already know and changing their opinions whenever the evidence calls for this. This suggests that Du Bois came later in life to think of the black intelligentsia, narrowly construed, as the appropriate leaders of black folk, for only they will have the requisite knowledge and worldly experience to assess the current condition of African Americans and to guide their efforts at self-development in the postindustrial era of global capitalism. Indeed, in his review of E. Franklin Frazier's *Black Bourgeoisie* (1957), Du Bois, although largely agreeing with Frazier's account of the self-delusions and folly of the new black elite, criticized Frazier for failing to "point out the voluntary abdication of the Negro intelligentsia from holding and reasserting that leadership which is theirs by right."[58]

In the post–World War II period, Du Bois also became convinced of certain Marxian or Marx-inspired theses: (1) that the products of labor should be distributed according to need, not by chance, privilege, or power; (2) that industry should be controlled and managed by the state in light of scientific knowledge; (3) that all goods should be owned and distributed to promote the general welfare; (4) that all should be educated according to ability; (5) that each should work in accordance with the requirements of economic efficiency; and (6) that the state should take on the responsibility for health, housing, social security, and facilities for recreation and human intercourse. To these economic measures, he added the following liberal principle: "There should be the widest possible area reserved for liberty of thought and of action and for creative ideas."[59]

Du Bois insisted that this program—whether one calls it liberalism, socialism, or communism—was the consensus of the civilized world at the time, even within much of the United States. He hastened to add, however, that the program had received consistent opposition from capitalists and their apologists. According to bourgeois ideology (classical liberalism), individual free enterprise spurred by the profit motive and with minimal state interference in the market is the only viable and just method for promoting the general welfare. Du Bois thought that this view not only is incompatible with social justice but had been falsified by two world wars and several economic crises, including the Great Depression. He believed that further such wars and crises would be forthcoming if we continued to follow the principles of laissez-faire capitalism. And he claimed that knowledge of such facts was being concealed by a commercially owned and monopolized press and by the suppression of dissent. Thus, it was the duty of the black intelligentsia, he maintained, to resist these reactionary efforts by those in power. In particular, an educated and self-sacrificing social-scientific elite could play a leading role in this global struggle. This new black leadership must (1) understand contemporary global economic conditions, (2) coordinate and direct an alliance of blacks with other progressive forces in the United States and around the world, and (3) have a vision of a "new world culture." To carry this project forward, blacks would need a new special organization that would take the primary responsibility for instituting, directing, and funding this effort.

Returning now to the problem of the new black elite, it was clear to Du Bois that this group is not especially well suited to play a leadership role in this new radical democratic politics. These persons are, first of all, concentrated in the professions (for instance, medicine, law, business, and technology); and because they benefit from the status quo, they are prone to accept conservative ideology and mainstream American values, including prejudice against Communist countries and Third World nations. Because they are relatively economically advantaged, they share few economic interests with the working classes and the poor and generally aspire to the ranks of the wealthiest strata in the country. They tend to be apolitical, complacent, and hedonistic. And despite their own education and achievement, they often suffer from an inferiority complex about black ability. Hence, Du Bois urged the black working classes not to rely exclusively or even primarily on the petite bourgeoisie or the new professional elite for its leadership. Those from among the black elite who are chosen for leadership must show themselves to be committed to a progressive economic agenda that would work to the benefit of all, not just the privileged few.

Black Pride and Black Militancy

Du Bois's approach to class divisions within the greater black population can also help us better understand the significance of black pride for black solidarity. Du Bois maintained that his new black radicalism would require the deliberate cultivation of race pride, by which he meant pride in the achievements of all persons of African descent. Blacks cannot make common cause if they are ashamed of their blackness, so they need to learn that blacks are a people with a history of accomplishment, both in Africa and in the African dias-

pora, comparable to any other people of the world.[60] Knowledge of
these accomplishments will encourage pride among blacks, especially among those who suffer from an inferiority complex and thus
are ashamed of being black. He admitted that some, like Marcus
Garvey, would be tempted to exaggerate the accomplishments of
the black race, claiming that blacks represent the first and greatest
of races. Du Bois encouraged blacks to avoid distorting their history, but he nevertheless urged them to take moderate pride in
black accomplishment, rooted in well-established historical facts.

This argument appears to be invalid, though. One can come to
firmly believe that he or she has no reason to be ashamed of being
black without holding that blackness is something to be proud of.
The fact of blackness—whether this fact is a matter of nature, social
convention, or some combination thereof—would seem to have no
bearing on the question of noteworthy achievement. Indeed, for
those who forthrightly reject racial essentialism and biological determinism, this stance might seem quite natural. Consistency might
even require it. If cultural traits are learned and achievement is neither determined nor limited by one's race, then why should blacks
have any special pride in their specifically *racial* identity? However,
it may be that, against the background of racial degradation and
stigma, *demonstrating* that one is not ashamed of being associated
with blacks does require, if not quite black pride, then something
quite similar. If there were no racial stigma, then this valorization of
blackness may indeed be unnecessary, even obnoxious. But given
that there is such prejudice, proving to others, and perhaps more
importantly to oneself, that one is not ashamed of being classed
with other blacks may only appear to be extreme and irrational race
pride—a kind of racialist chauvinism. In fact, though, making it
clear to oneself and others that one is not embarrassed to be associated with other blacks could function to sustain self-respect under
conditions of racial oppression. Racist ideology, while in many ways
shifting with sociohistorical circumstances and political contingen-

cies, has consistently deprecated black ability, especially with respect to intellect and moral character. The tendency for such propaganda to seep into the consciousness of blacks themselves, causing them to doubt themselves, is of course a core theme of *The Souls of Black Folk*. The onset of this inferiority complex must be actively and self-consciously fought, for if not effectively combated, it can undermine blacks' sense of their own worth as persons. Yet, it is possible to sustain black pride without believing that achievement is determined, to any significant extent, by race membership. The reason one can be proud in the face of antiblack ideology is that one realizes that if blacks seem not to have progressed as far as other races, this is not because of anything inherent in their nature as a racial group. Rather, such apparent differential achievement is the result of a long history of oppression and deprivation, for which blacks have consistently demanded redress and which they have struggled together to overcome.

These reflections on the meaning of black pride, which are by no means meant to be exhaustive,[61] have relevance for our discussion of the problem of class division among blacks. It might be that the public exhibition of black pride is necessary to strengthen or rebuild bonds of trust between members of the black population, a group that is now sharply differentiated by economic class and social status. Let us suppose for a moment that Du Bois was correct in his speculation that many elite blacks are ashamed of being black because blackness is typically associated with the condition and behavior of the black poor. In light of this, poor blacks will naturally want some assurances that black elites, especially those who would lay claim to leadership, are not ashamed to be associated with them. Such assurances are required if black solidarity across class lines is to be possible. The most severely disadvantaged within the black community will quite reasonably want some evidence that black elites have an unshakeable faith in the ability of all blacks to flourish and excel if given the opportunity. But even if Du Bois was wrong about the prevalence of racial self-contempt among the black elite, many working-class and poor blacks nevertheless *suspect* that black elites are prone to such self-hatred, a fact that Garvey exploited to discredit various middle-class black leaders, including Du Bois. Some black elites might, of course, vehemently deny that they are ashamed of being black, and they might justifiably resent the suggestion that they are somehow deficient in black pride. Yet unless they publicly identify as black and express their loyalty to the black community as a whole, their protestations will not be seriously entertained. This identification of the black elite with everyday blacks must also openly eschew the assumption that the former are somehow the "true" representatives of blackness over against the "niggers" of the race.

Extrapolating a bit, an analogous point could be made about the tendency of some whites to regard black progressives as unreasonably defiant or arrogant. Black militancy necessarily involves, almost by definition, being willing to use political methods that whites might find unacceptable or even offensive if black liberation requires as much. When members of the black elite exhibit these traits of militancy, this need not therefore be understood as some form of irrational racial chauvinism. It could be more charitably interpreted as an attempt on their part to demonstrate publicly that they are not servile and obsequious. This militant attitude is a public signal that they can be trusted in the collective black struggle, that they will not compromise the principles of the black movement for freedom and equality in order either to avoid white disapproval or to advance their individual positions within the white world.

There is therefore a sound basis for the demand that black elites publicly express both their pride in being black and their militant commitment to black progress. These are necessary to assure the black working class and black poor that their interests will not be sacrificed or compromised if black elites play a prominent role in defining the black political agenda and in publicly articulating the aspirations of the greater black community. But it is crucial that these expressions of black solidarity on the part of the elite not be taken as *sufficient* for their qualification for black leadership. The reason for this is relatively straightforward and, in a sense, obvious, though its implications are often underappreciated. Black elites are well aware of the fact that many blacks of more modest means and education are suspicious of the motives of the highly educated and affluent; that is, they recognize that non-elites often suspect that the educated elite is largely a self-hating, self-interested, and servile lot. Thus, if members of the black elite are so inclined, which no doubt some are, they can exploit black loyalty and mutual trust by disingenuously performing the widely venerated role of "race man" or "race woman." Under the cloak of black pride and militancy, they can surreptitiously advance their own narrow economic interests while giving the false appearance of promoting the interests of all blacks.[62]

Of course not all bourgeois-minded black elites will be so shameless and calculating, and their cupidity will rarely be so unrestrained. Some of the new black elite no doubt genuinely believe that they are committed to the black working classes and may even be solicitous of the latter's approval in order to feel affirmed in their self-identity as black persons, especially if they regard working-class and ghetto black folk as quintessentially black, as some seem to. But because their material interests and desire for status have a perhaps unconscious influence on the formation of their political opinions, they will nevertheless be inclined to accept relatively conservative measures to address economic inequality and poverty, possibly even sincerely believing that these measures are good for all black people. Because of these conflicts of interest within the black population, the black working class and the ghetto poor must also demand, as Du Bois suggested, that their leaders embrace and demonstrate their commitment to progressive political and economic principles of justice, not just to black cultural pride and militant rhetoric. Thus in order to develop a mutually recognized basis for group solidarity across socioeconomic divisions, blacks must discover some common political principles that all can reasonably accept despite this class heterogeneity. In the chapters that follow, I will outline principles that could serve this purpose.

3

Black Power Nationalism

The concept of Black Power rests on a fundamental premise: *Before a group can enter the open society, it must first close ranks.* By this we mean that group solidarity is necessary before a group can operate effectively from a bargaining position of strength in a pluralistic society.

—Stokely Carmichael and Charles Hamilton, *Black Power* (1967)

This right of self-determination has always been denied. It is a right which blacks have always fought for. The first black newspaper in America [*Freedom's Journal*] published its first edition on May 16, 1827. In its lead editorial, it stated, "We wish to plead our own cause. Too long have others spoken for us."

—Julius Lester, *Look Out Whitey!*
Black Power's Gon' Get Your Mama! (1968)

The vast majority of African Americans do not favor forming a separate black nation-state.[1] Despite their justified grievances, they generally recognize the United States as their home. Of course, many do have ambivalence, and at times hostility, toward their country. They have become disillusioned with some of their nation's more lofty ideals or, rather, by the failure of their government and compatriots to live up to them.[2] Given the historical experience of blacks in America and the persistence of racism, this ambivalence should hardly be surprising. Though these sentiments rarely translate into a desire to expatriate, the idea of group self-determination still resonates among African Americans. Many desire not simply to enhance their autonomy and political influence as individual citizens, but to increase their independence and political empowerment *as a group,* to move toward a form of collective self-rule less radical than a separate sovereign republic.[3]

This more moderate goal has a long history and a number of advocates, who hold that black empowerment should be rooted in the fact that African Americans could become, or already are, the overwhelming majority in certain neighborhoods, municipalities, and states within the United States. If effectively organized, such concentrations of blacks could enable them to make progressive changes in the way their government responds to black interests, but without having to dramatically transform the formal structure of U.S. governmental institutions or appropriating a portion of its territory to create a separate black state.

Du Bois fervently defended a version of this view during the Depression era. His vision rested on the fact of forced racial segregation, which ensured that a high concentration of blacks of diverse socioeconomic standing lived in the same communities. With the end of Jim Crow, however, such a conception of black solidarity would have to be rooted primarily in voluntary self-segregation. Thus, today such a project would require the development of a new black migration movement, where a significant number, many of whom are now dispersed throughout the country and some of whom live in predominantly white communities, would commit themselves to what has been called "community nationalism."[4] This would mean that blacks would abide by the principle that they should live in black communities, a commitment that would require a number of them to move to new locations. While not bringing about an independent black government, this program could arguably contribute to the establishment of a meaningful, if limited, form of collective self-determination for black America.

It could, for example, increase black political power by creating or strengthening voting blocs in local, state, and national elections. It could provide safe locations for a robust black public sphere, where matters of common concern could be regularly and openly discussed face-to-face without the interference of nonblacks. If a sufficient number of wealthy and middle-class blacks adhered to this program, this might also help lift severely disadvantaged blacks out of dire poverty. By investing in these communities, the black elite could help revitalize the local economies in poorer black areas; and through their greater political clout, these more affluent blacks could push for policy initiatives that aid in developing the infrastructure of central cities. Should community nationalism therefore constitute the content of contemporary black solidarity?

The Legacy of Malcolm X

Philosophical scrutiny of the idea of black group autonomy is no mere intellectual exercise. Under current social and political conditions, there is every reason to believe that black leaders and activists will aggressively and urgently advocate this conception of black politics or something quite similar. Blacks, who are largely liberal to left in their political orientation, find themselves in an increasingly conservative political era, where the Republican Party cultivates and exploits antiblack sentiments to maintain power and the Democratic Party, given the influence of neoliberal elements within it, is loath to publicly advocate for policies that are explicitly designed to reduce racial inequality, for fear of losing white support.[5] Many African Americans are convinced that the broader public has abandoned poor black communities, and that black urban ghettos now face a crisis that our government is unwilling to adequately address. Moreover, black Americans often suspect that their fellow citizens

fail to support reform because of racial prejudice and see evidence
of this in the general trend toward conservative political ideology,
the gutting of welfare programs, and public withdrawal of support
for affirmative action.[6] The situation has been exacerbated by the
recent public turn away from domestic problems toward a focus on
national security and foreign policy, a shift that will leave even
fewer resources with which to fight poverty and improve education
in urban communities. In what is widely perceived to be a political
environment inhospitable to claims against the state on behalf of
African Americans, a return to calls for black control over community institutions is inevitable.

Acceptance of the principles of community nationalism is not
limited to those who came of age before or during the Black Power
movement. Many of the post–civil rights generation are also at-
tracted to these ideas, which have been an element of black political
culture at least since the Sixties and became even more entrenched
during the Reagan era. This is readily apparent in the culture of
hip hop.[7] Rap artists and groups such as Boogie Down Produc-
tions, Public Enemy, X-Clan, Paris, The Coup, Dead Prez, Mos Def,
and Talib Kweli give lyrical and sonic expression to these political
ideas—updating them, as they see it—to suit the needs of black
communities in post–cold war America. Rappers such as Chuck D
and KRS-One have written books defending the ideals of community nationalism.[8] Perhaps most importantly, community nationalism has come to the hip-hop generation through the autobiography
and recorded speeches of Malcolm X (1925–1965), a figure who has
attained iconic status in the post–civil rights era.[9]

The most influential exponent of black nationalism during the
early 1960s followed the teachings of Nation of Islam leader Elijah
Muhammad, who regarded African American emigration to Africa
as a long-term political goal and held that in the meantime blacks
should seek institutional autonomy and collective self-determination within the borders of the United States.[10] This would require

not only that blacks select the politicians who represent them but that they control the businesses, schools, public institutions, and law-enforcement agencies in their communities.

Like many nationalists before him and since, Malcolm X claimed that white nationalism in the United States and global white supremacy in general are the central problems facing people of African descent.[11] He argued that there was a direct parallel between the political struggles of blacks in America and anticolonial liberation movements in Africa, Latin America, and Asia, sometimes suggesting the possibility of international solidarity among all "dark peoples." Articulating a now familiar theme from Delany, he argued that the U.S. government should be viewed as a colonial power in relation to blacks in America and that blacks should oppose this illegitimate control over their communities.

Like Garvey, Malcolm X was suspicious of middle-class black leaders who advocated racial integration.[12] He believed that the black elite functioned largely to contain the black masses. Indeed, he maintained that whenever the revolutionary masses begin to fight for their freedom through militant collective resistance, whites call on their puppet Uncle Tom leaders to infiltrate the movement, take it over, and dissolve its militancy. These "so-called black leaders," as he often called them, would transform the black insurrectionist movement into nonviolent protest, a mere public spectacle. Whites in power, he insisted, were prepared to make minor concessions to blacks in order to keep the system of white supremacy intact. In light of this circumstance, he argued that privileged blacks sought integration, even if that meant living without true racial equality, because they feared that their standard of living would decline if blacks separated from whites. Thus, also like Garvey, Malcolm X aimed his message at the working class and ghetto poor, for he was convinced that they were revolutionary in spirit and generally regard the United States as a white nationalist imperial power.

Malcolm X frequently pointed out that even though blacks had helped vote in the Democrats (Kennedy-Johnson and a majority in both houses of Congress), those same officials had done very little to help black people, especially the most disadvantaged blacks.[13] He suggested that the Democrats had no intention of helping the masses of black folk, and claimed not only that these politicians were hypocrites but that they had conspired to limit the voting power of blacks, through, for example, gerrymandering districts in the North and failing to protect the voting rights of blacks in the South, where blacks constitute a majority in many districts.

Malcolm X believed that, politically, blacks should behave like a family: In public they should speak with one voice and show a unified front; any internal disputes should be worked out behind closed doors and out of the view of whites.[14] This meant that blacks needed a racially exclusive public sphere for political debate, a space where only blacks could participate in the discussion. He also thought it essential that blacks exclude all whites from their political organizations, for he believed that white Americans suffered from a practically incurable form of paternalistic racism and were an inherently divisive force among blacks.

Initially quite hostile to Christianity and favoring Islam, Malcolm X believed that Christianity's pacifism, messianism, and ethic of universal love encouraged blacks to capitulate to injustice and suffer in silence. But toward the end of his life he argued that blacks should put aside religious and ideological differences and recognize that they had a common oppressor.[15] Antiblack racism, he argued, negatively affects all blacks, regardless of faith or party affiliation, and thus blacks should unify to resist racial oppression on nonsectarian and non-ideological grounds. Although he continued to believe in the necessity of autonomous black institutions, he did come to relax his opposition to alliances with progressive whites.

Malcolm X's ideas of internal colonization, black communal self-determination, skepticism toward the black elite and the Democratic Party, and racially autonomous political organizations influenced a generation of black activists and have had a significant impact on the contemporary political culture of African Americans. As Manning Marable remarked, "Dead at the age of 39, Malcolm quickly became the fountainhead of the modern renaissance of black nationalism in the late 1960s."[16] Indeed, shortly after his assassination in 1965, many of Malcolm X's ideas were developed and promoted by several black leaders under the slogan "Black Power," a phrase popularized by Stokely Carmichael. This slogan carries strong negative connotations for many, largely because of the fraught historical context of its original invocation and perhaps because of its association with Malcolm X and militant forms of black nationalism.[17] But by ignoring its connotation and focusing on its philosophical content and social-theoretic underpinnings, we can begin to see the contemporary relevance of this political outlook.

Institutional Racism and Black Autonomy

To facilitate this critical reconsideration, I turn to the classic statement and defense of black political empowerment found in Carmichael (Kwame Ture) and Charles Hamilton's *Black Power* (1967). There are of course alternative conceptions of community nationalism. Yet most are still rooted in the philosophy of Black Power (even if they do not go under that controversial label) and hence are generally variants of the position defended in this influential book.[18]

Despite the legal gains of the civil rights movement, in particular the Civil Rights Act (1964) and Voting Rights Act (1965), Carmichael and Hamilton believed that continuing racism and black poverty demanded greater black solidarity. They defined racism as "the predication of decisions and policies on considerations of race for the purpose of *subordinating* a racial group and maintaining control over that group."[19] They also made the important and now

well-known distinction between overt acts of racism—aimed at racial subordination by means of murder, physical injury, the destruction of property, or other blatant forms terrorism—and covert
institutional racism that functions to subordinate low-status racial
groups through the hidden operations of established and respected
forces in society (such as the criminal justice system, the public education system, or corporate America). Institutional antiblack racism works through the subtle operation of a complex and powerful
racist ideology, which systematically leads, sometimes without the
full conscious awareness of those under its influence, to the subordination or neglect of vital black interests.

Carmichael and Hamilton claimed that although overt racism
had decreased, institutional racism remained endemic. Though this
analysis had new elements, they articulated it within the familiar
idiom of black nationalism. They claimed that blacks in the United
States constitute an internal colony, that blacks stand as colonial
subjects in relation to white society. Thus, they thought of institutional racism in America as a form of neocolonialism. They acknowledged that the analogy is not perfect, since colonial subjects
are usually geographically separated from the colonial "Mother
Country," and the colony is typically a source of cheaply produced
raw materials. Yet they insisted that blacks in America are forcibly separated into segregated communities and that the black population serves as a cheap source of labor, exploited by whites at
the expense of blacks. So blacks are, essentially if not strictly, in a
colonial relationship with the white majority. African Americans
constitute, as Delany would say, an oppressed nation within a nation.

In keeping with this theme, Carmichael and Hamilton thought
of American white nationalism as simply an outgrowth of European imperialism. Like Delany, they maintained that this expansion
was not initially motivated by racism, but a racist ideology soon

formed to provide a convenient rationalization for the subordination and exploitation of non-Europeans, particularly Africans. Because both white elites and the white working class have vested interests in the continuing subordination of the black population—a
point that Du Bois often emphasized—these two segments of the
white population frequently put aside their differences in order to
buttress white privilege and maintain collective control over their
black colony. It is in their relation to blacks that a relatively diverse
and often internally antagonistic white population becomes a more
or less unified group or, in the idiom of the Black Power movement,
"the white power structure."[20]

Note that these considerations are advanced largely from a pragmatic nationalist point of view: they emphasize the unjust treatment of blacks in America rather than a shared and intrinsically
valuable black national identity. There is, however, a classical rationale for Black Power politics implicit in Carmichael and Hamilton's
argument, a rationale based on the intrinsic value of group autonomy: namely, that concentrated and thereby increased political
power would enable blacks to exert greater influence on, or even
to control, the operation of those institutions that have the greatest impact on their well-being and freedom. Such political power
would allow blacks to exercise significant autonomy over their own
lives, to realize, to some extent at least, the goal of self-government
despite the persistence of institutional racism.

Community control over public services—education, social services, welfare provisions, housing, security, transportation—could,
if properly managed, effectively meet black needs. Not only would
this enhance black group autonomy, but to the extent that it pro-
motes a strong sense of cohesion, it may even be more efficient:
Blacks living in the same community would have greater knowledge
of and concern about their own needs than nonblack bureaucrats
from outside. Because of their tendency to produce networks of so-

cial support, living and working together would also make it easier for blacks to mobilize in times of crisis. Moreover, as blacks see concrete results from their collective political activity, overall civic participation would likely grow. Finally, to increase self-respect and dignity it would be necessary to eschew white paternalism. This program of communal solidarity would have the upshot of avoiding this "politics of deference" by reducing black dependence on white goodwill.

Yet black liberation, according to Carmichael and Hamilton, cannot be achieved by withdrawing from American domestic politics. Rather, it depends crucially on the ability of blacks to gain greater power and broader participation within established U.S. political institutions. With such political empowerment, blacks would be able to choose their own leaders and hold them accountable. To accomplish this, they insisted, Black Power requires blacks first to "close ranks," to cultivate group solidarity and organizational independence *before* seeking integration.[21] This means blacks must control their own communal institutions, which entails, among other things, preventing nonblacks (and especially whites) from exercising power over or within these institutions. Blacks must seek to define and control their political destiny, perhaps even form their own independent political party. This institutional autonomy need not be racially exclusive; black organizations and institutions may include some nonblack, even white, members. Yet it is essential that blacks lead, fund, and make policy for these organizations and institutions.[22] Committed nonblack allies should participate only in a supporting role.

Carmichael and Hamilton maintained that, contrary to a widely accepted national myth, American politics has always operated on the basis of ethnic-group power politics, and so community nationalism is really nothing new. If blacks are to be successful in this (sometimes covertly) tribal environment, they must not allow themselves to be misled by the ideology of bourgeois individualism but rather should come together on the basis of racial solidarity so that they can bargain from a position of strength.

Black Power was meant to be a direct challenge to white privilege, to white paternalism, to white power. However, Carmichael and Hamilton repeatedly emphasized that the goal is not the domination or exploitation of other ethnoracial groups, not even whites. The point instead is to gain an equitable share of social and political power, the *fair* share that continues to be denied to black Americans despite the passage of the Voting Rights Act. Black Power is not, therefore, a racist ideology. Although it advocates race-consciousness and black political independence as a strategy, it does so not for the purpose of subjugating whites but in order to create greater black political empowerment. Moreover, a political power base is sought, not in order to deny other groups their rights or to impose unfair burdens upon them, but rather to make the civil rights of blacks truly effective and to ensure that black interests are not politically marginalized. This form of empowerment would enable blacks to choose political leaders who are not beholden to white interests. Without such independence, nonblack supporters of the black cause could withdraw their support (or threaten to do so) whenever they perceived a conflict of group interests, thereby obstructing black advancement. On this view, then, Black Power politics is required to realize American ideals of democracy and equality in a society still plagued by institutional racism and rife with ethnoracial division.

With this summary of the basic tenets and justification of Black Power politics as background, in the next few sections I will argue that this philosophy is not one that blacks should accept today. I begin with some of the internal weaknesses in this conception of solidarity; I then turn to some of the external obstacles to its success. My general argumentative strategy will be to move us closer to a tenable conception of black political solidarity by demonstrating how we should *not* conceptualize such solidarity.

Reconstructing Black Residential Communities

The first thing to note is that the philosophy of Black Power faces a collective action problem that is analogous to an obstacle that would inhibit mass black emigration outside the borders of the United States in order to build a stronger black republic in, say, Africa, Jamaica, or Haiti. The difficulty is convincing the first stream of black elite and middle-class persons to leave more affluent and often predominantly white communities in order to live in or near poor black communities. Since the decline of the Black Power movement, an increasing number of blacks, despite the persistence of racism, have managed to raise significantly their socioeconomic standing, in terms of income, wealth, education, occupational status, and home ownership. Since 1970 the residential segregation of blacks has declined as middle-class and affluent African Americans have moved into formerly all-white areas of cities and suburbs.[23] Many of these better-off blacks now do not live in black communities, if they ever did, and some are understandably reluctant to sacrifice their standard of living by residing in poor communities. The mass exit of well-off blacks has had an enormous impact on the concentration of poverty and joblessness within those communities, resulting in forms of social dislocation and urban decay previously unknown there.[24] The explanation for this tendency of upwardly mobile blacks to leave black neighborhoods should not be reduced to racial self-hate. This out-migration might happen not because these communities are mostly *black* but because many are severely disadvantaged—in terms of job opportunities, availability of adequate housing, access to quality education, physical safety, social services, modern amenities, and venues for amusement and recreation.[25] As with earlier migrations from the South, it is reasonable to suppose that most blacks left those communities to take advantage of better conditions elsewhere.

A collective action problem arises for Black Power politics because some African Americans have been able to improve their socioeconomic position, sometimes quite substantially, despite continuing racial barriers and sometimes with the help of affirmative action and minority set-aside programs. Although antiblack racism negatively affects all blacks, its specific impact on blacks' life prospects can vary considerably—in scope, degree, and kind—across different sectors of the population. One consequence of this intraracial socioeconomic differentiation is that it is generally at odds with the basic interests of affluent blacks to live in predominantly black communities, because many of these communities have high concentrations of poverty.

If a number of well-off blacks were nevertheless to move to such communities, the reduction in the concentration of poverty would likely improve social conditions there, thus making the move more attractive to other affluent blacks. But the problem is that those black elites who make the *first* move have no assurances that others will follow, and so those well-off blacks who might otherwise be inclined to commit themselves to Black Power politics will typically stop short of moving to poor black communities. Instead they will opt, perhaps with regret, to assist the least advantaged in the black population through less personally risky measures, and from a distance.

Some might argue that a sense of solidarity *should* be sufficient to motivate more-affluent blacks to help those more disadvantaged, even if that means moving to low-income communities.[26] Their presence would expand the tax base, which could be used to improve schools and the social infrastructure; they could use their political clout and social capital to press the local government to make needed reforms; they could function as role models and mentors for youth in urban environments; and they could provide the required leadership to rebuild essential black social institutions and revitalize black civil society. Thus, in the spirit of solidarity they should assist those blacks in need. To not help when one clearly could exhibits a kind of callous indifference to the severe plight of fellow blacks.

But what exactly is the normative basis of this duty of the black elite? Two of the core elements of group solidarity suggest themselves. First, recall from Chapter 2 that *loyalty* typically includes a willingness to exert extra effort to help members of the group and to advance the group's interests. Clearly the poorest members of the black population could benefit from assistance from its more advantaged members, and this would in turn advance the goal of racial equality. Second, *special concern,* the disposition to assist and comfort those with whom one identifies, could underwrite the duty of the black elite to help those struggling to survive in America's ghettoes. This kind of concern should not be understood as simply fulfilling one's impartial moral obligation to help those in need—which we all, regardless of our racial identification, should be sure to carry out—but as a special obligation to other blacks in the collective fight for racial justice. This obligation is not special in the sense of *greater* but in the sense of *peculiar,* a distinctive duty that springs from the identification that solidarity entails.

Insofar as blacks are committed to group solidarity, this sense of unity can and should move them to aid each other in times of need. Yet it is unreasonable and unrealistic to expect blacks to discharge this duty by voluntarily moving to or remaining in such severely deprived social environments when they have no assurance that others will follow.[27] At a minimum, those blacks who have children owe their offspring a much better start than inner-city life typically affords. Although it may be morally *permissible* for parents to sacrifice the interests of their children in order to advance the interests of their ethnoracial group, especially when that group is oppressed, it is not clear that this is morally *obligatory.* Indeed, some would argue, plausibly I think, that it would be irresponsible to put one's offspring in harm's way by raising them in dangerous and impoverished social environments when suitable alternatives are available. Whatever obligations African Americans owe to each other in virtue of their political solidarity, it is not at all clear that these racial duties always, if ever, trump the obligations parents have to their own children.

But a more decisive consideration is this: Attempting to build communal self-determination on the assumption that black elites will come to recognize and be moved by such austere moral demands is a hopelessly utopian political program. It is imperative that blacks make an honest assessment of the limits of their unity rather than exaggerate its liberatory potential. Black Power politics must face the regrettable though undeniable fact that most people are not inclined to make tremendous sacrifices or take great risks for a cause from which neither they nor their offspring can expect to benefit.[28] There is no reason to believe that blacks are special in this regard, that they are somehow endowed with greater moral resolve than the members of other racial groups. Insofar as Black Power includes a residential requirement, some blacks would have to give up and risk a lot to carry it forward, and it is unhelpful to dismiss this circumstance with insistent (and often self-righteous), though clearly impotent, calls for greater unity and group responsibility.

In claiming that Black Power faces a collective action problem that a sense of solidarity cannot be expected to overcome, I do not mean to suggest that people are incapable of acting contrary to self-interest in order to benefit others. Many, if not most, are capable of such altruism, and group solidarity would be impossible if we were never willing to put aside our narrow self-interest to advance the interests of others. I only assume that *most* people do not freely make *great* sacrifices for people with whom they do not share intimate bonds, and that moving to or remaining in the ghetto would constitute a great sacrifice for most affluent blacks.

Class, Community, and Accountability

Some will be unconvinced by the above argument. So let us continue on the assumption that the collective action problem is solvable. Perhaps the sacrifice of a few highly motivated and dedicated middle-class blacks is enough to substantially increase black political power and community control. Maybe continuing housing discrimination will force more members of the black middle class to move closer to the black poor.[29] Perhaps by a fortuitous confluence of events, a large group of blacks in sufficient concentration will find themselves in residential proximity. Or maybe Black Power does not require geographical proximity after all, but only strong black organizations and committed black officials who are willing to advocate for blacks regardless of where they themselves reside.[30]

Whatever way the residential question is resolved, it should be clear that black community empowerment, of the sort Black Power theorists envisaged, cannot occur without significant contributions from black elites and the black middle class. There are several reasons for this. First, highly educated and financially secure blacks possess vital skills, economic resources, and information networks that are needed to effectively challenge white privilege, resist unjust state action, and reduce black poverty. Second, to the extent that black empowerment entails community control over vital social institutions and the administrative apparatus, black communities will need teachers, attorneys, managers, social workers, entrepreneurs, civil servants, and others from the professional-managerial class. Third, black elites, for a variety of complex reasons, tend to participate more than working-class and poor blacks in electoral politics—for example, in voting, being active in political organizations and campaigns, and discussing the relative merits of political candidates with their friends and family.[31] And fourth, it will be from among this more privileged group that black political leadership will largely come, particularly those who stand a chance at being elected to state or national public office.

Because blacks as a group cannot effectively challenge institutional racism unless at least some elites play a leadership role in the effort, the difficulty becomes how to provide an independent institutional base for elite political participation while ensuring that these leaders are *accountable* to black communities and not beholden to outside interests. If black political independence is to be achieved, this will require breaking the "client relation" that ties black leaders to external sources of patronage and thereby divides their loyalties.[32]

Carmichael and Hamilton were acutely aware of this problem. Indeed, their attempt to grapple with it led to their indirect-rule thesis: The white power structure controls black communities through local upper- and middle-class blacks who promote or protect the interests of the white machine and often neglect or sell out the interests of everyday black people. Such black politicians have no autonomous effective power. They are merely puppets for the white regime, a role that they sometimes rationalize by insisting on the need to be loyal to the Democratic Party in a rigid two-party system. Carmichael and Hamilton go on to say of this group of would-be black leaders: "It is crystal clear that most of these people have accommodated themselves to the racist system. They have capitulated to colonial subjugation in exchange for the security of a few dollars and dubious status. They are effectively lost to the struggle for an improved black position which would fundamentally challenge that racist system."[33] They claimed, following Malcolm X, that the white power structure is only too willing to offer selective favors and minor concessions in order to maintain its rule, and thus what has to be faced up to is the fact that a person cannot be an effective and trustworthy black leader and also have socioeconomic security. Well-paying jobs and social status will have to be sacrificed if the racist system is to be effectively challenged.

Now, it would indeed be wise to choose political leaders with a demonstrated commitment to forgo material advantages when this is necessary to advance the interests of their constituents. And, again, these persons may be in sufficient supply so that blacks no longer need to rely on white patronage. However, even if this practical difficulty could be solved, there is another that may be an even bigger obstacle: Class differences among blacks could undermine the possibility of a *democratic* form of solidarity, a form of group politics that is inclusive and respects equally the legitimate concerns of all black people. The problem is that if blacks are to find endogenous institutional sources of support for black political leadership, this will inevitably come, at least in large part, from more-affluent blacks, for again it is they who possess the necessary resources, in terms of education, highly valued skills, financial assets, political influence, and social networks. What this means is that no matter how self-sacrificing and dedicated black leaders and public officials are to improving the lives of the most severely disadvantaged among their people, they must inevitably seek patronage from this relatively privileged group of blacks. Without this support, they will not be able to alter the way the state and its related institutions operate vis-à-vis black interests. So although some black elected officials and activists can perhaps avoid being beholden to white interests, they cannot escape being beholden to black elite interests.

The trouble with this arrangement, as we observed in Chapter 2, is that the interests of elites will often be quite different from, and at times even in conflict with, the interests of more economically disadvantaged blacks. For instance, the black poor, for obvious reasons, are primarily concerned with securing employment that pays an adequate wage and finding affordable and decent housing, while black elites, because they already possess those basic material goods, are more often concerned with improving the public image of the group, removing racial obstacles to career advancement, or reducing (or compensating for) the psychological costs of being racially stigmatized.[34] In addition, to the extent that black elites view the behavior of the black poor, rather than, say, structural factors or irrational racial prejudice, as the source of the persistence of antiblack contempt, this will put these two segments of the black population at odds, threatening to undermine altogether the possibility of black solidarity. This problem of how to enlist the help of black elites while ensuring that they do not have a disproportionate influence on leadership or the construction of the black agenda is perhaps the biggest internal challenge to community nationalism.

In response to this concern, it is not sufficient to simply note that there are members of the privileged classes who are dedicated to the cause of black empowerment. Such "race men" and "race women" do exist, as Du Bois emphasized, and their hard work and sacrifices should be acknowledged and appreciated. As Du Bois came to recognize, however, there are also black elites who are dishonest, opportunistic, easily corrupted, or narrowly self-interested. It is difficult to establish what proportion of the black elite falls into this latter category, but we have reason to believe that they are a significant segment, certainly substantial enough that caution here is warranted. These self-serving individuals often effectively conceal their duplicity such that sorting the trustworthy from the untrustworthy within the ranks of the black elite is a particularly difficult task. Hence, although we should not deny that there are persons of integrity among the elite who would support black leadership without exploiting their power, we also must face the fact that many within this class are willing and able to use their positions and influence to secure their own interests at the expense of more disadvantaged blacks. This insight, which we owe to the radical democratic wing of the Black Power movement, is one that blacks would do well to take seriously.

Unfortunately, as Adolph Reed has pointed out, too many theorists and would-be spokespersons obscure the depth of these inter-class cleavages by employing the rhetoric of "the black community."[35] This expression can be benign, or nearly so, as when it is used simply to refer to the black population in a particular locale or to the black population as a whole, or when it is invoked to suggest the existence or value of black solidarity. But the idiom can also give the false impression that the black population (or some particular black subgroup) can, or should, speak with one political voice on all matters that affect blacks. It is not difficult to understand why Black Power advocates would exaggerate the degree of black cohesiveness, because the realization of their philosophy requires that blacks possess a determinate collective volition regarding their status and future in America. But identifying or cultivating a black plural subject capable of expressing the comprehensive political aims of black people taken as whole would be no small feat, for there are, as should be clear, conflicting interests and sharp ideological disagreements within the group. Some advocates of community nationalism implicitly assume that there exists, or could exist, a well-integrated black collective agent that is class-transcendent, pro-feminist, culturally cohesive, racially endogamous, trans-regional, and ideologically unified. This plural subject is sometimes spoken of as if it has its own aims, interests, and projects, and as if it already had the, perhaps unrecognized, capacity to act autonomously in pursuit of them. Lerone Bennett, for example, in his neglected but insightful book from the Black Power era, *The Challenge of Blackness* (1972), assumed that this kind of black solidarity is a realistic possibility, indeed a potentially revolutionary force: "If we [black people] pooled all our resources and energies, if we correlated all our forces and created one black superpower, we could end this thing or this country in a few weeks or a few months. A united black community, speaking with one voice and acting with one will on issues of politics, welfare, education, and housing, could turn this country upside down."[36]

Yet in reality there can be no such black superpower. At best, some individual (or some group) would presume to speak for the whole. This would-be black voice would have to assume or pretend that blacks share sufficient interests in common that his or her (or their) declarations about the collective will of blacks are uncontroversial or capable of garnering consensus. To be sure, blacks do share important interests in ending racism, eliminating racial inequality, and eradicating ghetto poverty. The problem is that many advocates of community nationalism try to reduce all forms of black disadvantage to racial oppression or white supremacy, thus linking every important political question that arises for blacks to this form of subordination. But racism, institutional or otherwise, is not the only significant obstacle that blacks now face, and for many it is not even among their more urgent political concerns.

Black Corporatism and Black Diversity

Harold Cruse has famously argued that blacks should arrange themselves into the institutional framework of a national corporate unit, rather than rely on Democratic Party elites, spontaneous collective action, or free-floating spokespersons for the race.[37] "Black corporatism" holds that the black population should be organized into a single corporate person with recognized authority to speak for all blacks. For example, blacks could form a new (or fortify an existing) political party, a national organization, or a federation of such associations. This would facilitate the formation of a collective will, enable coordinated action, and create institutional mechanisms for leadership accountability.

Unfortunately, advocacy of black corporatism sometimes amounts to defending what Wilson Moses calls "authoritarian collectivism," which he defines as "a belief that all black people could and should act unanimously under the leadership of one powerful man or group of men, who would guide the race by virtue of superior knowledge or divine authority."[38] In principle, though, corporatism need not be elitist, patriarchal, autocratic, messianic, or sectarian. Blacks could choose leaders from all social classes and genders; blacks could be neutral on matters of theology; and they could hold their representatives accountable. But even though democratic group self-organization is possible, at least in theory, there are serious grounds for doubting the desirability of blacks' forming themselves into one corporate body.

There are numerous fault lines among blacks that make it difficult to define a political agenda tied to specific policy initiatives without disadvantaging certain segments of the black population. Many of the political concerns of these marginalized subpopulations are what Cathy Cohen calls "cross-cutting political issues," which she usefully defines as "those concerns which *disproportionately and directly* affect only certain segments of a marginal group. These issues stand in contrast to consensus issues, which are understood to constrain or oppress with equal probability (although through different manifestations) all identifiable marginal group members."[39]

One of the most salient cross-cutting issues affecting black political cohesion is sexism, which remains a problem among blacks, as of course it does throughout the country and world. Given this, black corporatism would likely exacerbate institutional patriarchy. Black men are still thought of as the "natural" leaders of black people, they (provided they fulfill their responsibilities "as men") are widely thought to be the highest authority in black households, and the prevailing norms of family structure encourage women's economic dependence. This patriarchal ideology is already reinforced by concrete institutional power, as, compared to black women, black men continue to disproportionately occupy positions of authority in government, law, business, and the clergy. If blacks were corporately organized so as to speak with one voice, that voice would almost certainly prove to be biased in favor of male interests.[40]

A second cross-cutting issue is the political role of black churches and Christian leaders, which continue to have tremendous influence in U.S. politics, often defining the black agenda of some local communities. Given their organizational power and accepted legitimacy, black churches often drown out non-Christian voices within the greater black community.[41] Moreover, black churches, as is characteristic of many religious institutions, often have a strong male bias, if not an outright patriarchal stance on gender roles and women's rights. The clergy is overwhelmingly made up of men, and many Christians oppose the ordination of women. This unequal access to recognized leadership positions effectively marginalizes the interests and concerns of black women and silences their voices of dissent.[42] This circumstance could only be exacerbated by black corporatism, in which some organization would claim the right to speak for all, regardless of gender.

Third, given the persistence of prejudice toward homosexuality within the black population, corporatism would likely further marginalize the legitimate political interests of black nonheterosexuals, a subpopulation seeking equal civic status under already difficult circumstances.[43] When framed within the prevailing "official" conception of a domestic family unit (that is, a group of two or more persons residing together who are related by birth, marriage, or adoption), the interests of this doubly stigmatized group are often neglected, because few nonheterosexual partnerships are recognized civil unions with the same rights as traditional marriage contracts. The marginalization of gay, lesbian, bisexual, and transgendered persons is exacerbated by religious proscriptions against "homosexual acts," and worsened yet still by the HIV/AIDS crisis within the population that disproportionately affects and further stigmatizes gay men and, increasingly, heterosexual and bisexual women. Thus, nonheterosexuals and those infected with HIV/AIDS could not reasonably depend on corporatist black solidarity to secure their distinctive interests under these conditions.

Fourth, strong norms of racial endogamy exist among blacks, and these are at odds with the interests of the increasing number who have nonblack or multiracial parents, partners, or children. Even though the legal proscription against interracial marriage was lifted in 1967, interracial intimates still have to contend with continuing social disapproval of such relationships. Large segments of the black population not only prefer in-group marriage but also strongly object to racial exogamy and transracial adoption, at least where blacks are involved. Among those of known multiracial lineage who are categorized as black by the so-called one-drop rule (the social criterion for disambiguating racial identity that holds that a person is black if she or he is known to have at least one black ancestor), some desire multiracial social affiliations, a mixed-race social identity, or both. Some blacks are reluctant to recognize such persons as full-fledged members of the community and thus are not inclined to take their distinctive concerns seriously. Black corporatism could only worsen the marginal position of interracial intimates and those of multiracial lineage, putting them in an impossible position vis-à-vis racial politics.[44]

Finally, because of variations in local and regional conditions, different black communities will have different needs. Those in metropolitan areas but outside the central city often have a high number of middle-class blacks in proportion to poor blacks, relatively high property values, decent public schools, and low unemployment. In inner cities and rural areas, in contrast, poverty is highly concentrated, property values are low, schools are greatly underfunded, public infrastructures have deteriorated or are underdeveloped, and unemployment is high. Moreover, income and wealth vary by region in the United States; and there is a particularly large socioeconomic gap between black southerners and blacks in other parts of the country.[45] Region also powerfully affects the outcome of elections, with the South and parts of the Midwest being considerably more politically conservative than the West and

Northeast. Black corporatist politics could therefore marginalize the interests of those in less affluent or more conservative parts of the country.

In addition to the difficulties posed by cross-cutting issues, there is the problem that an effective form of black corporatist politics would seem to require that African Americans share a broad political ideology. However, as Michael Dawson has convincingly shown, blacks do not share such an ideology.[46] Though black Americans overwhelmingly vote for Democratic representatives (which does not necessarily mean that they *identify* as Democrats or fully embrace the party's agenda), they do not have a common vision of the ideal society; they do not share a conception of social justice or the common good; they do not agree on the basic principles that should regulate the relationship between government and citizens; and, finally, they do not agree on what kinds of economic inequality, if any, are justified in a truly just social order.

In short, Black Power corporatism would mean that many within the black population would be taking on enormous risks to erect an organizational structure with the authority to speak for the group. These are risks that the bonds of identification, trust, and loyalty among blacks are unlikely to be able to withstand. These concerns have long been present. Yet in the past, most blacks believed that these concerns were outweighed by the desperate need to defeat white supremacy, a deadly social force that denied the rights and severely reduced the life prospects of *all* blacks in the United States. Because racism and white domination were the most serious threats to their well-being and freedom, closing ranks on terms that were less than equal or fair was a sacrifice many were willing to make. Those who felt marginalized in the collective effort lacked the power to effectively press their claims for better treatment, for they had no viable alternative to racial group organization. However, with the legislative and judicial gains of the civil rights movement and the overall improvement in the racial climate in America, fewer blacks are willing to sacrifice or subordinate their other interests in order to advance the social position of blacks as a whole. Many marginalized black individuals are now able to demand as a condition of cooperation that their interests be taken seriously. Although racism still negatively affects all blacks, the material conditions of most have dramatically improved.[47] These social changes have shifted the context for black political struggles. In order both to protect against elite dominance, patriarchy, and the tyranny of the black majority over minority subpopulations and to enable political solidarity, blacks must reject the strategy of political centralization.

This rejection would not be tantamount to rejecting black solidarity as such. This unity, fragile as it sometimes is, could continue to serve as a political resource in the broader quest for social justice. But black solidarity, insofar as it is still tied to the Black Power paradigm, must be reformed and refined, not only to deal with new social realities but also to better conform to democratic principles. Blacks earnestly desire to be regarded as social equals in America, not just formally but substantively. This is, or at least should be, a principled stance, rooted in a commitment to equal justice for all. The commitment of blacks to equality should therefore be modeled or prefigured in the social institutions through which they seek full social inclusion and equal standing. That is, as Cornel West has consistently urged, blacks should regard each other as equals, and their political practices and social organizations should reflect this democratic commitment.[48] This, unfortunately, is not yet a reality.

To make political cooperation possible under these less than ideal circumstances, certain practical constraints should be instituted and generally recognized. In particular, it is essential that blacks have multiple and independent sites of organizational power and democratic accountability, where ideally the membership of such organizations overlaps to some extent. Such a decentralized network would enable the voices of all blacks to be heard and the legitimate interests of minorities within the minority to be protected. Without such protections, interclass conflicts, patriarchy, and majority black opinion will remain menacing forces, capable not only of restricting individual freedom but of undermining the prospects for mutually beneficial and fair black cooperation in politics.

Advocates of Black Power nationalism could agree that these are serious concerns. They might, for example, reject the idea that one institutional structure could represent the interests of all blacks, and might even concede the necessity of having several independent parties, civic associations, and political organizations. Yet proponents of Black Power may nevertheless insist that there must be some acceptable institutional means for coordinating black subgroups when their interests and goals overlap. Public activism is more effective when it operates through well-organized institutions with strong leadership. Given that blacks are a minority with relatively little power in national politics, their ability to effect meaningful social change hinges on their capacity to coordinate their efforts. Thus, a *multi*corporatist approach could empower blacks through greater group self-organization without running afoul of the demands of equality, tolerance, and individual liberty. Each democratically organized corporate body could opt out of or publicly dissent from any broader effort that it did not support. Such a progressive and inclusive form of pragmatic black nationalism would not dilute the collective power of the community by unnecessarily inhibiting its ability to organize itself independently.

This would be a more defensible vision of black political empowerment. Yet such a multi-organizational vehicle, insofar as it aims to express the political will of black people taken as a whole, also has significant weaknesses. The main problem with this suggestion is that once blacks shift their focus from race matters to broader issues of social justice or the public good, they should not want all, or even most, of the political organizations they participate in to be exclusively or primarily black in their membership or leadership. In fact, there are at least two reasons to reject any black multicorporatist solution that entails closing racial ranks within political institutions.

First, black membership in multiracial organizations could provide some protection from encroachments from the black majority, black men, and black elites. By supplying an alternative mode of political organization, multiracial associations could act as a check on the illiberal, undemocratic, and inegalitarian tendencies of some black political groups. Armed with the threat of defection to a multiracial political group, the marginalized would be in a stronger position to effectively demand tolerance and equal concern from fellow blacks without having to withdraw their allegiance to group struggle for black liberation. As a result, black organizations would either lose members or become more inclusive and democratic. Should marginalized groups still fail to receive the treatment they deserve, the members of these groups could then choose to advance their interests and ideals exclusively through multiracial organizations.

Second, at least some of the needed political associations would be significantly more effective in advancing the cause of social justice if they were racially inclusive and open to nonblack leadership. For example, the problems of poverty, high unemployment, joblessness, and failing schools are not peculiarly "black" issues—though blacks clearly suffer disproportionately from these disadvantages—but problems that negatively affect millions of nonblacks as well. Making progress in these areas will require multiracial cooperation. Even if blacks were better organized and more cohesive, they would still lack the power to successfully correct these forms of unfair disadvantage by themselves; and, as I noted earlier, there will be many blacks who do not have a direct stake in improving the life prospects of the economically disadvantaged. Similarly, bringing about gender equality and greater women's empowerment are not tasks that black women alone can carry out, not even with the help of sympathetic black men.[49] And attempting to eliminate sexism and gender inequality among blacks without attacking it in the larger society is surely futile. A fortiori, some of the interests of blacks who are not Christians, heterosexuals, or Democrats cannot be adequately secured by all-black organizations, as these would inevitably be too small. Finally, the concerns of biracial persons and interracial intimates for what Naomi Zack calls "microdiversity" must, ipso facto, be addressed by multiracial cooperation.[50]

If these points are conceded, it is difficult to see how multicorporatist Black Power politics could be democratic and egalitarian, inclusive and sensitive to intragroup minority concerns, respectful of individual autonomy, and yet politically effective in advancing the broad range of black interests within the current political environment. Black America is not now, nor has it ever been, a homogeneous mass. The black population is almost as pluralistic as the broader United States itself. To ensure that all subgroups and individuals are treated fairly within the institutional framework of Black Power, blacks would need something comparable to their own constitutional democratic regime, with all the rights and protections that such an arrangement generally entails. The establishment of such a regime is neither realistic nor, for the vast majority at least, a desirable outcome.

This discussion reveals a basic weakness in the philosophy of community nationalism or Black Power. The entire outlook is premised on an alleged social fact that no longer obtains: that for any (or almost any) black person, he or she will have more basic interests, political values, and urgent needs in common with other blacks than with any other group with which he or she might realistically make common cause in the political realm. This was true from the slavery era through Reconstruction. It might even have held throughout the age of Jim Crow. But it is not true in the post–

civil rights era, and blacks must come to terms with the political
significance of this fact.

Navigating the Racial Divide

Even if it were possible to effectively mobilize a multicorporatist
Black Power program without running afoul of democratic values or compromising broader egalitarian concerns, this form of
black solidarity may not be pragmatically desirable because of factors that are exogenous to black communities. Thus far I have discussed this program without much consideration for how other
ethnoracial groups would be likely to respond to its institutional
realization. It is reasonable to assume that Black Power politics
would engender a countermobilization on the part of nonblacks,
and not just whites, seeking to protect their own interests. Indeed, if
Carmichael and Hamilton were correct about the essentially ethnic
basis of American politics, we should fully expect this kind of resistance. With increased political centralization and organizational
autonomy, openly aimed at advancing black interests, we would
also likely see a rise in white nationalism, where some whites increase their collective power through greater group self-organization and solidarity, as they have often done in the past and, to some
extent, continue to do even now.[51]

Such resistance would not come solely from racists, however.
Some potential allies would also be alienated by this nationalist
program and may consequently become (further) disillusioned
with the ideal of racial integration, indifferent to black problems,
or disaffected from black people. Nonblacks would naturally view
their relegation to "supporting roles" within black political organizations as a sign that their help in the struggle for racial justice is
unneeded or unwanted; that their commitment to racial justice is
in question; that blacks are more concerned with advancing their
group interests than with fighting injustice; or that blacks do not
seek a racially integrated society. Moreover, because those who have

status and exercise power within institutions generally have a stake in preserving these institutional structures, even if they no longer serve the goals for which they were initially established, nonblacks have well-founded reasons to worry that black political organizations may, through sheer inertia or opportunism, become ends in themselves. Thus, although institutional autonomy might increase the organizational independence of blacks, the overall power of the group could be reduced because of isolation from other progressive forces. This situation would be particularly disastrous for blacks who live in minority-black electoral districts, for they cannot elect effective political representation without the support of like-minded nonblack citizens.

As Lani Guinier and Gerald Torres have warned, meaningful multiracial cooperation cannot occur if politics is viewed solely as a racially competitive arena.[52] In view of the tremendous power advantage the white majority has in electoral politics, the substantial growth in Latino and Asian American populations, and the need for nonblack allies, the form of group empowerment that community nationalists and black corporatists desire would prove counterproductive.[53] I agree, therefore, with William Julius Wilson that, given both the increasingly polarized racial divide that now exists in the United States and the need for multiracial alliances to combat rising economic inequality and urban poverty, we must not rely on racially exclusive strategies for improving the life prospects of black people.[54]

These external and strategic considerations will not, however, be compelling to the classical black nationalist. For him, black group autonomy is not merely a strategy for expanding the freedom and securing the material well-being of blacks but an end in itself, a principled stance rooted in the desire for collective self-actualization for the black nation in America. On this view, nonblack resistance to black autonomy is something to counter and defend against. Yet blacks should not acquiesce to such opposition,

for this would undermine their most basic political goals. The pragmatic nationalist, on the other hand, does see black solidarity as
merely a means, as a possible avenue for bringing about racial justice. Thus, the fundamental issue is which strategy—multiracial
organizations or black institutional autonomy—is more likely to
secure the basic interests and rights of blacks. According to the
pragmatic nationalist, blacks must choose the institutional means
that are most likely to be effective in the given sociopolitical context. Given that the present context includes the active presence of
powerful nonblack groups, their values and interests must also be
taken into account. In a strategic context, all rational parties should
consider how each of the others would respond to their activities
and choose courses of action accordingly. What this means is that if
needed allies will react to Black Power politics with hostility or mo-
bilized resistance, then blacks must calculate whether in using such
measures their interests will be advanced or compromised.

In light of such pragmatic considerations, one might be tempted
to conclude that blacks should both reject race-specific political
solidarity altogether and abandon demands for state-sponsored
measures that are explicitly and exclusively aimed at helping African Americans. Because many nonblacks are weary and sometimes
resentful of African American demands for racial justice, perhaps
blacks should rely solely on multiracial coalitions to advance their
goals and advocate for class-based or race-blind policies that would
benefit large segments of the U.S. population. Such a stance arguably would better enable blacks to garner allies in the fight for social
justice.

I think blacks should resist this suggestion. This concession
would make blacks needlessly vulnerable to antiblack racism, and
blacks would quite rightly be suspicious of any would-be ally who
would require this as a condition of political cooperation.[55] Racism is still a reality in America, where subtle forms of racial prejudice and implicit bias operate, both institutionally and infor-

mally, to attenuate black rights and limit black opportunity. On this point, Carmichael and Hamilton were absolutely correct. The non-black allies of blacks cannot reasonably expect African Americans to forgo all forms of group solidarity given the ever-present threat of race-based ill treatment and blacks' relative lack of institutional power.[56]

Civil rights laws, even if more adequately enforced, cannot protect blacks from all manifestations of racism. For one thing, there is no legal prohibition against some forms of unfair discrimination, neglect, and exclusion, such as the forms that occur within private associations and in informal settings, and there are subtle forms of cognitive bias that the formal and often crude mechanisms of law cannot readily detect.[57] When the law does punish racial offenders or correct racial injustice, the redress can be slow in coming or too late to be of much comfort to the victims, as it often is in housing and employment discrimination. Even when justice is swift, irreparable damage has sometimes already been done, as in cases of racial violence. It would therefore be irrational for blacks to unilaterally abandon group solidarity and depend exclusively on interracial efforts to protect themselves from all forms of race-based mistreatment. Some form of black solidarity, at least as a last line of defense and a means of mutual support, is needed to ensure that the interests of blacks are looked after, to make sure that blacks "have each other's back" in sometimes hostile social environments where interracial coalitions are unstable and where it is often difficult to distinguish friend from foe.

Moreover, contrary to the arguments of Carol Swain, fear of white backlash, even vicious white nationalism, is not a sufficient reason to avoid black political assertion, a lesson we should take from Du Bois's critique of Booker T. Washington.[58] As a matter of principle, no oppressed group should surrender to injustice simply because of fear of resistance. Blacks should demand, without compromise or apology, the enforcement of their rights as free and

equal citizens of the Republic; and they should defend themselves
by all morally permissible means against any attempt to harm their
legitimate interests.[59] To do any less would mean shamefully submitting to an undignified social existence, making them complicit
in their own oppression. In addition, would-be black leaders who
fail to speak publicly about what they think is just and fair, even
when, perhaps especially when, they face opposition, cannot expect
to sustain or gain the loyalty and trust of the broader black population, for blacks would regard these so-called leaders as cowardly
and obsequious, as mere accommodationists. Furthermore, because
there is no agreement among blacks or Americans more broadly
about what racial justice precisely consists in or how best to achieve
it, there must be open debate about these questions if there is to be
any hope of garnering such consensus. Remaining silent about or
downplaying the significance of racial injustice is thus a threat to
the dignity, political unity, and equal citizenship of black Americans.

So, for example, if black leaders are convinced that race-specific
public policy is needed to provide adequate redress for black Americans disadvantaged because of wrongs perpetrated against them
or their ancestors, these leaders should not shrink from asserting
this publicly simply because it is unpopular among whites. Nor
should they fail to defend race-conscious measures they believe are
necessary to ensure equal opportunity in education and employment. And if they are persuaded that race-based redistricting is a
fair and effective remedy for discriminatory efforts to dilute the
voting power of blacks, this too they should openly defend.

On pragmatic grounds, blacks might decide not to aggressively
press their agenda if the political context is unfavorable. Yet this decision would be a matter of political strategy. It concerns how best
to bring about racial justice given the sociohistorical context of action. Such political calculation and decision making should be seen
as separate from determining, say, what justice consists in, under

what conditions we should regard justice as having been adequately realized, or what means for effecting social change are morally legitimate. These latter questions should be determined on grounds of principle, and they should not be subject to compromise or negotiation even if this would reduce the likelihood of backlash.

Blacks are certainly entitled to organize as a corporate unit (or several such units) in order to advance a political agenda. Indeed, this entitlement is a component of their basic constitutional right to freedom of association and freedom of speech. Thanks to the courageous efforts of activists in the civil rights movement, Black Power is a program that blacks are now free to carry out as a political strategy, as a means to improve their well-being and enlarge their political power through greater group self-organization. Its legitimacy is no longer in question. What is in question are its wisdom and effectiveness. Here the political calculation of the benefits and costs of the program is entirely appropriate. Indeed, it is crucial that blacks openly discuss what different segments within the population would likely stand to gain from this program; who within the population will, or should, bear the burdens of carrying it forward; and who will suffer most should it fail or backfire.[60]

4

Black Solidarity after Black Power

Blacks must be clear about what they ultimately want, and can reasonably expect, from group solidarity. Do blacks want to maintain themselves indefinitely as a distinct, politically autonomous subnation and to view their autonomy, not simply as a means to full and equal civic standing within a multiracial democratic polity, but as an intrinsic goal? Or should they, following the principles of pragmatic nationalism, regard themselves as a community burdened by the stigma of race and racial inequality, collectively seeking to bring about a society where individuals are no longer unfairly disadvantaged because of their racial classification?

At this historical juncture, the classical position is untenable; black Americans still seeking group autonomy must take a pragmatic approach. But, as we have learned, even this more moderate vision has limitations. Black Power politics, in both its communal and its corporatist forms, is wrought with collective action problems engendered by the geographical dispersal of the greater black community and the residential segregation of its most disadvantaged members. Class divisions pose a problem for democratic representation and accountability, and such intraracial conflict threatens to undermine black political solidarity altogether. Organizational centralization is no solution, for this would threaten the legitimate interests of women and other marginalized groups within the broader black population. Moreover, it would be difficult to build stable bonds of political solidarity within such a diverse black population, where differences in culture, gender, sexuality, religion, region, intraracial identity, and political ideology create divergent interests, values, and priorities. Finally, by pressing their case for racial justice in a racially exclusive way, blacks would also run the risk of increasing an already tense racial divide and isolating themselves from needed progressive allies. These considerations suggest that if black political solidarity has a future in the United States, its content must be rethought.

Solidarity without Institutional Autonomy

I believe that the contemporary sociopolitical context calls for *trans-institutional* black solidarity—a form of group unity that does not depend on organizational separatism but rather extends across social organizations within which blacks (could) participate. No doubt, maintaining some black-only or black-controlled organizations is still useful and has its place within the larger social reform effort. Such institutions foster a shared sense of social responsibility and trust among blacks; they offer opportunities for public debate and building consensus; they provide contexts for black youth to develop a strong sense of self-worth; they demonstrate that blacks are capable of independent achievement; and they provide vehicles for resistance and self-defense when interracial solidarity breaks down. Yet it is equally important that these autonomous organizations be supplemented with greater black participation in multiracial associations that are sympathetic to black political interests.[1]

This means that, contrary to what many Black Power theorists have argued, black political unity should not be defined by institutional autonomy. Rather, it must be constituted by a joint commitment on the part of individual blacks to maintain solidarity with one another regardless of the racial composition of the political organizations in which each participates. This political sensibility, which might be called "pragmatic black consciousness," is as mobile as the individual who exhibits it, and it can have a positive impact on political dynamics through a variety of institutions, not just black ones. In this way, black solidarity would not be limited to the institutions and organizations that blacks effectively control or lead but would expand to every arena, formal and informal, in which politically conscious blacks have influence. The core of black solidarity—the identification, special concern, loyalty, trust, and political principles—is not, nor can it be, inherent in the institutional structures that blacks participate in or control. Although it surely needs to be cultivated and reinforced through interaction and cooperative efforts, this core must lie in the souls of individual blacks themselves.

To give just one example of how such solidarity might function trans-institutionally, consider the Congressional Black Caucus (CBC). Established in 1969, the CBC consists of black members of the United States Congress who work together to promote legislative initiatives designed to improve the lives and protect the rights of black and other marginalized citizens. These public officials are able to represent the broad range of interests of their multiracial constituencies while also voicing the specific political concerns of black America. Though members of the CBC form only a small minority in a white-dominated legislative body, their unity with one another and with other black citizens enables them to influence federal legislation and to ensure that black interests are not ignored. They have worked individually, together, and with other egalitarians in Congress to push for full employment, raising the minimum wage, equality of educational opportunity, enforcement of civil rights laws, increasing federal funding for urban development and public education, tax cuts for low-income families, and other measures that advance the causes of racial and economic justice.

Blacks situated in other multiracial organizations or institutions could operate analogously, maintaining their solidarity with other blacks while also working to promote causes for which there is no black consensus.

This decentralized form of black solidarity requires a broad division of labor. By this I mean not simply the assignment of responsibilities within an organization, but a broader division of efforts across black society as a whole. While some offer broad political visions, others articulate the concrete measures necessary to realize them. Those focused on tactics are balanced by those driven by principle. While some run for public office, others run their campaigns and yet more act as watchdogs, keeping the public informed and their leaders honest. There must be loud, militant agitators and those who work quietly behind the scenes. Some will have a talent for facilitating public debate, others will be better at influencing public opinion. Some shall seize the tool of law to defend the vulnerable, while others form private associations to help the needy and neglected. Some can fund-raise, others can fund. Some are born to educate, some to inspire, some to cajole. There can be team players and mavericks, traditionalists and innovators, leaders and followers. Few, if any, have the talent, motivation, temperament, and resources to play all these roles effectively. Not even the most revered race men and race women in black history—leaders like Frederick Douglass and Ida B. Wells-Barnett, Martin Luther King Jr. and Fannie Lou Hamer—performed all of these roles, and only a handful of people can be expected to devote themselves to black progress as if it were a calling.

Through such a division of tasks, black heterogeneity can serve an emancipatory purpose. Yet in urging each to play a complementary role within the collective struggle, I am not suggesting that someone or some group should be empowered to assign each their task. To avoid intragroup domination and unjust restrictions on individual freedom, black solidarity should be voluntary, nonhierarchical, and largely spontaneous. Across the population as a whole, this would therefore be a relatively uncoordinated form of group cooperation, one dependent on individuals moved by a sense of justice, group self-identification, and self-interest to contribute to the effort in a responsible way. Of course within individual organizations, responsibilities may be assigned. But provided one has joined voluntarily and may freely exit, this more coordinated intra-organizational division of labor is not incompatible with individual autonomy.

Three important consequences follow from this conception of solidarity that distinguish it from Black Power politics or community nationalism. First, it holds that black empowerment depends on the political will of individuals to use whatever talents, resources, and influence they possess to push for social reform, and on the willingness of progressive nonblacks to work cooperatively toward a more just social order—both highly contingent factors, to say the least. Second, such solidarity would not ensure that the black population in the United States could speak truth to power with one unified voice, for there would be no person or recognized corporate vehicle with the authority to represent the interests of all blacks. Third, blacks would moderate the demand for race-based organizations, for they would seek to join multiracial political organizations and to accept nonblacks as equal members in many of their own institutions.

These three consequences would undoubtedly lead some to see this as a toothless, and thus worthless, form of political solidarity. However, blacks must face up to the fact that organizational unity and group cohesiveness cannot deliver all that Black Power theorists promised. This does not mean that black solidarity is not worth sustaining and cultivating. Blacks continue to need the protection that such solidarity affords, and they can use what unity they do have to demand, encourage, and work toward greater racial justice. What they cannot do is expect that black solidarity would or could secure all or even most of the wide-ranging political interests of blacks. Pragmatic black nationalism might be less ferocious than Black Power, but that does not make it worthless or politically impotent, just more realistic. Blacks should emphasize the continuing importance of black political unity while also recognizing its limitations and its diminished—though not extinguished—progressive potential since the decline of the Black Power movement.

Others may charge that I have abandoned the nationalist tradition. For them, black nationalism is inconceivable without some form of racial separatism. But I would suggest that the integration/separation dichotomy should never have been regarded as the sine qua non of black nationalism. At one time, blacks might have been able to avoid racial oppression by physically moving away from states or neighborhoods controlled by whites. Today, geographical or institutional separation offers little escape from white influence. In fact, it might now be more pragmatic for blacks to be *dispersed* in order to exert influence within the multiracial institutions and informal networks that largely determine blacks' life chances. In this way, black dignity can be affirmed, black unity preserved, and black freedom attained, without relying on institutional autonomy or exaggerating the liberatory potential of group unity. Pragmatic nationalism is not a group-undermining form of "liberal individualism," as some might suppose. It is simply the form of black political solidarity most appropriate to the twenty-first century.

Ideological and Structural Causes of Black Disadvantage

I will now lay some of the philosophical and social-theoretic foundations for this alternative conception of solidarity. To begin with, any viable form of black political solidarity must distinguish the different sources of black disadvantage. There are (a) disadvantages that all blacks face because of contemporary racism; (b) disadvantages that some blacks face because of inherited handicaps attributable to past racial domination; and (c) disadvantages that some blacks face because of nonracial structural factors that have a negative impact on the life prospects of blacks.[2]

Racism is an *ideology,* a set of misleading and irrationally held beliefs and assumptions that serve to bring about and reinforce structural relations of oppression.[3] These social illusions, like the belief that blacks are intellectually inferior, are socially reproduced through norms that are embedded in the culture. These ideas are typically accepted, often unconsciously, because of the subject's unacknowledged desires or fears. For instance, some white workers have embraced racist beliefs and sentiments when they have been anxious about the entrance of lower-paid blacks into an already competitive labor market.[4] Racist ideologies emerged with and legitimized the transatlantic slave trade and European domination over "darker" peoples. These peoples were "racialized" in an effort to justify their subjugation and exploitation; that is, the idea of biological "race," the linchpin of the ideology, was used to impute an inherent and inalterable set of physical characteristics to the subordinate groups, an "essential nature" that supposedly set them apart from the dominant group and that explained why they could legitimately be exploited. Although racial ideology has far fewer explicit adherents or proud defenders in the United States today than it once did, and its content and form have shifted with historical and political circumstances, it continues to be expressed, often in implicit and unconscious ways, through the attitudes and conduct of many.[5] Racist ideology engenders and rationalizes discrimination against, neglect of, and outright hostility toward those it socially marks as "black," with consequences for virtually every sphere of social life. These familiar forms of racism, whether expressed in the operation of institutional structures, the mass media, or everyday social interaction, cause many of the burdens that blacks presently shoulder. Moreover, susceptibility to being harmed by racism is still a central feature of the black experience in America.

But some obstacles to black freedom and self-realization have their sources elsewhere. Some of these obstacles are structural disadvantages—such as inequalities in wealth, opportunities, and political power—that are the direct result of discriminatory treatment perpetrated in the past. Racial disparities in wealth and education, for instance, partly derive from a history of chattel slavery, land expropriation, destruction of property, forced segregation, and state-sanctioned racial discrimination. These historical injustices continue to have a negative impact on the life prospects of many African Americans despite the fact that these practices have been effectively proscribed. For example, because previous generations of blacks were largely prevented from accumulating wealth and gaining a formal education, many blacks born after the fall of Jim Crow have inherited few, if any, financial assets or educational advantages, putting them at a distinct disadvantage in relation to their white counterparts, many of whom have even benefited from past racial injustice.[6] In the absence of efforts to remedy these historically engendered inequities, blacks would continue to be relatively disadvantaged in our market-driven society even if racism were to be completely eliminated.

In addition, though, racial inequality has been exacerbated by social dynamics that cannot be attributed to the workings of racist ideology, such as a postindustrial U.S. economy that generally dispenses high rewards to persons with a college education and miserably low wages to those without; stagnation and decline in economic sectors that rely heavily on low-skilled workers; and changes in the tax code that favor individuals and households with significant financial assets. None of these developments rely directly on contemporary expressions of racism to produce their far-reaching social consequences. Yet they disproportionately impact blacks in a society where deep racial inequalities in education, employment opportunities, and wealth already exist, and they worsen racial inequality and create new forms of disadvantage. Consider the following example offered from Melvin Oliver and Thomas Shapiro:

> Four IRS mandated benefits can flow from home ownership: (1) the home mortgage interest deduction; (2) the deduction for local real estate taxes; (3) the avoidance of taxes on the sale of a home when it is "rolled over" into another residence, and; (4) the one-time permanent exclusion of up to $125,000 of profit on the sale of a home after the age of fifty-five. Put quite simply, since blacks are less likely to own homes, they are less likely to be able to take advantage of these benefits. Furthermore, since black homes are on average less expensive than white homes, blacks derive less benefit than whites when they do utilize these tax provisions.[7]

The racial consequences of this ostensibly race-neutral tax scheme are clear: It disadvantages blacks in their attempt to accumulate wealth and other desirable social goods. But if racist ideology, including racial stereotypes and implicit racial bias, played no role in its enactment—for instance, by corrupting the decision making of lawmakers—then it is misleading to characterize the negative impact of the tax scheme on blacks as a form of racism.[8] Indeed, such a characterization would be unhelpful in that it fails to identify the primary source of the problem (in this case wealth inequality) and leads to inappropriate remedies. Although blacks will disagree over which of these factors is the most significant in shaping their life chances, it is crucial that they recognize that black disadvantage is created by a complex set of ideologies, structural factors, and unintended social consequences, not just racism.

Agency, Responsibility, and Social Realities

Some will object that in emphasizing ideological and structural causes of black disadvantage I am ignoring *behavioral* causes. In particular, they will argue that some blacks among the working class and ghetto poor fail to take advantage of the employment and educational opportunities available to them and often irresponsibly engage in self-undermining activities—such as unprotected sex, street crime, illegal drug use, and consumption of luxury items—that further impoverishes urban communities.

To be sure, anyone who violates the rights of others should be held accountable, and those who make immoral choices are rightly criticized and sometimes punished for doing so, especially when these decisions impose unfair burdens on their children, families, or fellow citizens. But without denying that disadvantaged blacks should take responsibility for the choices they make—after all, rich or poor, we're all capable of making bad choices—it is unfair and callous for black elites to preach to those in dark ghettoes about how they ought to conduct their lives when we know that there are not enough jobs, that the public school system is in need of radical reform, and that racial discrimination remains a serious social problem. We also know that living in severely impoverished conditions shapes the attitudes of the poor toward work and education.[9] Hence, the poor often fail to develop the skills, credentials, and discipline needed to fare well in a capitalist economy. In addition, the combination of racism and poverty tends to severely damage the sense of self-worth and self-efficacy of its victims, a condition that is worsened by the lack of opportunities to be publicly valued and esteemed.[10] It should not be surprising that hopelessness, hedonism, and self-destructive behavior are the results.

Elites' criticism of the ghetto poor is also often presumptuous and condescending. Individuals who have demonstrated genuine concern for, and earned the trust of, poor blacks should certainly encourage them to take advantage of the meager employment opportunities that do exist, to study hard and stay in school, and to avoid activities that will likely exacerbate their situation. But such encouragement and practical advice is most effective when offered by persons on intimate terms with those who would benefit from hearing it. Simply being an affluent member of "the black community" hardly gives one the standing to berate poor blacks for their decisions or lifestyles. And self-righteous moralizing about the bad behavior of inner-city blacks will only alienate the severely disadvantaged from better-off African Americans, causing resentment and thus undermining the effort to build the kind of solidarity that would enable blacks to push collectively for the very social changes that would reduce such self-defeating behaviors.

Moreover, a one-sided focus on the behavioral causes of black disadvantage often gives rise to two tendencies that must absolutely be avoided if a more just society is to be achieved. The first is the temptation to substitute self-help programs for political action aimed at removing ideological and structural obstacles to equal opportunity. When political resistance to progressive change is formidable or stubborn, there is a dangerous tendency among elites to overemphasize self-help strategies or, worse, to opt for these strategies exclusively. Peer counseling, religious proselytizing, moral exhortation, and charitable giving, as worthy and worthwhile as they might be, do not constitute a politics. They are simply survival tactics.

The second tendency to be avoided is the use of the discourse of "personal responsibility" as a rationalization for not channeling public resources to those desperately in need. Providing these vital goods often requires sacrifices on the part of the better-off, and it is no surprise that some elites are reluctant to admit that justice necessitates these sacrifices. Yet a decent minimum standard of living must be guaranteed if we are to take seriously the principle of equal citizenship and to enable all members of our society to live with dignity and self-respect. Frustration with or resentment of the bad choices of some does not justify the withholding of the resources necessary to affirm their equal status among us.

Others might challenge the distinction between ideological and structural causes of black disadvantage, on the grounds that we are rarely, if ever, able to so neatly separate these factors, an epistemic situation that is only made worse by the fact that these causes interact in complex ways with behavioral factors. These distinctions, while perhaps straightforward in the abstract, are difficult to employ in practice. For example, it would be difficult, if not impossible, for the members of a poor black community to determine with any accuracy whether their impoverished condition is due primarily to institutional racism, the impact of past racial injustice, the increasing technological basis of the economy, shrinking state budgets, the vicissitudes of world trade, the ascendancy of conservative ideology, poorly funded schools, lack of personal initiative, a violent drug trade that deters business investment, some combination of these factors, or some other explanation altogether. Moreover, it is notoriously difficult to determine when the formulation of putatively race-neutral policies has been motivated by racism or when such policies are unfairly applied by racially biased public officials.

There are very real empirical difficulties in determining the specific causal significance of the factors that create and perpetuate black disadvantage; nonetheless, it is clear that these factors exist and that justice will demand different practical remedies according to each factor's relative impact on blacks' life chances. We must acknowledge that our social world is complicated and not immediately transparent to common sense, and thus that systematic empirical inquiry, historical studies, and rigorous social analysis are required to reveal its systemic structure and sociocultural dynamics. There is, moreover, no mechanical or infallible procedure for determining which analyses are the soundest ones. In addition, given the inevitable bias that attends social inquiry, legislators and those they represent cannot simply defer to social-scientific experts. We must instead rely on open public debate—among politicians, scholars, policy makers, intellectuals, and ordinary citizens—with the aim of garnering rationally motivated and informed consensus. And even if our practical decision procedures rest on critical deliberative discourse and thus live up to our highest democratic ideals, some trial and error through actual practice is unavoidable.

These difficulties and complications notwithstanding, a general recognition of the distinctions among the ideological and structural causes of black disadvantage could help blacks refocus their political energies and self-help strategies. Attention to these distinctions might help expose the superficiality of theories that seek to reduce all the social obstacles that blacks face to contemporary forms of racism or white supremacy. A more penetrating, subtle, and empirically grounded analysis is needed to comprehend the causes of racial inequality and black disadvantage. Indeed, these distinctions highlight the necessity to probe deeper to find the causes of contemporary forms of racism, as some racial conflict may be a symptom of broader problems or recent social developments (such as immigration policy or reduced federal funding for higher education).

The distinction between disadvantages caused by racism, on the one hand, and by race-neutral social factors, on the other, draws attention to the fact that blacks as individuals or as a group will often have common interests with members of nonblack groups. And given the magnitude of some social problems—such as increasing economic inequality, declining real wages, substandard public schools, urban poverty and joblessness, the scarcity of low-cost quality housing, and the high costs of adequate health care—multiracial efforts based on those common interests will be essential for progressive social change. Moreover, if the factors that create and sustain antiblack racism are rooted in the basic structure of U.S. capitalism, as radical democrats and socialists have often argued, we may find that the interests of blacks significantly overlap with the interests of other groups fighting for workers' rights and economic justice.[11] A narrow focus on racism as *the* cause of black disadvantage runs the risk of needlessly putting blacks in conflict with potential allies.[12]

Third, these distinctions can alert blacks to possible conflicts of interest within the group. A social obstacle caused by antiblack racism is potentially of concern to all blacks, because all are vulnerable, in one way or another, to this form of injustice. And although a social problem with a nonracial social explanation—for instance, that high unemployment among blacks is due to the unavailability of well-paying jobs for low-skilled workers—should be of concern to all, it might engender serious concern only in a subset of the black population. Even the fact that some blacks still suffer the effects of past racism will not necessarily move all blacks equally, for some have managed to secure a privileged social position within the current stratified order despite the legacy of racism.

The core suggestion here is that black solidarity can still be a useful tool of resistance when it comes to problems of race. Yet with other important political issues and social problems, the interests of different segments of the black population often diverge or even conflict. With these latter concerns, having someone or some group speak about *the* will of the black population not only would be misleading but would seriously threaten the legitimate interests of many. When we clearly distinguish the various sources of black disadvantage, we highlight fault lines within the greater black population that are often obscured when we talk loosely about the subordinate position of blacks in America. The point of stressing these internal sources of conflict is not to further fragment or undermine black unity. Instead, the aim is to demonstrate the necessity of making a realistic assessment of the progressive potential of black political solidarity. Once it has been rethought, pragmatic black nationalism can still play a positive role in contemporary U.S. politics.

The Content of "Black" Solidarity

The foregoing considerations raise a fundamental question: What are (or could be) the underlying basic principles of a specifically *black* political solidarity? The realm of domestic politics in a liberal capitalist democracy includes (1) the relations of dominance and subordination, legitimate or illegitimate, between the government and the inhabitants of the state's sovereign territory; and (2) the operation and internal structure of nongovernmental institutions (such as corporations, economic markets, schools, and political organizations) and of informal social networks that significantly shape how scarce but vital resources are distributed and how legitimate authority is obtained, structured, and exercised. I understand black politics to be collective action that aims to advance black interests by altering the constellation of benefits, burdens, and power within this complex domain. Given this, the fundamental question for us is, What are "black interests"? Are they the group interests of the U.S. black population qua irreducible national community? I have argued that either this conception of black interests assumes an untenable conception of black cohesiveness, or it wrongly supposes that it is possible and desirable for blacks to become a corporate body with would-be representatives who speak for the whole.

My alternative suggestion is that we conceptualize black interests in terms of the unfair social disadvantages that some individuals or groups face because they are (or their ancestors were) socially defined as members of the "black race." This is "identity politics" only in the sense that individuals who are widely regarded, and generally regard themselves, as members of a distinct social group participate in collective political action. It is not what some call a "politics of recognition."[13] That is to say, it does not seek to institutionalize or publicly affirm black ethnic, cultural, or national distinctiveness. Nor, I hasten to add, does it seek to abolish blackness as a positive social identity. Rather, this is a black politics whose aim is to remove or mitigate the ideological and structural obstacles to the equal civic standing and equal life chances of those who are socially classified as racially black. On this conception of solidarity, black politics is not simply a matter of promoting the interests of blacks, as if black people were just another "interest group" seeking advantages through traditional political processes. Black politics is instead about identifying, correcting, and ultimately eliminating race-based injustices. In this way, black political solidarity should be understood as black collective action in the interest of racial justice, not on behalf of an ideal of blackness.

Adolph Reed has argued forcefully against the "politics of authenticity," where some normative standard—whether petit bourgeois self-help ideology, grassroots radicalism, cultural nationalism, or Pan-Africanism—is posited as representing the "real" group interest of all blacks. He is also suspicious of attempts by would-be leaders to speak for the black population as a whole, especially when they lack an identifiable popular base of support that can effectively hold them accountable. But Reed maintains that limiting black politics to race-based problems artificially restricts the scope of legitimate political action. Alternatively, he defines black political activity as

> a dynamic set of social relations and interests that converge on some issues as consequential for broad sectors of the black population and that diverge from others, based on other identities and interest aggregations. This is a black politics that does not pretend to exhaust all, or even necessarily the most important, aspects of all black people's political concerns and activity. It is a notion of black politics in which black people, as individuals and as groups, organize, form alliances, and enter coalitions freely on the basis of mutually constituted interests, crisscrossing racial boundaries as they find it pragmatically appropriate.[14]

Reed's trenchant critiques of contemporary black political culture are often compelling. Yet black politics should not be understood as just any political intervention by a large group of blacks with mutually recognized shared interests. Take, for example, a group of black residents living in an all-black or predominantly black neighborhood who collectively protest the placement of a toxic waste dump near their community. Does this constitute *black* politics? I would argue yes *only* if their political action is based, at least in part, on their shared belief that public officials or the relevant corporations had acted on racial prejudice or bias (whether conscious or unconscious) and treated this community, because it is black, as if it were due less than equal concern and respect. However, if environmental racism is not the concern, and the community has simply come together to protect their interests in preserving an environmentally safe neighborhood, then their action should not be conceived as an expression of black politics.[15]

If we are to leave behind all residual traces of racial essentialism, we must allow that it is possible for blacks to act in concert without this being motivated by racial identification or a concern for how their actions would impact blacks as a group. I agree with Reed that we should not deny that blacks, both individually and collectively, can act politically in all sorts of ways without their actions springing from specifically racial concerns. But neither should we think that every political action carried out by a group of blacks is an instance of black politics, even if that group is large and race-conscious.[16] The failure to fully appreciate this point is often a symptom of a racial ideology that, as Barbara Fields points out, absurdly assumes that everything that blacks do or say is somehow "racial."[17]

Moreover, Reed's conception of black politics reduces it to an ad hoc basis, a kind of black *modus vivendi*.[18] He treats black politics as *solely* a matter of particular black individuals or groups responding to specific circumstances that affect their interests and negotiating a common basis for collective action. The consensus reached through such mutual adjustment is only as stable as the contingent circumstances that have brought about this convergence of interests. The virtue of this approach is that it conceives of black politics as pragmatic and voluntary. Yet its limitation lies in the fact that it treats black political solidarity as merely a matter of short-term alliances. This is not a kind of unity that blacks can rely on in the long-term struggle for racial justice. A mere black intragroup coalition politics would have the weakness of all coalition politics—instability. A shift in the constellation of power among the relevant groups leads, too often, to the withdrawal of needed forces or the exclusion of marginalized elements. Blacks need a form of solidarity that includes a standing readiness to act collectively in the political arena, a unity rooted in a set of principles that all can be reasonably expected to affirm. Without this, black politics lacks the foundation needed for continuous endeavor. Indeed, in the absence of this principled solidaristic disposition, it is not clear that we should be talking of "black politics" at all, as opposed to proclaiming its demise.[19] Reed's "black politics" embraces limited cooperation for mutual advantage, but not solidarity. This requires us to reject Reed's position, despite its several positive dimensions, because it fails to recognize that a meaningful form of black political solidarity is still viable in the post–Jim Crow era.

To address skepticism toward my thesis, we must distinguish between the interests that blacks share *because* they are black (such as combating racial discrimination) and the interests that some blacks may happen to share for reasons unrelated to their blackness (such as securing low-cost health care). The latter set of interests need not be shared by all or even many blacks and may significantly overlap with the interests of nonblack groups. The former set of interests potentially binds all blacks together, for these interests are bound up with eradicating the racial stigma and racial injustice that unfairly limit the liberties and opportunities of blacks. It is only these interests associated with racial justice that, I believe, should now be characterized as "black interests" in the relevant political sense of the phrase. Accordingly, I would urge that we define black politics, not only in terms of (1) the common racial identity of the agents who engage in it, but also, and more importantly, in terms of (2) the political interests those agents share because of the unfair social consequences that this ascriptive racial identity typically entails and engenders and (3) the mutual recognition of the need to work collectively to advance these shared interests in racial justice.

This limitation in scope might appear to have an ideological dimension, because it is rooted in a commitment to individual autonomy, a value that is associated with liberalism. But the constraint just as readily can be defended on conceptual and pragmatic grounds. Black political action is constituted by black collective interventions in the political realm on behalf of black interests. Under current conditions, the only interests that blacks share on account of their being black and that can also serve as a stable and legitimate basis for political unity are race-related ones—fighting racism, promoting racial equality, eliminating racialized poverty, and reducing racial antagonism.

Now, some who conceptualize black politics as any political intervention of a sufficiently large group of blacks tacitly invoke the idea that blacks, quite apart from their vulnerability to being harmed by racial injustice, form an inextricably linked black nation. On this familiar kinship conception of blackness, a core element of classical black nationalism, anything that would affect the interests of some group of blacks or, at the limit, any black person, should be of concern to all blacks simply because they are black. It is as if each black person were a family member whose interests are seen as intimately and inescapably bound up with the interests of all other members. But as I have discussed in previous chapters, this romantic vision of black unity, despite its prima facie appeal, is an unrealistic and invalid attempt to extend the idea of familial loyalty to racialized groups.[20]

Disproportionate Impact and Racial Equality

There is, however, a more plausible version of this kinship concept that should be considered. According to this view, any remediable social problem that *disproportionately* affects blacks (such as urban poverty, joblessness, or failing schools), regardless of whether it has been caused by racism, is a matter of black political interests.[21] Now of course blacks, as U.S. citizens and as human beings, should be concerned about these social problems and should do their part to correct them. But our focus here is the political basis of *black* solidarity, not the moral obligations of American citizens or persons qua moral agents. Ours is a question about what black political unity specifically requires and aims at, a form of solidarity that need not, and indeed should not, define all of the moral and political commitments that a black person takes himself or herself to have.

Our question might be put this way: What political principles can blacks reasonably expect all other blacks, because they are black, to commit to as a basis for group action? Given the differences in socioeconomic condition that currently exist, this "disproportionate impact" approach to black interests is not a reliable basis for political unity. Blacks simply cannot expect such broad support where material interests and racial classification diverge sharply. The very fact that a given social policy disproportionately affects the black population, as opposed to impacting all blacks, is a reason to think that some blacks will likely defect from the collective fight to resist it. For example, we have reason to believe that, on average, black elites will not have the same level of concern about social disadvantages that primarily affect working-class blacks (such as the unavailability of jobs that pay a living wage) as they will have about the closing off of opportunities for the more affluent (such as legal proscriptions against preferential treatment in higher education). This suggests that the alternative kinship conception is still implicitly tied to the dubious idea of an irreducible black nation. Its defenders often hold out the unrealistic hope that all blacks will be equally invested, or nearly so, in all forms of disadvantage that affect blacks.

Some endorse the disproportionate-impact view of black political interests because they are convinced that where an institution, practice, or policy disproportionately and negatively affects blacks, racism is the root cause. But, as I argued earlier, the causes of black disadvantage are diverse and complexly interrelated. It is simply a mistake to assume that racism, past or present, can explain every form of social disadvantage from which blacks disproportionately suffer. The dangers in this assumption are twofold: it can lead some blacks to expect allies within the broader black population where there are none or too few, and it can mislead them into thinking that their interests are always opposed to those of nonblacks. Either way, this assumption gives rise to self-defeating forms of classical black nationalism.

There is, however, an important aspect of the disproportionate-impact view that should be regarded as a matter of black interests, properly understood. Many policies and practices that have a disproportionate negative effect on blacks, regardless of whether these policies and practices spring from racist motives or bias, will worsen or reproduce racial inequality, such as higher rates of unemployment, incarceration, and poverty among blacks than among whites. This outcome would reinforce widely held racist assumptions, such as that blacks are "naturally" less intelligent, lazier, and more violent than the members of other racial groups. Social outcomes that seem to confirm racial stereotypes will inevitably perpetuate ideological illusions about "racial" differences, and the persistence of such a racist ideology does negatively affect all blacks. Given that blacks want to end or reduce racism, they should therefore also be concerned about *substantive* racial inequality. Demanding procedural equality and equal opportunity will not be suf-

ficient, because, as we observed earlier in this chapter with the case
of inequalities in wealth, a policy or practice can be race-neutral in
conception and implementation and yet still reproduce or worsen
racial inequalities. I am not suggesting that proportionate racial
representation or racial parity in all significant sectors of social life
is, in itself, a principle of justice. But if we are serious about erasing
racial stigma, then we must attend to racial outcomes and not regard their consideration as always opposed or irrelevant to social
justice.[22] Careful consideration of how a given policy, procedure,
or practice will impact the *relative* life prospects and political power
of different racial groups must be a component of any antiracist
agenda.

Of course, if so-called racial differences were not reified or natu-
ralized as they are in our racialized culture, blacks' being overrepre-
sented among the poor and underrepresented among the affluent
would not lead to stigmatizing assumptions about the inferiority of
blacks. But given the power and sheer inertia of racial ideology,
these suspicions linger, perhaps even among some blacks. Some
people even have the perverse disposition to cling to any "evidence"
that might appear to confirm black inferiority. Consider, for example, the "best-seller" status of such books as Dinesh D'Souza's
The End of Racism (1996) and Richard J. Herrnstein and Charles
Murray's *The Bell Curve* (1996). It would be nice to think that racist
beliefs could be eradicated simply by education, counterevidence,
or dialogue. And perhaps someday such beliefs will be generally regarded as silly superstitions of a bygone era. In the meantime, the
rights and opportunities of some are being unfairly limited by the
continuing existence of racist stereotypes and racial bias. To ensure
that the life prospects and political liberties of blacks are not thus
obstructed, blacks should regard themselves as having a pragmatic
stake in policies that would move the country closer to substantive
racial equality.

To give just one example of how this commitment might express itself, consider the distressingly high incarceration rates of young blacks, especially males. To the extent that these rates are due to institutional racism in the criminal justice system (for example, racial profiling, unfair sentencing, and racial bias in drug laws), blacks can work to reduce them on grounds of racial justice. But they should also fight to reduce them because high rates of imprisonment stigmatize all black youth as violent, undisciplined, lazy, and lawless, thus reducing their life prospects and perpetuating racial stereotypes. We should keep in mind, moreover, that black rates of imprisonment would be disproportionately high even if the criminal justice system were free of racial bias, because blacks, especially black children, are disproportionately poor. Because of desperation, the poor are more likely to commit crimes for which they will be caught and punished, and they are less likely to have the resources (for instance, money for bail or quality legal counsel) that will enable them to escape jail-time. So here we see why blacks should advocate for government policies and promote self-help strategies that will reduce substantive racial inequality. Such measures, when fair to all who will be affected by them, can contribute to the quest for racial justice.

Some will still want to retain a more expansive conception of black political solidarity than the one defended here. One way of making the case for this would be to insist that black interests are not limited to racial justice but also include any progressive agenda that a group of blacks attempts to advance *qua* black people. That is, the political intervention would be motivated by their self-understanding *as* black people *on behalf of* black people, whether or not the political concern could plausibly be construed as resistance to racial injustice. For example, fighting for socialism or gay rights, despite the fact that most blacks favor neither, could nevertheless be an expression of black solidarity, provided it was carried out in the spirit of unity.

But by leaving the normative content of political blackness

completely unspecified, we run into a difficulty discussed earlier: namely, not all blacks, given their diverse interests, priorities, and values, could reasonably be expected to endorse every political intervention undertaken "on their behalf" by a group of race-conscious blacks. Of course, individual blacks or black subgroups should advocate for whatever causes they believe in, and they should try to convince other blacks to join these causes. A problem arises, however, when activists or would-be spokespersons represent such political interventions as if they were expressions of the will of the black community. As African American history teaches us, some of the things done or said by blacks on behalf of blacks would be unwelcome by many of their intended beneficiaries. Recall, for example, the case of antebellum free blacks negotiating with President Lincoln over the resettlement of the black population to Latin America or Africa. We should also remind ourselves of Booker T. Washington's political program, which suggested to whites that blacks were willing to sacrifice their civil rights in order to advance economically. Or consider the more recent attempt by Ward Connerly to get state governments to no longer recognize "black" or other racial categories as relevant social classifications within the public sphere, despite the fact that this would inhibit the state's ability to enforce civil rights laws.

In the present context, in which many would welcome a solution to the long-standing "Negro problem" as long as it would cost them little or nothing to enact, prominent and well-connected blacks who propose such answers will inevitably be taken seriously by the wider public even if they lack broad support within the black population. Blacks currently lack an effective means to hold such persons accountable, as well as any means to effectively affirm or dissent from their public declarations in a way that will be heard by those in power.

Blacks do have some control over the public officials whom they elect to represent them, especially in majority-black districts, as these persons can sometimes be voted out of office if they are unresponsive to black concerns. But these representatives, as important as they are, will be insufficient to successfully carry the cause of racial justice forward in the current political climate, where far too many citizens are indifferent, if not hostile, to the calls of public officials for racial redress. Grassroots organizers, civil rights activists, civic associations, political organizations, intellectuals, and publicly engaged citizens, all acting in the spirit of solidarity, are therefore still vital.

Although black corporatism is not desirable as a means for creating democratic accountability within the context of the form of solidarity defended here, a public philosophy might be an attractive alternative. As I have emphasized, such a philosophy should not, and could not, be a comprehensive political ideology. Yet some common understanding of the scope and content of black political unity is needed, if only at the level of general principles. The elimination of racism, ghetto poverty, and racial inequality is in the interests of all blacks qua blacks. When black activists acting in the name of black people work for racial justice, such acts can reasonably be expected to garner consensus; and therefore these actions have some measure of legitimacy. These basic values could therefore function as "fixed points" of agreement, not in the sense of a bedrock foundation that should never be revised, but as principles that should be altered or discarded only after serious and careful consideration. They could serve as an implicit "Black Constitution"—as precepts that would informally regulate and sanction black political action. One concrete upshot of the establishment of such a public philosophy would be this: Any would-be black spokesperson who urged policies clearly incongruent with these principles would be met with a loud chorus of dark voices ringing out in collective dissent.

5

Race, Culture, and Politics

It is inconceivable that I feel alienated from the Western tradition; my people have contributed so much that is vital and good to it. I am alienated from the *people* who call themselves white, who think they own Western tradition.

—**Nikki Giovanni,** *Racism 101* (1994)

I have argued that a black public philosophy should include a commitment to antiracism, antipoverty, and substantive racial equality. Yet many advocates of black solidarity would urge that we also include a commitment to black cultural autonomy. At least since the late nineteenth century, prominent black intellectuals, artists, and activists have advocated various forms of black cultural self-determination. And as William Van Deburg has observed, cultural nationalism, perhaps more than any other ideology of the Black Power era, continues to have an enormous impact on African American self-understanding, political consciousness, and social institutions.[1] Moreover, the cultural politics of difference (or multi-culturalism), which many progressives embrace, has some striking similarities to the cultural nationalism of the Black Power movement. Thus many have come to think of this "politics of recognition" as an enduring component of black politics.

In light of its continuing currency, I want to critically evaluate the principal claims of black cultural nationalism. The focus of this inquiry, as before, will be on the philosophical presuppositions and political significance of the doctrine. I will argue that black Americans should not embrace black cultural nationalism as a component of their public philosophy and that contemporary black politics should not be understood on the model of multiculturalism.

Black cultural nationalism (though not always under the label *nationalist*) takes a variety of forms, as it has had numerous proponents of various ideological stripes at different historical moments. Canonical representatives include W. E. B. Du Bois, Alain Locke, Amiri Baraka, Harold Cruse, Haki Madhubuti, Maulana Karenga, and Molefi Asante.[2] Rather than discuss each historical variant, I offer a general characterization—a sort of Weberian ideal type or heuristic construct—comprised of eight tenets.[3] These tenets should not be regarded as the necessary and sufficient doctrinal commitments for one to count as a bona fide cultural nationalist. Nor do they aim to get at the "essence" of black cultural nationalism. The tenets are merely meant to articulate, in a relatively abstract and schematic way, what I take to be the main concerns of those who seek black cultural autonomy. But my aim is to characterize this popular philosophy in such a way that any proponent of black cultural autonomy would endorse some substantial subset of the tenets and would be generally sympathetic to them all.

There will be some who subscribe to a number of the following tenets yet do not think of themselves as nationalists of any sort. With regard to such persons I see no need to insist on the designation *nationalist,* a label to which many would object. Some would prefer to be regarded as "cultural pluralists" to distinguish themselves from versions or aspects of the doctrine that they reject. Again, my point is not to debate political labels but to critically engage with substantive positions that are widely accepted among those who identify with, or at least have some affinity for, the nationalist tradition.

Tenets of Black Cultural Nationalism

Each of the following eight tenets of black cultural nationalism has embedded within in it both factual (descriptive) and normative (evaluative) presuppositions. In this section I will make these assumptions explicit and outline the basic rationale behind each tenet. Part of the aim will be to suggest how they fit together to form a coherent outlook—a black nationalist philosophy of culture.

1. Distinctiveness: There is a distinct black culture that is different from (and perhaps, though not necessarily, in opposition to) white culture. The "black" culture in question is sometimes understood narrowly to mean indigenous African American culture (that is, the culture of African slaves in North America and their descendants). Alternatively it may be thought to include cultures from the broader diaspora (for example, from parts of Latin America or the Caribbean) or from sub-Saharan Africa. The relevant "white" culture is conceived variously as WASP, Anglo-Christian, Euro-American, European, or Western. Within these categories, some would also distinguish between high, middle-brow, and popular culture or, alternatively, between fine art and folk expression. For simplicity, I will use the terms *black* and *white* to denote all conceptual variants, and I will not invoke a high/low or fine/folk distinction. The account of the specific characteristics of and differences between black and white cultures varies with the particular advocate of black cultural nationalism. Yet it would not be unfair to say that such accounts generally characterize black culture as fundamentally oral, communal, harmonious, emotive, spontaneous, spiritual, earthy, experiential, improvisational, colorful, sensual, uninhibited, dialogical, inclusive, and democratic. White culture, by contrast, is often viewed as essentially logocentric, individualistic, antagonistic, rationalistic, formal, materialistic, abstract, cerebral, rigid, bland, repressed, monological, elitist, and hegemonic. These are, as I say, typical ways of representing the differences between the two cultures. Other, perhaps more nuanced, ways of distinguishing them are of course possible.[4]

2. *Collective Consciousness: Blacks must rediscover and collectively reclaim their culture, developing a consciousness and a lifestyle that are rooted in this heritage.* It is thought that this would enable blacks to form an identity on their own terms, autonomously and endogenously. Some cultural nationalists concede that black culture, especially the African American variety, has been eroded or suppressed by other ethnonational groups, in particular those of European descent. But rather than acquiesce to this cultural imperialism, they insist that this loss of cultural distinctiveness is all the more reason for blacks to self-organize and perhaps to self-segregate in order to revive their heritage or construct a new independent culture without the interference of nonblacks.

3. *Conservation: Black culture is an invaluable collective good that blacks should identify with, take pride in, actively reproduce, and creatively develop.* Black culture is held to provide many benefits for blacks, including these: a basis for psychological integration, sources of self-esteem and group pride, a repertoire of valued social roles, a stock of useful skills and techniques, conventions of social intercourse, artifacts of aesthetic worth and historical import, images of symbolic significance, distinctive styles of expression, a venerable intellectual tradition, and common narratives that contain vital sociohistorical knowledge. The loss or decay of this culture would be tragic, as it would mean the disappearance of an irreplaceable and multifaceted, shared social good. As they (could) benefit in countless ways from its existence and would be harmed

by its extinction, blacks must do their part to preserve black culture. This may involve, among other things, contributing to the establishment and maintenance of cultural institutions, such as schools, churches, archives, and media and entertainment outlets, that store and disseminate black cultural knowledge and artifacts.

4. Rootedness: Unlike white culture, black culture provides a stable and rich basis for feelings of community and for the construction of positive and healthy individual identities. Some have maintained that many blacks suffer from self-alienation and dislocation as a result of living (or attempting to live) in accordance with the values and norms of a white culture that disparages the ability, beauty, and moral character of black people. Authentic black culture, they contend, offers a sense of rootedness within a unified community, a space that feels more like home. This culture provides an existential defense against madness and self-destruction in a world hostile to the very presence of black peoples. An identity fortified by black cultural traditions will be more self-affirming and better integrated, and thus blacks should accept cultural blackness as an integral component of their sense of self.

5. Emancipatory Tool: Black culture is an essential tool of liberation, a necessary weapon to resist white domination, and a vehicle for the expression of nationalist ideals. A role for—or the role of—black artists, intellectuals, and cultural critics is thus to produce works that represent and affirm the authentic black experience and that inspire ordinary black folk to work for freedom and independence. Some black nationalists have no faith in the emancipatory potential of white culture, for they believe (or at least suspect) that it is inherently biased against black interests or that it is contrary to the true sensibility of blacks. Some maintain that no dignified fight for self-determination can be carried out using the culture of the oppressor group. Hence, the struggle for cultural self-determination must be prosecuted using cultural weapons taken solely (or almost exclusively) from the black world. And those resources should be used for the uplift and advancement of black people, not simply for self-expression or personal gain.

6. *Public Recognition: The state should refrain from actions that prevent the endogenous reproduction of black culture; and non-blacks, perhaps with encouragement from the state, should cultivate tolerance and respect for black culture.* The vast majority of black Americans are not immigrants or the descendants of immigrants but the descendants of African slaves, forced into exile in the Americas. Although the United States did not appropriate their native land, the people of African descent in America have themselves been annexed to the United States. They thus have no obligation to assimilate, as perhaps voluntary immigrants or refugees do. As a stigmatized minority culture threatened by white cultural imperialism, black culture has a right to protection and social recognition. The government may even have an obligation to support black cultural infrastructures through public finance or tax breaks.

7. *Commercial Rights: Blacks must become the primary producers, purveyors, and beneficiaries (financial and otherwise) of their culture.* Nonblacks have reaped tremendous profits from the exploitation of black culture (especially its music and vernacular style). Moreover, blacks are rarely given full credit for their innovations that have contributed to American culture, and they are almost never appropriately compensated for them. However, if blacks are to have cultural autonomy, then they must be the ones to decide if and how their culture is to be used for commercial ends, and they should be the ones to gain profit and recognition from this use.

8. *Interpretive Authority: Blacks are (or must become) and should be regarded as the foremost interpreters of the meaning of their cultural ways.* This claim has a dual basis. First, some white teachers, scholars, and art critics have taken up the task of explaining the sig-

nificance and value of black cultural practices to the rest of the world. Because of their white privilege and the general disparagement of black cognitive abilities, white interpretations of black culture are sometimes accepted (even by some blacks) as more authoritative than black interpretations. Second, white interpretations of black culture typically contain considerable distortion and misrepresentation, leading to greater stigmatization and widespread misunderstanding of the distinctive ways of black life. But even knowledgeable whites with genuine good will toward blacks often mischaracterize black culture simply because, given their whiteness, they are incapable of being fully incorporated into the culture they wish to represent. Their ineradicable outsider-status prevents them from fully understanding and thus appreciating the culture from the inside.

Responding to the Legacy of Cultural Imperialism

Black cultural nationalism is often criticized on the grounds that no black culture exists (or could exist) separate from so-called white culture. This challenges the very coherence of the idea of black cultural autonomy. Although I would reject the crude, ahistorical, and Manichaean visions of black/white cultural difference put forward by cultural nationalists, I do not deny that it is coherent and useful to speak of specifically black forms of cultural life. For purposes of the argument to follow, then, I assume that there is such a culture (or cultures) along with a white counterpart (or counterparts). My focus will be on how blacks should think about and relate practically to these cultures.

First, it is important to note that not all persons designated as *racially* black self-identify as *culturally* black. The significance of this fact should not be underestimated. The cultural nationalist is speaking not merely to those black individuals who already have a robust and committed black cultural identity, but also to those who are tempted to assimilate, who only marginally identify as culturally black, or who are not culturally black at all. Thus whether the collective consciousness tenet is ultimately defensible will depend crucially on whether the cultural nationalist claims merely that it is permissible and laudable for blacks to identify with and reproduce their culture or that blacks have an *obligation* to embrace black culture.

Most will agree that blacks should be free to develop and maintain their cultural identities without being inhibited by unjust measures or artificial barriers. But it does not follow from this that their cultural identities must be rooted in *black* culture, no matter how cultural blackness is defined. Keep in mind that cultural autonomy is a right that blacks may exercise or, if it is denied that there is such a right, a legitimate goal that blacks may strive for. It is perfectly consistent with such a right or goal that those blacks who do not desire this form of group self-determination are free to cultivate an alternative cultural identity, even to assimilate completely to white culture. On straightforward grounds of freedom of association, and provided they respect the autonomy of individuals to opt out, blacks are entitled to self-organize to preserve black culture by establishing separate educational, religious, and artistic institutions and by maintaining historical societies and museums over which blacks committed to the cause would have control.[5]

However, a familiar argument for a positive obligation to develop a shared consciousness in black culture goes as follows. American slaveholders prevented slaves from reproducing their African cultural forms, and historically blacks have often been misinformed or prevented from learning about their African heritage. Such actions deprived generations of the knowledge of their ethnic or national origins. Moreover, racist ideology maintains that blacks have no worthwhile culture of their own—neither past nor present—and that therefore they should allow themselves to be assimilated into a "civilized" culture. Part of the oppression that blacks have experienced thus involves the malicious deprecation of their culture. This assault on the value of black cultural contributions has been so thoroughly damaging to the self-esteem of blacks that many fail to identify with and take pride in their unique cultural heritage. Hence, in order to reclaim their self-respect and dignity as a people, blacks must participate in, celebrate, and identify with black culture. Once we fully understand this, we will see that a collective identity, rooted in black cultural traditions, is a constitutive part of black liberation.

Historically, and even now, this has been a very influential argument. And, like so many others, I have been tempted to accept its conclusion. But this urge must be resisted, powerful as it is, for while much of what the argument suggests is true and important, it simply does not follow that the best or only response to the issues it raises is to make a common cultural identity a fundamental aim of black political solidarity. Blacks can restore and maintain their dignity in the face of the legacy of white cultural imperialism and the devaluation of black culture(s) without adopting a collective cultural consciousness. For decades now, blacks have fought white supremacy and the cultural stigma it imposes by celebrating, both privately and publicly, black history and cultures. This has been done through a variety of vehicles, including Black History Month; cultural festivals; black periodicals, books, and documentaries; African American museums and archives; the BET network; black religious and political organizations; black private schools and colleges; black studies programs at predominantly white universities; and, more recently, numerous sites on the Web. These are all essential efforts to educate blacks and nonblacks alike about black history and black struggles, to instill in blacks a sense of pride, and to cultivate a greater appreciation for the cultural contributions of black people to this country and world. And there is no doubt that blacks should be informed about their history and cultures—as should nonblacks—for, at a minimum, this will help them better understand the nature of their subordination and the possible routes to freedom. Yet none of this requires embracing a common cultural *identity*. One can acknowledge the importance of learning black history and appreciating the beauty of black cultures without treating cultural blackness, however delimited, as defining who one is as a person or allowing it to set the boundaries of one's lifestyle or self-understanding.

The Blackness of Whites

By focusing on the collective good that black culture provides to those who benefit from it, tenet 3—the conservation principle— suggests a different basis for a positive duty to embrace black culture. It is not at all clear that just because blacks (could) benefit from the existence of black culture, they thereby incur a duty to actively preserve it; but if we do suppose that they have such a duty, parallel reasoning would suggest that they also have an obligation to preserve many aspects of what is sometimes regarded as white culture. Perhaps the cultural nationalist can concede this. After all, it is consistent with tenets 2 and 3 that blacks have an obligation to adopt a cultural way of life that is rooted in both black and white cultures. Indeed, some have maintained that the creative and dynamic synthesis of European (or Euro-American) and African (or Afro-American) cultural elements is precisely what is unique about the form and content of modern black cultural expression.[6] This emphasis on hybridity is certainly a more nuanced view of the meaning of diasporic blackness than is typically advanced by cultural nationalists. The difficulty with this position, however, is that, on this reasoning, nonblacks would also have a duty to preserve black culture, as they too have benefited in countless ways from its existence.[7] Ralph Ellison has famously emphasized this important point:

> The problem here is that few Americans know who and what they really are. That is why few of these [ethnic] groups—or

at least few of the children of these groups—have been able to resist the movies, television, baseball, jazz, football, drum-majoretting, rock, comic strips, radio commercials, soap operas, book clubs, slang, or any of a thousand other expressions and carriers of our pluralistic and easily available popular culture. It is here precisely that ethnic resistance is least effective. On this level the melting pot did indeed melt, creating such deceptive metamorphoses and blending of identities, values and lifestyles that most American whites are culturally part Negro American without even realizing it.[8]

Moreover, there are aspects of black culture that whites have played a constructive role in maintaining and developing—such as musical forms and literary traditions. Do their efforts make the culture any less black? Or are we operating, absurdly, with a reverse "one-drop rule" of culture—with a criterion that holds that a cultural trait is black if and only if blacks *alone* invented it and it is white if *any* whites had a hand in its creation? To say that a cultural trait is black or white depending on which racial group played the larger role in creating it is still somewhat arbitrary, coming quite close to a racialized conception of culture. But even if we accept this majority-contribution criterion for ethnocultural provenance, this would not entail that blacks alone have an obligation to perpetuate black culture. Because many nonblacks benefit from the existence of black culture (whether or not they have contributed to its creation), it would seem that these nonblack beneficiaries should also play a role in sustaining it. Certainly it would be perverse to insist that those nonblacks who now play a constructive role in perpetuating the culture should cease to do so.

Perhaps the underlying worry is that some whites may have a corrupting or disproportionate influence on the development of black culture and thus that it is essential (as tenets 7 and 8 suggest) that blacks lead and maintain control over this conservation project, ensuring that there are at least some all-black or black-led cultural infrastructural institutions. Yet even if we concede that the fate of black culture should rest largely in black hands, this would not, by itself, entail a duty on the part of blacks to embrace a black cultural identity. Granted, if black culture were to come under unjustified siege or suppression and as a result were threatened with extinction, then there arguably would be an obligation on the part of blacks to act to preserve it, especially if the state refused to help and if, because of race prejudice, nonblacks failed to see why it was worth the trouble. Here the obligation to keep black culture alive would spring from the obligation to resist the injustice of cultural intolerance. However, discharging this duty does not require one to identify with the culture as specifically or exclusively one's own, as a part of who one "really" is. While maintaining an alternative cultural identity, one could simply contribute funds and other resources to those institutions committed to black cultural preservation and development. Or one could, in a suitably post-ethnic spirit, periodically participate in black cultural practices, just as one might do with respect to the cultures of other groups.

Culture as Group Inheritance

But there is a deeper, and quite old, philosophical question here. Should a person value the elements of a culture because they are intrinsically or instrumentally *valuable;* or, rather, should she value them because they are components of *her* culture—that is, because *she* is black and because these elements are a part of *black* culture? If she should value them because they are valuable, then there is no reason to think that she, as a black person, has a special stake in black cultural forms, a stake that is different from that of the members of other racial groups. All who view the culture as beautiful or useful, regardless of their racial identity, have a reason to value and preserve it. But if she should value it because she is black, then in what way, if at all, does the proprietary claim *(It is mine)* justify or entail the evaluative claim *(I should value it)?*

Henry Louis Gates Jr. has argued that the proprietary claim itself should be questioned: "I got mine: The rhetoric of liberal education remains suffused with the imagery of possession, patrimony, legacy, lineage, inheritance—call it cultural geneticism (in the broadest sense of that term). At the same moment, the rhetoric of possession and lineage subsists upon, and perpetuates, a division: between us and them, we the heirs of *our* tradition, and you, the Others, whose difference defines our identity."[9] Gates suggests that we abandon this discourse of cultural possession, the lynchpin of cultural nationalism. In his view, by accepting the proprietary premise, native-born blacks who are descended from African slaves, having been dispossessed of their African ethnic culture, inevitably end up affirming their status as cultural outsiders and interlopers in the place of their birth and the only home they have ever known.

In seeking to ground the evaluative claim in the proprietary claim, the cultural nationalist must avoid this trap of cultural self-marginalization. Consider a few ways that this might be accomplished. First, she could take the short road: blacks created the culture, so they should value it. But surely the fact that blacks created the culture does not, in itself, give them a reason to value it. We do sometimes create things that lack value; and it would be more than a bit paradoxical to insist that people should value things that lack value, to insist that they embrace junk. This is not to say that valuing something that lacks value is irrational. People sometimes *confer* value on otherwise worthless things, such as items that would be considered junk if not for their sentimental value. But as to the question of whether a black person should value the elements of a culture simply because these elements are a part of *her* culture (in a sense yet to be specified), it would seem that the value of the culture is a necessary condition for justifying this normative claim. Let's proceed, then, on the assumption that black culture is valuable, objectively speaking. So the question becomes this: Assuming the intrinsic merit or instrumental value of a cultural form, is there a *further* reason to value it that springs from a proprietary claim? Perhaps a black person should value black culture because of its role in making her who she is. So Sarah Vaughan might have valued black culture because its musical traditions contributed to her becoming a great jazz vocalist, which, we may assume, was a constitutive component of her identity. But nonblacks could value the culture for this same reason, because many of them have been positively impacted by black cultural traditions. Moreover, many blacks will not feel this way, for the culture may have had little impact on who they have become. Thus, although this account may provide those who already have a strong black cultural identity with a reason to value black culture, it does not give blacks, in virtue of their racial classification, a special reason to value black culture. Here the culture does not belong to me in virtue of my membership in a racial group; it belongs to me, when it does, in virtue of the fact that it is a part of me.

A third possibility is that we can value a culture because we have *participated* in its maintenance or development. Here we value it because its reproduction is a product of our efforts. So, for example, by participating in black rhetorical repartee—what Gates calls the vernacular art of signifyin'—one contributes to keeping this lively and enjoyable practice alive.[10] As one's contribution is a source of pride, one would therefore have a reason, apart from its intrinsic merits or utility, to value the culture. But, again, many nonblacks participate—to good effect, one might add—in black culture, while some blacks have made little or no contribution to the preservation or advancement of black culture. Some, arguably, have had a negative impact on it. Thus, some nonblacks could have an achievement-based reason to value black culture, notwithstanding the fact that the culture is not "theirs," and some blacks will lack such a reason, despite the fact the culture ostensibly "belongs" to them.

A fourth possibility is to hold that individual blacks have a reason to value black culture, quite apart from whether they have made any contribution to it, because it is the product of the imagination and efforts of *their* people. On this view, it is because blacks view themselves as constituting a distinct ethnoracial community that they can rightly take pride in the achievements of the other members of the group, in much the same way that a child might take just pride in his mother's achievements even though he has had little to do with her success and, indeed, may have been a hindrance to it. It is this sense of "we-ness" or shared belonging, rooted in mutual recognition, that underpins the special claim that all blacks have on black culture. Whites may indeed have benefited from, been shaped by, participated in, or contributed to black culture. But because they lack the descent relation and somatic characteristics that classify someone as racially black, they are not recognized members of the black nation and thus cannot possess this unique reason for valuing "its" culture.

The fact that black racial identity has its origins in the ideological fiction of "race" does not undermine the idea of blacks as a people. Other national identities are derived from similar myths— think of American narratives about being a free and democratic country even while it allowed slavery and denied women the franchise. The trouble with the position under consideration is not that blacks are not a people but rather that it does not follow that blacks have a *duty* to embrace black culture simply because they are racially black. At most, black peoplehood makes it permissible for blacks to take special pride in black culture and thus to value it as uniquely their own. Such identification is their birthright. Yet it does not entail that blacks cannot fully participate or find fulfillment in white culture. Those who do not strongly or primarily identify with blacks as their people, or with black culture as uniquely theirs, have no special obligation to take up a black cultural identity. In this way, being entitled to identify with black culture as one's own entails having the freedom *not* to exercise this right. Thus, without denying who one is as a black person, one may reject or simply ignore one's black cultural heritage.

Instability, Hybridity, and Rootlessness

Tenet 4, which emphasizes the value of rootedness, suggests an additional reason why blacks should cultivate a black cultural identity. It insists that black culture can provide blacks with a more stable and healthier basis for communal fellowship and identity construction than white culture can. Before considering the plausibility of this claim, we should note that cultures are never static but change with the sociohistorical context.[11] Such contextual factors will include prevailing economic conditions, state policy, material interdependence of cultural groups, those groups' relative isolation or integration, social pressures to assimilate or remain separate, and the number and kinds of cultural groups living in close proximity or otherwise having access to each other's cultural ways. We should also keep in mind that there has been significant black immigration to the United States in recent years from Africa, Latin America, the Caribbean, and Europe, and that these black peoples have quite diverse cultural and national identities. Their presence in America has clearly altered the contours and content of the greater black cultural milieu, reshaping our sense of the scope of black diasporic culture.

Given the external and internal forces that create cultural dynamism and hybridity, there cannot be a stable or rooted black cultural identity in contemporary America. This does not in itself mean that blacks cannot cultivate and sustain feelings of community among themselves. However, it is by no means obvious that black culture will be a unifying rather than a divisive force. And even if black culture, properly understood and appreciated, would promote a greater sense of community, not all blacks will want to realize the value of community through ethnoracial affiliation. They may find it more appealing to attain the value of community by means that are not based on race (for instance, through occupational groups or religious organizations), or they may consciously seek interracial community.

We must also come to terms with the fact that the increasing commercialization of culture, especially youth culture, has had a profound effect on the meaning and content of black culture, in the States and around the world.[12] Symbolic blackness, particularly in the form of ghetto outlaw images, is a tremendous source of profit in the world market, exacerbating the already contentious debate over what constitutes authentic black culture and what represents cultural exploitation and "selling out." As Paul Gilroy puts it: "Black culture is not just commodified but lends its special exotic allure to the marketing of an extraordinary range of commodities and services that have no connection whatever to these cultural forms or to the people who have developed them."[13]

Furthermore, the cultures of the world are becoming increasingly hybrid. To find favorable markets—for labor, goods, services, or investment—people are perpetually on the move, migrating when possible to where they are likely to acquire material advantages or to avoid material disadvantage.[14] Information networks also distribute ideas, sounds, and images across the globe in an instant. Thus, cultures are inevitably changing, sometimes dramatically and rapidly, because of cultural imposition, diffusion, emulation, and fusion. Although the cultural bases of black social identities are not, and cannot be, stable, the velocity and scope of global cultural exchange has made a vast array of cultural resources readily available to blacks, especially to those in the United States. Blacks can therefore construct their identities using cultural materials drawn from diverse sources.

Of course, the availability of this broad array of cultural resources will not guarantee that blacks will avoid social alienation, existential angst, or identity crises. As Durkheim and Weber have taught us, increasing anomie and meaninglessness are among the unfortunate *general* consequences of modernity, and the struggle to avoid being overcome by them is indeed formidable.[15] Yet, attempting to bring about or maintain a pristine and homogeneous black cultural community against the currents of globalization will create, not integration and fulfillment, but rather frustration and disappointment. We should therefore avoid thinking of social estrangement and melancholia as somehow peculiarly black issues that require a distinctive black response. These are no doubt serious threats to our sense of belongingness and happiness, but they are features of the human condition in the modern world.

Some contend, however, that there is a peculiar threat to black psychic health best remedied by a wholehearted embrace of black culture. This is the problem of internalized oppression, the so-called black inferiority complex. The ideological attack on blacks involves the devaluation not only of black cultures but also of the intelligence, physical beauty, and moral character of black people. At various times, blacks have been viewed as childlike, stupid, and lazy, and thus in need of white paternalism.[16] At other times, blacks have been depicted as wild, vicious, and impulsive, and therefore in need of being contained. Worse yet, and this is the heart of the matter, these negative images have also seeped into the consciousness of many blacks, often without their being aware of it.

Part of the remedy for this self-alienation is to be found in the strategies already mentioned: spreading accurate information about black history and cultural forms; using various forms of cultural expression to resist and subvert antiblack racism; and engaging in the relentless critique of the doctrine and practice of racial domination. However, there is more that can be done. Black people can also bond together to *collectively* combat their racial oppression. Indeed, the need to overcome the self-contempt produced by antiblack racism is an important justification for black solidarity.[17] Given the widespread internalization of antiblack race prejudice, it becomes necessary for black people to be a significant, if not the primary, force behind their liberation from racial subordination. It is not enough for black people to be freed from their subordinate position by their nonblack allies and sympathizers. They must participate, in a meaningful way, in freeing themselves. The collective struggle for self-emancipation, even if unsuccessful, can itself enhance the participants' self-esteem and self-respect.

This was well understood by those blacks who voluntarily fought in the Union Army war against the slaveholding Confederate States. The same can be said of those who walked miles to work in order to boycott segregation on buses in Montgomery, who worked to register black voters in violent Mississippi during Jim Crow, and who marched through southern towns in nonviolent protest for their civil rights, often risking mob violence, police brutality, and even murder. Moreover, fighting together to free themselves from racial exclusion and domination is one way, in addition to the ones already mentioned, for blacks to strengthen their conviction that the doctrine of white supremacy is a vicious lie.[18] No doubt, blacks should have a liberated consciousness, one that is as free as possible from the devastating effects of racist ideology. However, in freeing their minds from the grip of such degrading and essentialist images of themselves, they don't need to, nor should they, replace these representations with another essentialized group identity, no matter how healthy or group-affirming some may think it to be.

There is a tendency among some black nationalists to exaggerate the "problem" of black cultural homelessness. As suggested by the quotation from Giovanni that opens this chapter, blacks rightly feel alienated by white racism, but not all blacks feel out of place in or ambivalent about white culture. In fact, although some are reluctant to admit this, many blacks do not feel particularly at home in even the most revered black cultural spaces. For example, the traditions and modes of expression that are characteristic of many black churches are widely thought to be paradigmatically black.[19] There is no reason, however, to assume that those committed to other faiths or to no religion at all will find peace and security in black churches simply because these institutions embody black cultural traditions.

Moreover, white and black cultures are not the only alternatives. Some blacks may choose to identify with another ethnoracial culture altogether (for example, black Puerto Ricans who identify culturally as Latino/a or black Jews who are committed to Judaism). Or some may simply opt for a more self-consciously hybrid ethnocultural identity, notwithstanding the (unsubstantiated) charge that such identities are incoherent and anomic.[20] There is, furthermore, no need to accept every element of a culture. Those components that are obnoxious, immoral, pathological, or otherwise unappealing need not be embraced, regardless of their putative racial origins. Just as it is a mistake to assume that we must choose between white and black cultures, it is also an error to assume that we are faced with accepting all or nothing from a culture.[21]

Now, the cultural nationalist may nevertheless insist that blacks *should* feel more comfortable within black culture, notwithstanding its dynamism, fuzzy boundaries, hybridity, and diverse roots. But why should they? If the different cultures of the world are learned and reproduced through socialization or acculturation, as they surely are, rather than genetically predetermined, then no culture is more "natural" to a particular individual than any other.[22] A person's comfort with a culture will depend on, among other things, which culture(s) she was initially socialized into, which cultures she has subsequently come in contact with, the freedom she has to experiment with different ways of living, and her temperament. It will not depend solely, if at all, on what race she belongs to.

Tools Are Tools

Tenet 5 maintains that black culture is an important emancipatory tool, one that black artists and intellectuals should make use of, perhaps exclusively, in the collective struggle for freedom and equality. Certainly cultural expression has an important role to play in black liberation. One way to fight against the dissemination of racist ideology is through cultural forms, such as literature, film, music, theater, dance, humor, painting, sports, theology, speech, dress, and hairstyle. Black people have a long and remarkable history of using various cultural practices, not only to express themselves aesthetically and spiritually, but to resist and subvert the forms of racial domination that oppress them.[23] Insofar as the cultural nationalist's interest in expressive culture is explicitly instrumental, the question for us is which cultural resources will make effective weapons of resistance or vehicles for propaganda. But if this is so, blacks should use the cultural resources that would advance black interests and discard or avoid whatever would impede them, regardless of the ethnoracial pedigree of these resources. Celebrating the emancipatory potential of black culture should not be allowed to blind blacks to the instrumental value of ideas and practices that lack black origins.

There is, however, a more plausible version of this tenet. It holds that white cultural forms are acceptable as tools in the struggle, particularly among the black elite and middle class, but black political mobilization requires black artists, cultural critics, and intellectuals to use familiar black cultural forms (for instance, the idiom of the black church and black popular music) to inspire working-class and poor blacks to progressive action. There are at least two ways to defend such a view. The first assumes that many blacks regard white culture with suspicion. Thus if black artists and intellectuals are to energize and inform everyday black people, they will have to do so with cultural tools that have greater legitimacy among these folk. If

this assumption about working-class and poor blacks is sound—
which by no means is obvious—then, on pragmatic grounds, it
may make sense for cultural elites seeking to start or energize a
mass movement to work within cultural idioms that are more to
the liking of most black people. Yet insofar as the intelligentsia want
to play a leadership role, they must be willing to challenge prejudices among blacks. False assumptions about white culture—or
black culture—must be questioned. Indeed, as Du Bois maintained,
such courage is a qualification for leadership, and it is one criterion
by which we can distinguish the true leader from the demagogue.
As Henry Louis Gates Jr. and Cornel West put it: "Being a leader
does not necessarily mean being loved; loving one's community
means daring to risk estrangement and alienation from that very
community, in the short run, in order to break the cycle of poverty,
despair, and hopelessness that we are in, over the long run."[24]

According to a slightly different view—one to which both Gates
and West seem sympathetic—white culture is not necessarily problematic from the standpoint of most black people, but it is unfamiliar or opaque to many working-class and poor blacks. If the black
intelligentsia are to get their message across to most black people,
they will therefore have to "speak their language"—that is, use a
cultural idiom that most black people can more readily understand.
Again, this may at times be pragmatically necessary. Yet, in account-
ing for this communication gap, we should not exaggerate the extent of black/white cultural differences. Blacks and whites have a lot
of experience interacting with each other, if not in common residential communities and schools (due to de facto segregation),
then certainly in the workplace, marketplace, and public sphere.
Misunderstandings between members of the two groups certainly
happen. It must nevertheless be relatively rare that dialogue breaks
down because blacks fail to understand the cultural ways of white
folk.

Most importantly, we must be careful not to confuse differences in cultural traditions with differences in education. What is sometimes regarded as "white culture" is simply that variant of post-industrial, mass culture that prevails in the United States—that familiar set of standardized meanings, assumed common knowledge, and basic competencies that the vast majority of adult citizens must master if they are to live minimally decent lives in liberal capitalist America. This common culture, which is largely transmitted through educational institutions, allows citizens from diverse ethnic and class backgrounds to communicate with one another, coordinate their actions, carry out commercial transactions, and conduct their common affairs. Because of substandard public schools and unequal educational opportunity, far too many people and a disproportionate number of blacks have underdeveloped verbal and cognitive skills, deficient knowledge of history and world cultures, little familiarity with different political traditions, and low reading levels. Rather than emphasize the need to recognize black cultural difference, then, it is more urgent for black progressives to push for reforms in our failing public school system. This I take it is one of the insights that Du Bois wanted to convey with his Talented Tenth doctrine, though the point may have been obscured by his vanguardism and cultural nationalist leanings (see Chapter 2).

Some will be made nervous, if not put off, by this emphasis on educational problems over intercultural misunderstandings. They will fear that it gives comfort to racists who disparage black cognitive ability and who maintain that black underachievement is due to the cultural pathology of blacks. Others will take it to be an expression of elitist contempt for the "uncultured masses." However, I would not suggest for a moment that blacks are intellectually inferior to whites, or that black expressive culture is any more an obstacle to learning and educational achievement than any other such culture. Nor do I think that educated blacks are inherently or culturally superior to blacks with limited education. Rather, the point is that the need for equal educational opportunity regardless of race—or gender, class, ability, national origin, and region—is a pressing one and that the demand for such opportunity must be a central component of any progressive black agenda. The first impulse of the pragmatic nationalist must of course be to defend black humanity against insult. To do any less would show a lack of self-respect, group pride, and commitment to defending the dignity of the least advantaged in the black population. But if such solidarity is not to be merely symbolic or, worse, reactionary, then it must distinguish between the depredations of white cultural imperialism and differential educational opportunity. With educational reform and, just as important and not unrelated, the expansion of economic opportunities, there is no reason why blacks cannot maintain their cultural distinctiveness and yet develop the basic repertoire of skills and knowledge needed in a complex market society. Such reform would constitute tangible black empowerment. Not only would it equip black youth to compete in a global economy, but it would provide them with the skills and knowledge needed to understand their world and the political measures needed to change it for the better.

Ethnocentrism, Cultural Intolerance, and Race Prejudice

This leads us to tenet 6, which demands both state-sponsored protection of black culture from the forces of white cultural imperialism and public recognition of the equal worth of black cultural contributions. There might have been a time when such measures were justified, but they have little pertinence today. To see why, first it is necessary, drawing on Oliver C. Cox, to distinguish between ethnocentrism, cultural intolerance, and race prejudice.[25] *Ethnocentrism* "is a social attitude which expresses a community of feeling in any group—the 'we' feeling as over against the 'others.'"[26] This is simply a matter of group solidarity (see Chapter 2), which is not always expressed as "racial" unity. Such in-group sentiments and partiality can be rooted in cultural traditions, religious practices, national origins, shared experience, or common aspirations. This group preference need not be antagonistic toward those outside the group, and both dominant and subordinate groups in a stratified society can be, and typically are, ethnocentric. Yet it is clear that ethnocentrism is often joined with hostility or prejudice toward various out-groups.[27]

One such form of out-group hostility is *cultural intolerance,* which Cox defines as "social displeasure or resentment against that group which refuses to conform to the established practices and beliefs of the society."[28] Here the dominant group is unwilling to tolerate, and thus actively suppresses, the culture of a subordinate group because it regards these beliefs and practices as detrimental to national solidarity or a danger to the dominant group's privileged position.[29] Whites would be culturally intolerant toward blacks, then, if they had negative attitudes toward blacks because blacks refused to adopt the shared beliefs and practices of the white majority and to abandon their distinctive cultural identity. Such intolerance would yield were blacks to assimilate into or be absorbed by the dominant culture, leaving behind all traces of black culture.

Race prejudice, according to Cox, is based on somatic characteristics. It is characterized by an emphasis on obvious, visible, physical characteristics like skin color and hair type. In the case of blacks, such traits carry the stigma of inferiority. Quite apart from anything blacks believe or do, these physical characteristics communicate diminished social status. Cox rejected the use of the term *racism* to refer to race prejudice, for he feared that this usage (associated as it was at the time of his writing with the Nazi "philosophy" of racial antipathy) would mislead us into thinking of racial antagonism as merely a matter of dogma or rationalizations. Instead, he insisted, it should be viewed as a materially based form of oppression that is facilitated by the social attitude of race prejudice. I think the worry here is well founded. Yet if we conceive of racism as an ideology that functions to stabilize systems of oppression, as I have urged (see Chapter 4), this in no way precludes the careful study of the ideology's material basis—it invites it.[30] Thus, I will continue to speak below of race prejudice as a form of racism. Such prejudice is not "instinctive" or "natural." The social significance attached to relatively superficial bodily traits is the product of the spread and solidification of racist ideology.

White racism should not be confused with white cultural intolerance. In addition to being subject to race prejudice, those Native American, Latino/a, Asian, Jewish, Hindu, or Muslim persons who maintain their distinctive religious, ethnic, or national identities are often unfairly disadvantaged in the United States by Anglo or Christian cultural intolerance. As a condition of being fully recognized as equal citizens, they are pressured to give up beliefs and practices, often related to religion and language, that set them apart from most whites. Being English-speaking Christians, the vast majority of native-born black Americans are not oppressed by cultural intolerance, but by racism. African Americans are not currently subject to pressures to assimilate to the cultural ways of white people—though obviously some of their African ancestors were. Rather, because of race prejudice they are *inhibited* in their attempt to assimilate and thereby are prevented from becoming equally valued citizens of the United States. Indeed, those black Americans who have adopted the beliefs and practices of the dominant culture nevertheless remain vulnerable to race prejudice.

Black "difference," where this has negative implications for the life prospects and civic status of African Americans, has mainly to do with a somatic profile that is associated with African origins and that signifies inferior social status. If African American cultural difference is similarly stigmatized, which at times it surely has been and to some extent still is, it is not primarily because of the qualitative differences between blacks' beliefs and practices and that of most whites but because African American culture is associated with blacks.[31] Indeed, the mere fact that other Americans readily adopt or consume the distinctive aspects of African American culture should enable us to see that it is not the intrinsic features of black life that ground antiblack beliefs and attitudes. Nevertheless, the slightest perception of black cultural difference (such as a dropped -g in a gerund or a "be" where one would normally expect an "is") can serve as a convenient *excuse* for antiblack prejudice in an era when explicit expressions of racism are not generally tolerated.

Now, historically some whites have explicitly sought the degradation of blacks by denying them access to education. Some whites have also rebuffed attempts by blacks to take on what is regarded as a white cultural identity. These were attempts to keep blacks "in their place," subordinated to the white majority, not to absorb them culturally. What is at issue here is not expressive culture but the cultivation of a repertoire of economically and politically valuable skills. To the extent that whites possess these skills and blacks do not, black progress toward racial equality is impeded. The sad fact is, some whites would be quite content, some would be enthusiastic, if blacks were to insist on remaining "different," as this would buttress white privilege and exacerbate black disadvantage in at least three predictable ways. First, to the extent that blacks are successfully portrayed as not meeting widely accepted standards for college admission and employment, blacks would more easily be excluded from highly valued positions in society. Second, because of their relative lack of educational and social capital, some blacks would become or remain a cheap source of labor to be discarded when the economy is receding or when low-skilled laborers from poor countries are recruited to do the same work for lower wages and fewer benefits. And third, black economic disadvantage could be rationalized by pointing to the inability or unwillingness of African Americans to conform to mainstream norms.

Some black nationalists are not, however, primarily concerned with cultural intolerance. Instead, their main demand is that black culture be given public and equal "recognition." They justify their position by pointing to the fact that nonblacks often regard black culture with disdain or as inferior to other ethnoracial cultures. But it is hard to imagine what legitimate steps blacks could take to extract the desired form of recognition from the state or their fellow citizens. In a society that rightly treats freedom of expression as a basic liberty, the only way to engender the wanted recognition is through education and persuasion. The state could, and no doubt should, require a curriculum in the public schools that includes the teaching of the history and cultures of the society's diverse citizenry.[32] Yet if the root cause of contempt for black culture is not a lack of knowledge of the culture but race prejudice, then such educational efforts, while perhaps welcome on other grounds, are unlikely to achieve the desired goal of equal public recognition.

The cultural nationalist could nevertheless demand that the state impose sanctions on those who publicly express derogatory opinions about black culture, thereby reducing the number of unfair or ill-informed assaults on the value of black culture that African Americans must endure. But this, even were it justifiable and effectively enforced, would be insufficient. Such opinions, along with explicit expressions of racism, already receive widespread unofficial public censure under the strictures of so-called political correctness. Yet the shared sense among blacks that their culture is underappreciated or wrongly devalued remains. What must be acknowledged here is that the desire for public recognition is not simply a desire that nonblacks refrain from *expressing* their disdain for black culture, but a desire that, as a matter of *conviction,* they actually value black culture as having a worth equal to that of other ethnoracial cultural contributions. This latter goal cannot be forcibly extracted from nonblacks through state action but must be achieved, if it can be, through changing beliefs and attitudes—something that cannot be accomplished without defeating racism and altering the social conditions that sustain and encourage it.

Perhaps the demand for recognition is not so much a matter of getting whites to respect black culture as it is of making sure that blacks do. In that case, the politics of recognition should be understood as a demand that the state grant certain black corporate bodies authority over blacks for the purpose of perpetuating black culture. The government could, for example, require black children to attend black-controlled schools where they will learn about black history and culture from black teachers and from a black perspective. Here, "recognition" would entail two components: (1) compelling black kids (at least those whose parents cannot afford private instruction) to attend black schools, and (2) no, or very limited, government regulation of the curricula, employment practices, and the admissions and expulsion policies of such schools. But this proposal faces the problems discussed in Chapter 3. To insure just treatment of job applicants, employees, children, and parents within this arrangement, blacks would need their own democratic constitutional regime to regulate compulsory public education in the black nation. Again, as I argued in Chapter 3, such a corporatist regime is neither practical nor desirable.

Production, Distribution, and Rewards

Tenet 7 takes up the question of black exploitation. But rather than concern itself with the exploitation of black labor as such, the commercial rights thesis is concerned with the exploitation of black culture. Understanding the meaning of black cultural exploitation depends on making sense of the idea of a culture belonging to black people, understanding the way in which a culture is exclusively or predominantly theirs, such that an exploiter can be said to have wrongly appropriated and used it. We found that a cultural element could be said to belong to the culture of black people if (1) the cultural item is rooted in or derived from traditions initially developed and commonly practiced (either in the past or presently) by black people, and (2) blacks identify with each other as a distinct people, forming a ethnoracial community of descent. This makes cultural possession a matter of cultural provenance and the communal relations that exist between the originators of the culture and their descendants.

Tenet 7 can then be broken down into three claims about the primacy of blacks in relation to their culture. The first requires that blacks be the primary *producers* of their culture. This does not necessarily exclude nonblacks from participating in the culture; it only requires that blacks be the predominant agents behind its reproduction and development. This is about cultural control or influence, not participation as such. It does not matter, in principle at least, how many nonblacks participate in black culture or how few blacks do, provided blacks retain primary control over how it is practiced and extended. The point of this aspect of cultural autonomy is to preempt the threat of cultural distortion or erosion due to nonblack involvement in black practices. This threat has three main sources.

The first and most obvious is antiblack race prejudice, which leads some nonblacks, even some of good will, to view black cultural practices as inferior. Such prejudice could lead some, perhaps unconsciously, to want to change black culture so that it more closely resembles what they take to be superior cultural forms—that is, white modes of cultural expression. The second is the dominance of white cultural practices. Given the greater cultural capital of whites in relation to blacks—their greater capacity to appropriate (both symbolically and materially) so-called legitimate culture—what may start out as egalitarian cultural exchange or voluntary fusion may quickly turn into cultural domination.[33] The third, and most controversial, is the alleged inability of nonblacks to fully appreciate the meaning of black culture because they lack the key to unlocking its peculiar significance—namely, the black experience, the experience of navigating a racialized and antiblack social world in a body that is indelibly marked as black. The potentially corrosive effects of antiblack sentiment, white cultural hegemony, and systematic misunderstanding can be contained, according to the black cultural nationalist, if blacks have the power to monitor and shape the ways in which their culture is reproduced and developed.

The second claim requires that blacks be the primary *disseminators* of their culture, which can be understood as their having primary control over the public and private circulation of the culture. If we set aside questions about who profits from the diffusion of black culture, the point of the present requirement would seem to be to prevent cultural misrepresentation or perversion. But if blacks maintain control over their cultural practices and nonblacks distribute only what is culturally inauthentic—a watered down appropriation or pathetic imitation—then such items are not "really" elements of black culture at all but merely some bastardization thereof. Baraka expresses this thought with regard to the blues tradition:

> Blues as an autonomous music had been in a sense inviolable. There was no clear way into it, i.e., its production, not its appreciation, except as concomitant with what seems to me to be the peculiar social, cultural, economic, and emotional experience of a black man in America. The idea of a white blues singer seems an even more violent contradiction of terms than the idea of a middle-class blues singer. The materials of blues were not available to the white American, even though some strange circumstance might prompt him to look for them. It was as if these materials were secret and obscure, and blues a kind of ethno-historic rite as basic as blood.[34]

The worry expressed in the second subclaim of tenet 7 thus becomes this: the uninformed or naive will mistake the fake stuff for the real thing, coming away with a distorted view of the value of the original or failing to recognize its black origins altogether. Viewed this way, the concern is less with distribution than with interpretation and authentication, the proper province of tenet 8, to be discussed below.

The third claim focuses more directly on the question of cultural exploitation, for it concerns who *benefits* from the production and dissemination of black culture, especially who gains financially. It demands that blacks be the primary beneficiaries of the production and dissemination of their culture. To properly understand this claim, it is important to distinguish between different ways that a person or group might benefit from a culture. There are benefits of intrinsic enjoyment or private consumption (use-value); there are benefits of esteem or prestige (status-value); and there are the financial benefits gained through the commercial use of the culture (exchange-value).

With respect to use-value, cultures should be shared, as Du Bois preached over a century ago, and black culture, too, is to be experienced and appreciated by all. Not even the most militant black cultural nationalist would want blacks alone to enjoy the richness of black cultural forms. In fact, many would argue that all peoples would be better off if they adopted elements from black culture. Separating the status-value of black culture from the money that is to be made from its commodification, the benefits of prestige are derived from people's beliefs about the worth of the culture. Black cultural nationalists want blacks to be esteemed because black cultural contributions are regarded as valuable, and they want this admiration to be grounded in an accurate understanding of what is distinctive and praiseworthy in the culture, not in superficial or mistaken judgments about it. To the extent that *black* opinion is the desired source of this esteem—that is to say, the mutual recognition among blacks of the value of their shared cultural ways—blacks could advance this goal by observing tenet 2: by their growing in their knowledge, appreciation, and affirmation of black culture. To the extent that *nonblack* opinion is the desired basis for such prestige, realizing the program embodied in tenet 8—blacks coming to be regarded as the foremost interpreters of the meaning and value of black culture—would achieve this goal. Nonblacks would then be obliged to defer to black judgment on the worth of a putative instance of black cultural expression, thereby ensuring that those who deserve the prestige associated with black culture are the only ones to receive it. What is at stake in tenet 7, then, is not who may legitimately benefit from the use-value or status-value of black culture but who may legitimately gain pecuniary benefits from its exchange-value.

We should also distinguish between the exploitation of black (creative) labor and the exploitation of black culture. Though there is considerable disagreement over what "exploitation" generally entails, most people who have given serious thought to the matter would agree that the labor of individuals, creative or otherwise, should not be economically exploited.[35] The powerful should not forcibly extract labor from those who are economically or otherwise disadvantaged. This way of benefiting from the labor of others is not only unfair but arguably an insult to human dignity. When corporations use their monopoly over productive assets to compel aspiring but economically desperate artists to work for them exclusively, this is often exploitative. But the cultural nationalist who defends tenet 7 wants to go further. He contends that when nonblacks use black culture for financial profit, not only is the labor power of black artists and performers exploited, but all black people are being exploited. The basis of this claim is that the traditions that enable these artists and performers to invent marketable, expressive culture ultimately spring from black *collective* creativity, from a long-standing tradition that has been reproduced and developed over generations.

Now, even if we allow that black cultural traditions are a resource that belongs to blacks as a people, they are not a resource in the same sense that land, oil, and other material assets are resources. The commercial appropriation or adaptation of a cultural practice by another group is not necessarily a financial loss to the originators of the practice, even if the cultural interlopers fail to share the profits with the originators. The commercial use of black culture by nonblacks does not, in itself, preclude a similar use by blacks. Blacks would be so precluded only if they were excluded from acquiring the necessary productive assets, financial capital, and means of distribution needed to profit from the use of their culture. But here the issue would be economic inequality and class subordination, not cultural self-determination per se.

In fact, the broader distribution of elements from black culture by nonblack capitalists may actually increase the demand for them, thus allowing blacks to gain more financially from their use than they otherwise would. Consider, for example, the commercial success of hip-hop music. Many rappers from the ghetto, given their lack of access to capital, would not have been able to make millions of dollars from record sales had corporate America not created a global market for the genre. Moreover, this wide exploitation of black culture has at times increased black access to the products of their culture—for instance, the "race" records from the 1920s made the blues widely available in black America.[36] Furthermore, sometimes taking up the cultural practices that originated with an ethnic group that is not one's own can be a form of homage, a way of acknowledging the value of the culture and paying tribute to its founders. Such homage can be done with integrity and respect even when it leads to financial gain for the outsiders.

Of course, one might worry that such use is often a misappropriation. That is, it might degrade the value of black culture in the eyes of others or it might not properly acknowledge the contributions of its original creators. Or one might contend that such commercial popularization has the effect of "diluting" the content and style of black expression, rendering these commodified cultural products inauthentic. However, these concerns, as we've said, are appropriately considered under tenet 8, which addresses the question of who has the authority to interpret, authenticate, and assess black culture.

The subject of all three components of tenet 7, then, is how blacks acquire and retain control over their culture. It is not clear, however, through what mechanisms blacks could gain and maintain the requisite kind of control. Complete exclusivity in the realm of culture is simply impossible. There is no way to fully control the flow of social meanings across time and space. No system of property rights could prevent cultural diffusion across racial lines in our modern high-tech world. Blacks might be able to prevent the U.S. government from interfering with black culture—though, as I argued earlier, this is not a serious worry anyway—but it is hard to see how they could keep global market forces from interfering with its development, dissemination, and consumption. Capitalists, by their very nature, are not patriots or nationalists but are driven by profit, whatever its ethnoracial pedigree or geographical source. Indeed, they must be primarily focused on profit or else their businesses would not survive. Given the exigencies of market competition, they must market their goods and operate their businesses in whatever part of the globe that will allow their capital assets to grow. Indeed, many successful capitalists have no intrinsic interest in the *qualitative* features of their products and services but treat anything that will return a profit as a commodity to be bought or sold. The products of cultural expression are sometimes profitable in their authentic form, even within the international market— think of how some consumers make a fetish of so-called authentic cuisine. But sometimes such products are more profitable when they have been altered from their original form, perhaps beyond recognition, to suit the tastes of consumers or the current vogue. Black capitalists in the culture industry will be subject to the same economic forces. There is little reason to expect, then, that they will be committed to keeping the culture pure of degrading elements when this would threaten the profitability of their enterprises.

However, even supposing there were blacks who were able and willing to exert this kind of control over the production and sale of black culture, we still would need to know how this could be done democratically. The capitalist system, to put it mildly, is not known for fostering democratic decision-making in the economic realm, and, as I discussed in Chapters 2 and 3, there are many perils associated with trusting the black bourgeois elite to represent the interests of the greater black community without some mechanism for accountability. Ultimately, then, the plausibility of tenet 7 depends on the soundness of the ideal of black group autonomy, either in its national self-government formulations or its Black Power articulations. But as we have seen, these forms of collective autonomy are themselves beset with difficulties and dangers.

Mysteries of Blackness and Privileges of Whiteness

Finally, we come to tenet 8, which demands that nonblacks defer to blacks on the meaning and value of black cultural forms. This clearly cannot mean that any nonblack person, no matter how knowledgeable about black history and culture he or she is, must defer to any black person, no matter how ignorant and misinformed he or she is. Thus we might interpret the tenet as holding that a "true" or "deep" understanding of black culture requires the interpreter to view it from the standpoint of the black experience, where the requisite black consciousness entails actually being black. The suggestion here is that a nonblack person can have only a superficial comprehension of the meaning and worth of black culture. If nonblacks want to get at the profound core of black culture, they will need to acquire it secondhand from those who are black. Blacks get their access to black culture through direct experience, in an unmediated form; whites get whatever access they do only inferentially, by analogical reasoning or black testimony.

It is true that participating in black culture as one who identifies and is publicly regarded as black will likely feel experientially different from the way it would if one were, say, white. But does the black experience really provide one with privileged insight into the meaning and value of black *culture?* Or, more plausibly, does it simply give one insight into the consciousness of black people, in particular into how they *experience* the culture? Of course, no one can have direct and complete access to the consciousness of others. Imagination, empathy, concerted attention, study, and dialogue can all help bridge the gap, yet they cannot close it completely. And if the point is to understand how black people experience their culture, then blacks have a kind of access to this knowledge that nonblacks cannot, a kind of access that philosophers call first-person authority. If, however, the point is to understand and appreciate the culture of black people, a culture that could exist independently of black interpreters (though not independently of the interpretations of its participants), then it is far from clear that being black is a necessary or sufficient qualification.

The confusion here is twofold. First, there is a hasty generalization from the fact of first-person authority—which concerns how an *individual* relates to the contents of his or her own subjective consciousness—to the claim that blacks have privileged access to their *collective* consciousness. Here again we find the implicit positing of a black plural subject, in this case underwriting the idea of a unique black experience that all blacks share. Although some rough generalizations may be possible here, there is no reason to think that blacks all experience their culture (or anything else, for that matter) in the same way. Differences in gender, class, sexuality, age, region, religion, values, political ideology, and many other things will all affect an individual's experience. However, even if there were something like a collective black experience, it would not follow from the presumption of "first-person-plural" authority that blacks thereby have privileged access to the meaning of black culture.[37] The only way such authority could be justified is if we simply assume that to (really) understand and (fully) appreciate black cul-

ture is to do so from the "black point of view." But this is just to beg
the question, because the possibility of nonblacks fully compre-
hending the richness of black culture (that is, as much as this is
possible for anyone) is precisely what is at issue.

It does seem plausible that being black gives one an advantage in
understanding black culture or, conversely, that not being black is a
handicap. Yet this is because blacks are often reluctant to accept
nonblacks into black practices as equal participants. Thus, to the
extent that blacks maintain some control over their cultural institutions and restrict access to participation in them, it will be easier for
blacks to come to understand and evaluate black culture for the
simple reason that they have greater freedom to enjoy and learn
about it. Accordingly, a more tenable reading of tenet 8 is that a
black person's interpretation of some putative item from black culture is, all other things being equal, more authoritative than a white
person's. The justification would then be the access advantage that
is afforded by being a recognized member of the black community.

This principle of "insider advantage" is better from a theoretical
point of view but is of negligible practical significance. For while
there might be a justified prima facie presumption that a black person's interpretation is to be given greater weight than a nonblack's,
further information about the relevant credentials of the parties to
an interpretive dispute could easily overturn this presumption. The
problem is that, once we acknowledge the relative advantages and
disadvantages of racial group membership for interpreting black
culture, things are rarely equal in all other relevant respects—such
as sociohistorical and cultural knowledge, active participation and
engagement, and aesthetic judgment and intellectual acumen. How
much weight should the black experience be given vis-à-vis these
other relevant qualifications? I'm not sure. But whatever weight we
give it, it should not function as a trump. This means that we can
never rule out the possibility that some nonblack person will have
as much, if not more, standing as some black person to judge the

meaning and value of a particular black cultural item or performance.

I would like to close this chapter by raising a final worry about tenets 7 and 8. The problem is that such arguments can be easily turned around to restrict the access of blacks to so-called white culture and to question the standing of blacks to interpret and evaluate nonblack modes of cultural expression. Should blacks be denied the opportunity to participate in, disseminate, consume, profit from, and assess white cultural ideas and practices? Because blacks lack the "white experience"—the experience of living with the bodily badge of whiteness and the privileges that this entails—does this disqualify them as equal participants in white cultures? Such arguments about the esoteric character of black cultural difference and the fundamentally alien character of white culture could lead us down this unfortunate path. Indeed, at a time when there is a black/white educational achievement gap—which in the absence of affirmative action will inevitably produce racial inequities in access to well-paying jobs—to suggest that there is some unbridgeable cultural gap between blacks and whites is to play right into the hands of those who would like to see blacks remain socially subordinate. Moreover, those of us who believe that we have important and original things to say both within and about the Western *philosophical* tradition should be especially concerned about the exaggerated claims of black cultural nationalism.

The black struggle for social equality has traditionally included the fight for each black individual to be viewed as an equal participant in the multicultural mix of America. This is a legacy of the civil rights struggle that should earnestly be kept alive, for it expresses a cosmopolitan ideal that is well worth striving for, though no doubt utopian at the moment. But cultural nationalism is not a suitable vehicle for bringing about this post-ethnoracial utopia, as its basic tenets are plagued by a number of conceptual and normative difficulties. My alternative suggestion is that blacks focus their critical analyses and political activism on lingering racism, persistent forms of socioeconomic inequality, unequal educational opportunity, and racialized urban poverty, for it is these that give rise to unflattering and disrespectful views of black people and thus of the cultural forms associated with them.

6

Social Identity and Group Solidarity

> We are one with you under the ban of prejudice and proscription—one with you under the slander of inferiority—one with you in social and political disfranchisement. What you suffer, we suffer; what you endure, we endure. We are indissolubly united, and must fall or flourish together.
>
> —Frederick Douglass, "To Our Oppressed Countrymen" (1847)

In an effort to liberate blacks from the burdens of racial injustice, blacks frequently call upon, even pressure, one another to become a more unified collective agent for social change. There are, of course, critics who think such solidarity irrational, impractical, and even morally objectionable.[1] Yet many people, both black and nonblack, continue to believe that black solidarity is essential to achieve the full freedom and social equality that American ideals promise. As we have seen, though, even among those who agree that black solidarity is important for bringing about racial justice, there is substantial disagreement over the precise meaning of this group commitment. Such disagreement can be quite fundamental, as can be seen by comparing classical and pragmatic nationalism.

Recall that, according to classical nationalism, black solidarity and voluntary separation under conditions of equality and self-determination is a worthwhile end in itself. On this account, blacks should unite and work together because they are a people with their own distinctive ethnoracial identity; and as a cohesive national group, blacks have interests that are best pursued by their seeking group autonomy within some relatively independent institutional framework. However, according to pragmatic nationalism, blacks should unite and work together because they suffer a common oppression; and given the current political climate they can make progress in overcoming or ameliorating their shared condition only if they embrace black solidarity. Here, black unity is merely a contingent strategy for creating greater freedom and equality for blacks.

Though similar in underlying motivation, the two strains within the nationalist tradition are importantly different. The pragmatic account, the least radical of the two, simply acknowledges the negative historical impact and current existence of antiblack racism in America and calls on those who suffer because of these injustices to act collectively to end them or at least to reduce their impact on their lives. The goal of this political program, then, is to free blacks from racism and its burdensome legacy, and it regards black solidarity as a necessary means to that end. The classical nationalist, on the other hand, maintains that blacks are a people whose members need to work together to bring about their collective self-realization as a people. Generally more pessimistic about the prospects for ending, or even sharply reducing, antiblack racism, this program seeks relief for black people through collective autonomy and self-organization and it calls for black solidarity to bring this about.

In previous chapters, I have highlighted the weaknesses in the classical program, problems that I believe are insurmountable. I have also tried to show that interpretations of pragmatic nationalism as community nationalism, political corporatism, or cultural nationalism are also untenable. My concern in this chapter will be to further clarify the practical implications of a viable pragmatic nationalism and to more sharply distinguish it from its classical rival. I shall do so by scrutinizing a doctrine that is often thought to be a component of any conception of black solidarity.

Collective Identity Theory

Collective identity theory holds that a shared black identity is essential for an effective black solidarity whose aim is liberation from racial oppression, and thus blacks who are committed to emancipatory group solidarity must steadfastly embrace their distinctive black identity. It is clear why the advocate of classical nationalism would accept this view, since it is the distinctive social identity of blacks that, on this account, constitutes them as a "people," which in turn grounds the claim of group self-determination. Without such an identity, the goal of black collective self-realization loses its rationale and much of its appeal. For the pragmatic nationalist, too, collective identity theory seems to have much going for it. In particular, it would appear to help with overcoming two serious obstacles to black collective action against racial injustice.

First, there is the familiar free-rider problem. Although many blacks, even some who are well off, are willing to make the relevant sacrifices to bring about racial justice, many are also complacent, narrowly self-interested, or simply weary of carrying on the struggle. Their inaction weakens the collective effort. It also breeds resentment and mistrust, as some are seen as benefiting from the sacrifices of others without contributing to what should be a group endeavor. Collective identity theory suggests a (perhaps only partial) solution: namely, by cultivating a common conception of who they are as a people, blacks can strengthen the bonds of identification, loyalty, special concern, and trust that would enable them to overcome these barriers to collective action. Such an identity could also give blacks a foundation for mutual identification across class lines, something that is sorely needed in this time of increasing intraracial economic stratification.

Second, there is the general problem that the mere acceptance of abstract principles of justice is often insufficient to motivate people to contribute the time and resources necessary for effecting meaningful social change. This difficulty affects the collective will of blacks as well, despite the fact that they, perhaps more than any other racialized group in America, desperately want to see an end to unfair racial disadvantage. We have noted several broad principles—antiracism, racial equality, equal educational opportunity, and antipoverty—that all blacks can be expected to support. But getting blacks (or any other group) to act upon these principles is another matter. Again, a collective identity would seem to help: viewing one another as black brothers and sisters with a shared social identity in blackness may, like the familiar motivating force of kinship relations, make blacks more inclined to help each other in a movement to eradicate racial injustice and its negative consequences.

Many influential theorists in the history of black political thought have defended or implicitly relied upon collective identity theory. The tendency to link the demand for collective self-definition with emancipatory black solidarity can be found in the writings and speeches of quite diverse black thinkers.[2] For purposes of illustrating this tendency, I will, once again, focus on Du Bois and his well-known essay "The Conservation of Races" (1897). In that early essay, Du Bois explicitly advocates a particularly strong form of emancipatory black solidarity: "It is our [American Negroes'] *duty* to conserve our physical powers, our intellectual endowments, our spiritual ideals; as a race we must strive by race organization, by race solidarity, by race unity *to the realization of that broader humanity which freely recognizes differences in men, but sternly deprecates inequality in their opportunities of development.*"[3] As was discussed in Chapter 2, Du Bois believed that black solidarity is necessary for overcoming racial oppression and insuring that blacks make their unique cultural contribution to humanity. He also insisted that blacks should "conserve" their racial identity rather than allow themselves to be absorbed completely into Anglo-American culture, for the goals of emancipatory black solidarity cannot be achieved without the preservation of a distinctive black identity: "We believe it the *duty* of the Americans of Negro descent, *as a body,* to maintain their race identity *until* this mission of the Negro people is accomplished, and the ideal of human brotherhood has become a practical possibility."[4] Although Du Bois often suggested that he would like to see black identity, in particular its cultural dimensions, preserved even beyond that time when social equality becomes a reality, here he emphasizes the "duty" of blacks to maintain their identity "until" such equality is realized.

Even in his early reconstruction of the concept of "race," Du Bois emphasized the link between racial identity and race solidarity: "[A race] is a vast family of human beings, generally of common blood and language, always of common history, traditions and impulses, *who are both voluntarily and involuntarily striving together for the accomplishment of certain more or less vividly conceived ideals of life.*"[5]

There has recently been a lively philosophical debate over the exact meaning of Du Bois's conception of race as defined in his "Conservation" essay.[6] Much of this debate has focused on the metaphysics of race—on what would make a group of people a "race," what it would mean for races to be "real," and, given what we now know about human variety, whether any races actually exist. In light of his avowed philosophical proclivities, it is safe to assume that Du Bois was concerned with such abstract ontological questions. Yet his interest in the reality of races was also based on his desire to lay a firm foundation for black solidarity, to forge or construct a collective black identity that would enable "the Negro" to become a more unified force for social change. Du Bois was convinced that a collective black identity—based primarily on a shared history and culture, and only secondarily, if at all, on a common biological inheritance—is a necessary component of an emancipatory black solidarity. Much of black political thought has followed him in this. Indeed, among advocates of black solidarity, collective identity theory is often regarded as a truism.

I will argue, however, that blacks should reject this conception of pragmatic nationalism, because cultivating a collective black identity is unnecessary for forging effective bonds among blacks, would create (or exacerbate an already) undue constraint on individual freedom, and is likely, in any case, to be self-defeating. I will urge the disentanglement of the call for an emancipatory black political solidarity from the call for a collective black identity. A black solidarity based on the common experience of antiblack racism and the joint commitment to bringing it to an end can and should play an important role in the fight against racial injustice. But a form of black unity that emphasizes the need to positively affirm a "racial," ethnic, cultural, or national identity is a legacy of black political thought that must now be abandoned for the sake of the struggle against racial domination and black disadvantage.

Before proceeding further, two caveats are in order. First, my concern in this chapter, as throughout the book, is with that form of group solidarity that has as its primary goal the liberation of black people from the burdens of injustice. Thus, when I speak of black solidarity I refer to this type of political or emancipatory solidarity. But of course not everything that could rightly be called a form of black solidarity is, strictly speaking, directly bound up with politics. There are other collective goals or values that might be thought to serve as a basis for building black unity. For instance, there is a form of black solidarity that has as its end the nurturing of communal relations among blacks, a solidarity that is not treated as a means to some other external objective but as valuable in itself. Some may seek solidarity with other blacks simply because they see intrinsic value in the social interaction and the feelings of community that it brings. Nothing I say here should be taken to preclude or disparage this type of *social* solidarity. The form of emancipatory political solidarity that I would defend is perfectly compatible with it. Indeed, sometimes black social solidarity can foster black political solidarity and vice versa. Second, like the cultural nationalists considered in Chapter 5, some blacks might want to work together to cultivate and preserve black culture. They may also see this collective project as important quite apart from its relationship to the struggle against injustice. Provided such a project is not treated as a necessary component of black political solidarity, it is not threatened by the rejection of the collective identity theory. It may, however, suffer from other conceptual and normative difficulties, as we have seen.

Modes of Blackness

Before submitting it to critical scrutiny, it will be useful to specify the collective identity theory in a bit more detail. This will require discussing a long-standing philosophical conundrum—the meaning of "blackness." According to collective identity theory, black people must embrace and preserve their distinctive black identity if a politically progressive solidarity is to flourish among them. Thus it is necessary to know what group of people the label *black* is supposed to be picking out here and what the nature of this "black identity" is that they must embrace and preserve. I want to approach these two questions by building upon the distinction introduced in Chapter 1 between "thin" and "thick" conceptions of black identity. Relying on this distinction, we will see, among other things, that the collective identity theorist urges the cultivation of thick blackness.

Recall that on a thin conception of black identity, blackness is a vague and socially imposed category of "racial" difference that serves to distinguish groups on the basis of their members having certain visible, inherited physical characteristics and a particular biological ancestry. There are widely shared, nationally variable,

intersubjective criteria for the classification of individuals into racial groupings. The prevailing (though not uncontested) thin conception of black identity in the United States, a conception that
has its social heritage in chattel slavery and Jim Crow domination, holds that *blacks* include both (1) those persons who have certain easily identifiable, inherited physical traits (such as dark skin,
tightly curled or "kinky" hair, a broad flat nose, and thick lips) and
who are descendants of peoples from sub-Saharan Africa; and (2)
those persons who, while not meeting or only ambiguously sat-
isfying the somatic criteria, are descendants of Africans who are
widely presumed to have had these physical characteristics. Thus,
on a thin view, blacks are persons who (more or less) fit a particular
phenotypic profile and certain genealogical criteria and/or who are
generally believed to have biological ancestors who fit the relevant
profile.

For those who meet these criteria, there is little room for choice
about one's "racial" identity. One cannot simply refuse to be thinly
black—as the African American folk saying goes, "the only thing I
have to do is stay black and die." If, say, one were to assimilate completely to so-called white culture, one's thin blackness would nevertheless remain intact, for cultural conversion provides no escape.
No amount of wealth, income, social status, or education can erase
one's thin blackness, which of course is not to deny that these advantages might mitigate some of its negative consequences. One
might alter her physical appearance so as not to "look black," or if
she doesn't look black, she might then conceal her genealogy—as
those who "pass" do—but in either case, she would still *be* black, in
the thin sense, even if never found out.[7] It is an individual's thin
blackness that makes her vulnerable to antiblack racism despite
her law-abiding conduct and good character, her commitment to
civic and personal responsibility, the extent of her assimilation to
mainstream bourgeois or mass culture, her middle-class income
and professional status, her educational success and intellectual

achievement, or her nonblack physical appearance.[8] Thus the category of thin blackness, as an official "racial" classification, is all that would be needed for the administration of civil rights laws and the enforcement of antidiscrimination statutes.

A *thick* conception of black identity, which usually includes a thin component, always requires something more, or something other, than a common physical appearance and African ancestry.[9] Here the social category "black" has a narrower social meaning, with specific and sometimes quite austere criteria for who qualifies as black. Unlike thin blackness, thick blackness can be adopted, altered, or lost through individual action. Drawing on the history of black social thought, five familiar modes of thick blackness can be distinguished.

First, there is the *racialist* mode.[10] On this conception, black identity is based on the supposed presence of a special genotype in the biological makeup of all (fully) black people that does not exist among nonblacks. On this view, an underlying cluster of genes, transmitted through biological reproduction, accounts not only for the relatively superficial phenotypic traits that satisfy the criteria for thin blackness but also explains more socially significant traits, such as temperament, aesthetic sensibility, and certain innate talents. It is the possession of this genotype that defines membership in the black race. There is of course a racialist conception that holds that the black essence significantly determines the native intelligence, reproductive traits and tendencies, and moral character of those who possess it. However, blacks generally regard this strong form of biological determinism as false and insulting, and so I shall proceed on the assumption that the collective identity theorist, as an advocate for black freedom and equality, does not endorse it either.

Second, there is the *ethnic* conception of blackness, which treats black identity as a matter of shared ancestry and common cultural heritage. On such an account, there is no assumption that two peo-

ple of the same ethnicity must necessarily share the same racial genotype. To be sure, as a result of their shared biological ancestry the
members of an ethnic group may share certain physical traits—for
instance, dark skin or the capacity to grow an Afro—and they may
even value their possession of these traits as part of their ethnic
identity. But these ethnic traits need not be viewed as indicating an
underlying biological essence that explains black behavioral or psychological dispositions. Indeed, the ethnic conception of blackness
is consistent with the complete rejection of racialism.

There are two dominant conceptions of black ethnicity among
black Americans. One emphasizes the fact that black Americans are
descendants of certain sub-Saharan African peoples, and it maintains that they share a culture that is traceable to the culture of
those ancestors. The other stresses both the experiences of blacks
with oppression in the New World and the rich culture they have
created in the context of that oppression since being forcibly removed from Africa. On either version, though, one does not have a
black ethnic identity, in the thick sense, unless one has the relevant
lineage and embraces, to some significant degree, the correspond-
ing cultural traits.

Third, there is blackness as *nationality.* "Nationality" has at least
two meanings. It is often used to mean citizenship in a territorially
sovereign state. A person would therefore have a black national
identity if he or she were a citizen of a (predominantly) black nation-state (such as Ghana, Haiti, or Nigeria). But "nationality" also
has a meaning that is quite similar to that of ethnicity. An ethnic
identity can be considered a national one when the people in question think of themselves and their culture as derived from a particular geographical location, where the relevant territory is considered an ancestral "homeland" and a source of group pride. In the
case of black Americans, this geographical region is, again, typically
(some part of) sub-Saharan Africa. However, I will treat black nationality, in both its senses, as a variant of the ethnic conception, for

the differences between ethnicity and nationality, as here defined, will not affect the argument to follow.

Fourth, there is the *cultural* conception of blackness. It rests on the claim that there is an identifiable ensemble of beliefs, values, conventions, traditions, and practices (that is, a culture or subculture) that is distinctively black (see Chapter 5). Though this culture is thought to be the creative product of those who satisfy the criteria for thin blackness, the continued reproduction of the culture does not depend solely on the activities of these blacks, because nonblacks may participate in sustaining and developing it as well. On this model, thick black identity is tied neither to race nor to biological descent. Anyone could, in principle, embrace and cultivate a black cultural identity, in much the same way that anyone could, again in principle, become a practicing Christian.

Finally, there is the historically influential *kinship* mode of blackness. This view conceptualizes black identity on the model of the family—recall Du Bois's conception of race as a "vast family" or consider the common use of "brother" and "sister" to affectionately refer to fellow blacks.[11] Of course blacks are not a family, not even an extended one, in any ordinary sense. And earlier I criticized the invocation of this idiom insofar as it is meant to underwrite contemporary black political solidarity (see Chapters 3 and 4). So what is it about familial relations that could plausibly constitute a basis or suggest an analogous foundation for a thick black identity? There seem to be three possibilities. First, one could understand blackness in terms of biological relatedness or genealogy—"blood ties." But then the kinship conception can be adequately expressed in terms of the racialist view, the ethnic view without the cultural requirement, or the thin conception of black identity.[12] Second, one could treat black identity as a matter not merely of biology but of the reproduction of a common way of life. But here the idea could be fully captured by the ethnic conception of blackness (perhaps with some additional racialist assumptions). Or third, like familial relations formed through marriage or adoption (whether formal or informal), blackness could be thought to rest on voluntary affiliation, custom, or (legal) convention. This form of blackness, however, would be simply a version of the cultural conception, a matter of *joining* the relevant group. The familiar kinship view is not, therefore, a conception of blackness distinct from the ones already considered, just a convenient (though often misleading) trope used to signify one or more of them. Now of course members of a family often share important experiences that contribute to their feelings of connectedness, trust, and loyalty. And in a similar way, black people have a common history of racial oppression and share a common vulnerability to racial discrimination. However, as I will argue below, these commonalities can form the basis for group solidarity without relying at all on a thick collective black identity.

There are several things to notice about thin and thick black identities and their interrelations. First, a person who satisfies the thin social criteria for being classified as black may nevertheless choose, with varying degrees of psychological difficulty and against various forms of social pressure, not to define his or her self-conception in terms of "blackness" at all. That is, such a person may choose not to subjectively identify with the label *black* or to conform to its associated behavioral norms.[13] Some nationalists contend that those so-called blacks who refuse to self-identify as black are denying something important about themselves, usually out of racially motivated self-hate. But a different, more respectable, reason for rejecting a black identity, one that does not necessarily involve self-deception or bad faith, is that one may believe that the designation *black,* with its typical connotations, is not an apt characterization of either who one is or who one would like to be. Or one might think that a black identity, while perhaps perfectly appropriate for some, is too limiting in one's own case. Yet another reason might be that one believes it to be an inherently invidious and repressive social distinction that should thus be repudiated on moral or political grounds. It should be clear, however, that the choice not to self-identify as black, whatever its rationale, does *not* dissolve the often constraining social realities that are created by the fact that *others* may insist on ascribing such an identity to one and consequently may treat one accordingly, whether for good or ill.

Second, black identity is not only multidimensional—involving the thin/thick distinction and often including various types of thickness—but the content of each mode is intensely contested. This circumstance makes possible the familiar but controversial discourse of black authenticity. It sometimes happens, for example, that an individual who satisfies the thin criteria for blackness possesses only a subset of the three modes of thick blackness under consideration—for instance, the thinly black person may (seem to) embody the racialist dimension without exemplifying the cultural dimension. There is intense disagreement among African Americans about whether anyone who identifies as black along one dimension should also, perhaps as a test of group loyalty or trustworthiness, identify as black along all the others—to be, in a sense, "fully" black. It is also possible for an individual to exemplify each of these modes but to different extents; for example, a person might have dark skin and love hip hop but have little fondness for or knowledge of African cultures and no interest at all in the blues. Recognition of this fact has also sometimes given rise to talk of "degrees" of blackness. Moreover, because the boundaries of each mode are both vague and fiercely disputed, there is often deep disagreement among African Americans about exactly when the label *black* applies in a given case, a circumstance that sometimes produces seemingly irresolvable questions about whether certain persons are "really" black.

Now given the thin/thick distinction, we can understand what it would mean to say of someone who is clearly black according to the thin criteria but who fails to satisfy the relevant criteria for thick blackness (whatever they turn out to be) that he or she isn't "really" black—a claim that is sometimes thought to be essentialist and par-adoxical, if not completely incoherent.[14] Here is how we might make sense of that familiar charge without relying on racialism and within the context of thinking about the relevance of a collec-tive identity for black solidarity. Though a person cannot choose whether to be black in the thin sense, she can, as we've said, decide what significance she will attach to her thin blackness. This includes deciding whether to commit herself to pragmatic black national-ism. But if she does so commit, either explicitly or implicitly, then she could rightly be criticized for failing to live up to obligations she has voluntarily accepted as a member of that solidarity group. For instance, she might be criticized for not being sufficiently faith-ful to the goal of racial equality.

Of course we all, whether black or not, have an obligation to re-sist racial injustice. The obligations of blacks in this regard are cer-tainly no greater than those of nonblacks.[15] But blacks would argu-ably have an obligation to pursue their antiracism *through* black solidarity if in its absence racial justice could not be achieved. Such an obligation would follow from the principle that if one wills the end, one also wills the necessary means, provided of course these means are morally permissible. If such a position is sound, then blacks who fail to commit to black solidarity are open to criticism. And thus if collective identity theory is correct, any thinly black person who does not affirm thick blackness as part of his identity, whether he has made a commitment to black solidarity or not, would be vulnerable to criticism. In this book, I leave open the question of whether a commitment to black political solidarity is strictly obligatory, for answering it would require resolving the dif-ficult empirical question of whether such solidarity is absolutely necessary to achieve racial justice. Instead I focus on what should and should not be required of those who *choose* to fight antiblack racism through black political solidarity, noting, as I have empha-sized throughout, that such group efforts are a legitimate and constructive means to effect social change. This leaves open the possibility that it is permissible for blacks to work for racial justice through some other means, whether group-based or not.

Thus, if we think of authenticity, not as a matter of acting in conformity to or fully realizing one's inherent essence, but as being faithful to the practical principles that one has freely adopted, then black "inauthenticity" could be understood as not living up to one's solidaristic commitments (whatever these turn out to entail). If the goals of black solidarity cannot be achieved without a thick shared identity, as collective identity theory maintains, then a person who has signed on to this emancipatory project, but fails to identify as thickly black, may rightly be criticized for being "inauthentic"— fraudulent or fake. By using the thin/thick distinction, then, we can more clearly discuss the discourse of black authenticity and what role, if any, it has to play in black solidarity.

Finally, it is clear that among those who satisfy the criteria for thin blackness, many spontaneously embrace a thick black identity without treating this as a conscious strategy and without being concerned for how this would impact black politics. Even for those who do deliberately choose to cultivate a thick black identity, they do so for the most varied reasons, many doubtless having to do with resisting racial injustice but some having more to do with cultivating self-esteem, wanting a rich and relatively stable conception of who they are, or desiring a strong sense of community. It is moreover probably rare that blacks consciously embrace a thick black identity solely for political purposes. In fact, in order for such an identity to have a positive effect on black solidarity, it may be necessary for some to embrace it for reasons apart from its political value. The collective identity theorist could concede all this but nevertheless insist that were a sufficient number of blacks, for whatever reason, to reject or distance themselves from thick blackness, this would seriously hamper, if not undermine, emancipatory black solidarity, especially given the collective action problems that blacks currently face. Indeed, the familiar policing of social identities that takes place among black Americans—which often frustrates those who seek greater freedom in the construction of their social identities—arguably functions to strengthen the bonds of solidarity necessary for effective resistance against racial oppression. It is for this reason that the advocate of collective identity theory urges blacks to accept a thick black identity, even if some will do so for reasons having little to do with antiracist politics.

Given the above distinctions and caveats, the collective identity theory can now be given a more precise formulation: There are persons who meet the criteria for thin blackness who also have available to them a black identity that is "deeper," that is, *thicker*, than their thin blackness, and these persons must positively affirm and preserve their thick blackness if collectively they are to overcome their racial oppression through group solidarity. Thus, for the remainder of this chapter, when I speak of the alleged need for a common black identity, I will be using the term *black* in the thick sense, and when I speak of "black people" or simply "blacks," I will mean "black" in the thin sense, unless otherwise indicated.

Is a Collective Identity Necessary?

On a racialist conception of blackness, with its commitment to a more-than-skin-deep racial essence, embracing and preserving black identity would entail, at a minimum, fostering intraracial reproduction between blacks and, perhaps more importantly, discouraging interracial reproduction between blacks and nonblacks. This practice of racial endogamy is supposed to help keep the black essence intact and protect blacks from the dangers of racial hybridity. However, this view has a number of well-known problems. For one thing, it is now generally acknowledged that no "pure" biological races exist. Indeed, many biologists and anthropologists question the very idea of "racial" difference.[16] But even if there are (or once were) pure racial groups, those Americans who are black by the prevailing thin criteria certainly would not qualify as such a group (or even a proper subset thereof), because most (by some estimates as many as 80 percent) have some European or Native American ancestry.[17] Limiting black solidarity to only "pure(er)" blacks would exclude many victims of antiblack racism, contrary to the point of the enterprise. It would also run the risk of creating a "reverse" color prejudice—a preference for darker skin rather than the more familiar but no less problematic preference for lighter skin—among those who identify or are identified as black. Harold Cruse has rightly emphasized this danger: "In the United States, the American Negro group is too large and mixed with too many racial strains for the ideology of black-skin supremacy to function within the group. It can lead to the reasoning that 'I'm blacker than you, and so is my mama, so I'm purer than you and your mama. Therefore, I am also more nationalistic than you, and more politically trustworthy than you and your mama, in the interests of Black Power.' But inside America this is a pure fiction."[18]

A racialist justification for the principle of black endogamy would be no more plausible if the more inclusive "one-drop rule" were adopted.[19] Such a conception of black identity would hardly justify prohibiting "race mixing" in the name of black solidarity. If anything, it suggests that blacks should make it their policy to produce "mixed" progeny, because this would only increase their numbers and thereby perhaps their collective strength.[20]

Given the obvious problems with its racialist version, most advocates of the collective identity theory have adopted the more plausible position that blacks should embrace and preserve their distinctive *ethnic* or *cultural* identity. Recall that the main difference between these two conceptions of blackness is that the ethnic version requires black ancestry while the cultural version does not. But because collective identity theory calls on blacks alone to embrace thick blackness, those who do so will have the appropriate ancestry by default; that is, the thinly black who have a black cultural identity will thereby be ethnically black. Thus for present purposes, the ethnic and cultural versions of collective identity theory come to the same thing, and I will therefore treat them as one "ethno-cultural" conception of blackness.

Yet perhaps this is too quick. The ethnic version of collective identity theory may urge blacks to *affirm* their black ancestry in some special way. Provided it is devoid of any racialist assumptions, there seem to be three important ways this affirmation could be carried out. First, one could honor the memory of one's black ancestors by embracing and passing on their cultural legacy. This view, however, is just a variant of the cultural version of collective identity theory. Second, it might be thought that because one's black bodily appearance is the result of one's black racial pedigree, one should honor one's black ancestors by being proud of that appearance and perhaps accentuating it. This might seem all the more important once one considers the fact that racists have often maintained that blacks are physically unattractive, even repulsive. Being proud of "looking black" can be expressed by, for example, wearing one's hair "natural" and prominently featuring one's other proto-typical "black features"—big lips, noses, and hips. Yet doing so would be a matter of observing certain norms of conduct or fashion imperatives, and thus this account of the alleged independent significance of black ancestry is also a variant of the cultural version of collective identity theory, one that attaches positive meaning to outward bodily appearance. Third, one might affirm one's black ancestry by honoring the sacrifices that previous generations of blacks have made for the benefit of future generations. Setting aside the option of paying such homage through cultural identification and preservation (see Chapter 5), I would argue that the best way to honor the heroic efforts of previous generations of blacks is to continue their struggle for racial justice and black liberation. This view, however, is consistent with a pragmatic nationalist conception of solidarity whether or not a thick identity is thought to be a necessary component, as either the thin or thick variant would urge blacks to work for racial equality and black freedom.

Now the ethnocultural version of collective identity theory requires blacks to identify with black culture, insisting that blacks view it as (at least partly) constitutive of who they are. Note, though, that if this ethnocultural identity is to have a positive impact on black solidarity—providing a basis for mutual identification, engendering a sense of special concern, reinforcing their commitment to common values or goals, and creating stronger bonds of loyalty and trust—then it cannot be a passive or merely internal acknowledgement of the value of black culture. Rather, blacks must actively perform or display their cultural identity for other blacks (and perhaps nonblacks) to see. They must demonstrate their knowledge and appreciation of black culture by, for example, participating in it, preserving or developing it, and exposing others to it, especially their children. However this is accomplished, there must be some means by which blacks publicly signify their allegiance to ethnocultural blackness.

There is a strong and weak version of the ethnocultural view. On the strong version, a collective black ethnocultural identity is a *necessary* component of black solidarity; that is, failing to cultivate such a collective identity would undermine the effort to build black unity. On the weak version, a collective identity is not claimed to be necessary for black solidarity, since blacks might get by without one, but it is thought that such an identity would strengthen the bonds of unity by giving blacks more in common than just their history of oppression and vulnerability to racism. However, I maintain that neither version is sound. Focusing on the strong version first, I will argue that there is little reason to suppose that blacks must share a collective identity in order for them to exhibit, as a group, each of the five characteristics of robust solidarity outlined in Chapter 2.

At the outset, it might be thought that if blacks are to *identify* with each other, they must share an ethnocultural identity (or at least they must *believe* themselves to share such an identity). Yet there are clearly other, and more politically reliable, bases for identification. Blacks could, for example, identify with each other because they believe themselves to suffer the same form of racial subordination, to have experienced the degradation and insult of antiblack racism, or to share a common interest in ending racial inequality and racialized poverty. The mutual recognition of such commonality could produce, and arguably already has produced, empathetic understanding of a deeply felt kind between blacks. Thus, quite apart from their supposed common "racial" characteristics, ethnicity, or culture, each could come to see and feel that a significant part of himself or herself is to be found in the others, so that it becomes meaningful to speak about and act on the basis of what "we" experience, "we" believe, and "we" desire.

In fact, members of oppressed groups often experience a common fate because of a social identity that they only *appear* to share, as it is not unusual for the dominant group to construct an identity for those it oppresses (and for itself) in order to justify the ill treatment and deplorable condition of the subordinate group.[21] Such imputed or ascribed social identities are sometimes entirely fictional, maliciously fabricated by oppressor groups. Consider, for example, the old myth that blacks are the descendants of Ham and thus are forever cursed to toil for the benefit of whites. But even when the ascribed identity is based in something real, members of the subordinate group may still find it more pragmatic to build solidarity on the basis of their common oppression and their desire to overcome it, for some of them might not value or identify with the ascription.

The special concern that is typical of solidarity groups often has little to do with a shared culture. Sometimes this concern is rooted in mutual identification itself, which, as I have said, does not require a common ethnoracial identity and often extends across lines of cultural difference. Consider the mutual concern that binds together some women in their fight to end patriarchy and gender discrimination. Such women come from a variety of ethnocultural backgrounds and yet are able, imperfectly to be sure, to identify with one another's burdens, fears, and pain.[22] But special concern does not even require such identification—that sense of "we-ness." Mere empathy is often sufficient. Such empathy is rooted in the feeling that "had things gone a little differently, I could be in your unfortunate position" or perhaps "I have been in your position, and thus I can understand what you are going through and may be well situated to lead you out of it." This kind of imaginative self-projection into the shoes of another can move individuals to the kind of special concern that is characteristic of solidarity, a form of caring that is not limited to those with whom one shares an ethnocultural identity.

Black solidarity does require a shared set of values or goals. But this normative commitment need not involve embracing black culture as the basis of a collective identity. One does not have to possess a black cultural identity—indeed one does not have to be black at all—to appreciate the value of racial equality, to condemn racism, or to abhor poverty. Of course, values are components of culture, and black cultural forms are among those that sometimes express or embody principles of social equality, which can be a legitimate source of black pride. Nevertheless, the basis of blacks' commitment to equality should be that this is what justice demands, not simply that such values are embedded in black cultural traditions. Now, to the extent that black culture expresses or embodies principles of justice, this might provide those who embrace a black ethnocultural identity with a *further* reason to cling to these principles. But if, as is not unreasonable to suppose, there were components of black culture that did not extol the virtues of racial justice but instead emphasized black supremacy or, worse, black inferiority, then blacks would of course need to reject these components of their culture and embrace social equality instead, whatever its ethnocultural roots.

Loyalty, too, can exist between blacks with a wide range of ethnocultural identities. Consider, for example, the loyalty that sometimes exists between the diverse members of labor organizations. Despite differences in age, race, gender, sexual orientation, religion, region, ethnicity, occupation, and many other things, some workers have been intensely loyalty to one another, especially when confronted with threatening or dire circumstances. Moreover, they often maintain this loyalty with little more in common than their shared vulnerability as workers and their will to improve their lot. There is no reason why blacks cannot do the same, for they, too, are vulnerable to a threatening social force—antiblack racism. And just as workers can unite in the name of economic justice without sharing a conception of the value of labor or a desire to preserve their "identity" as workers, blacks can unite in the name of racial justice without sharing a conception of the value of black culture or a desire to conserve ethnocultural blackness.

It is also clear that blacks can foster mutual trust among themselves without sharing a common ethnocultural identity. A common culture would undoubtedly create a type of familiarity and ease of intercourse that could contribute to the building of mutual trust. And, in general, it is easier to trust those with whom one shares a social identity. However, trust can be facilitated in other ways as well. On can, for instance, demonstrate one's trustworthiness by openly making efforts to advance the cause of black liberation. Working together with other blacks to accomplish limited, short-term goals—for example, collectively boycotting a known racist establishment or putting concerted pressure on political leaders to heed black concerns—can also foster trust. This makes the participants only minimally vulnerable to one another, while at the same time creating seeds of trust that can grow through future collective efforts. In any case, as I argued in Chapter 2, using one's talents and resources to promote an antiracist agenda is surely a better sign of one's trustworthiness in the struggle against racial oppression than expressing one's solidarity with other blacks through exhibiting pride in one's black ethnocultural identity.

Against this view, Laurence Thomas has argued that there can be no "genuine cooperation" among blacks until they develop what he calls a "group narrative"—defined as "a set of stories which defines values and entirely positive goals, which specifies a set of fixed points of historical significance, and which defines a set of ennobling rituals to be regularly performed"—for, according to him, such a narrative provides the basis for mutual trust.[23] Moreover, Thomas claims that a people cannot genuinely cooperate with each other simply on account of their desire to defeat a common enemy, because the existence of such an enemy cannot form the basis of mutual trust.

I disagree. First, if the civil rights movement did not constitute genuine cooperation among blacks, then I'm not sure what would. Thomas may not count the movement as genuine cooperation, because it did not operate on the basis of what he regards as "group autonomy"; that is, blacks were not generally regarded as the foremost interpreters of their history and cultural traditions. But unless the goal is black collective self-realization *as a people* or *cultural* self-determination, then the narrative-free black solidarity that held together the civil rights movement should be sufficient for the post–civil rights era as well. Second, Thomas's account of group narrative would seem to suggest that blacks need something comparable to an ethnic religion if they are to form bonds of mutual trust. But I see no reason to believe that, because, as I argued above, there are less restrictive and more reliable routes to that end.

Would a Shared Identity Help?

So far I have argued that a collective ethnocultural identity is not a necessary condition for the creation and maintenance of robust black solidarity. But, as I mentioned earlier, some collective identity theorists endorse a slightly weaker position. Instead of claiming that a collective black identity is necessary, they claim that, while perhaps not necessary for black solidarity, such an identity would create stronger bonds of unity. Prima facie, this seems quite plausible. Yet this weaker version is also unsound, as it is much more likely, at least presently, that the requirement of a common identity would weaken, if not undermine, black solidarity. There are a number of reasons for thinking this to be the case, some of which have already been reviewed.

For one thing, the push for a collective black identity would probably worsen existing intragroup antagonisms (recall the discussion from Chapter 3) and might even produce new ones. The types of internal conflict and competition among blacks that I have in mind would be likely to show up in several domains; here I mention four salient ones.

First, the imperative to conform to black culture would require individual blacks to possess the capacity to identify, if only implicitly and roughly, which elements are components of their culture and which are not. The problem is that there is no consensus on just what characteristics these are or on how they are to be distinguished from elements of white culture. In fact, what is culturally black is one of the most contested issues within the greater black population. Thus the question inevitably arises: Who has the authority and expertise to specify the content and define the parameters of black culture?

There is no black plural subject that can define itself culturally, only individual blacks who, perhaps working together or, more likely, struggling against one another, choose to cultivate this or that cultural identity—to take up various beliefs, values, practices, and modes of expression that they regard as "black." Even among those who most earnestly seek to maintain black cultural integrity (perhaps especially among them), there is often intense disagreement on just what elements constitute authentic black culture and which elements represent a bastardization or abandonment of the truly black. In light of this inevitable cultural friction, it is hard to imagine how an inclusive and democratic form of cultural autonomy could emerge. Should black Americans see themselves as essentially tied to Africa, and if so, what African culture(s) should be given privileged status? Can this shared identity include elements from European, Anglo-American, or Western culture and still be authentically black, or must it remain, in some sense, "pure"? How much, if any, of the cultural legacy of slavery—for example, southern Negro folk culture—should blacks embrace? Given historical migration patterns, should blacks from northeastern, West Coast, or midwestern urban centers or those with a southern sensibility be seen as more paradigmatically black? Should black identity be tied to a particular religious tradition, and if so, should this be Christianity, Islam, or some indigenous traditional African religion? Are there distinctively black norms of etiquette or black social values? Is there a black ethics, epistemology, or aesthetic? Are there uniquely black styles of dress, hairstyles, or modes of speech? While some of these are no doubt interesting questions, there is no reason to believe, and in fact every reason to doubt, that blacks can achieve anything like consensus on such matters. And the endless and often acrimonious disagreements over what constitutes the real meaning of blackness can easily become so all-consuming that blacks lose sight of the *sources* of their anxiety about who they are—such as antiblack racism, social exclusion, persistent racial inequality, and severe urban poverty—which should be the primary focus of their collective political energies.

Second, class differences among blacks will complicate any attempt to sustain a common black ethnocultural identity.[24] First of all, it is not clear that the black professional elite, the black middle class, the black working class, and the black urban poor share more cultural traits with each other as a group than they do with nonblacks of their respective economic station and educational level. Moreover, for decades now there has been an ongoing contest between blacks of different socioeconomic status over who has the standing to define black identity; that is, over who is best positioned to have the authentic black experience and to represent "the race" in the public eye. It is also clear that the growing physical separation of the black middle class from the black urban poor—the former sometimes living in the suburbs and the latter mainly in central cities—is likely to exacerbate this conflict. Given the increasing intragroup stratification of blacks and the well-known correlation between class position and cultural identification, we can expect this internal struggle over the meaning of blackness to continue and perhaps intensify. Yet if blacks were to drop the requirement of a common ethnocultural identity, which as I have argued is not necessary for the success of pragmatic nationalism anyway, this might reduce the negative effects that class differences have on black solidarity. I say *reduce*, not eliminate, for class differences among blacks pose a real and serious threat to pragmatic nationalism. My main point here, though, is that insisting on a common black ethnocultural identity can only worsen this already challenging problem.

Third, the requirement of a common black identity would surely aggravate the antagonism between black men and black women over the meaning of blackness as it relates to gender and the family. Historically, the content of black identity, including gender roles and norms governing family structure, has largely been prescribed by black men—that is, when it wasn't being defined by other ideological and structural forces within the larger society—most often leading to greater sacrifice and less freedom for black women. Moreover, the attempt to maintain a "positive" and cohesive group identity will likely have the effect, as it often has, of subordinating or ignoring the legitimate concerns of black women. Because black women are situated at the intersection of racial and sexist oppression, they have experiences and interests that are peculiar to their complex social condition.

But many black men fail to see, acknowledge, or take seriously these gendered experiences and interests. When black women voice, let alone attempt to aggressively deal with, their political concerns—such as sexual assault, domestic violence, inequality within the domestic sphere, degrading representations of women in the media, sexual and reproductive freedom, gender discrimination and harassment on the job, access to positions of leadership and authority—this is often wrongly seen as a divisive attempt to embarrass black men or as an imprudent move that threatens to worsen the public image of blacks. Rather than listening to black women and thinking of their concerns as integral to the freedom struggle, many black men have tried to silence them and have remained complicit in the perpetuation of patriarchy, often in the name of "unity." Given the prevalence of sexist attitudes and behavior among black men (and even some women), and the continuing unequal power relations between the sexes, male-centered conceptions of blackness are likely to predominate, though not, of course, without resistance. Witness, for example, the mixed reaction among black Americans, and especially black women, to the nomination of Clarence Thomas to the Supreme Court or to the call for a Million Man March on Washington. Though black feminist perspectives are growing in influence, even among some black men, until greater strides are made against (black) male hegemony, a shared and progressive view of what it means to be black is unlikely to develop.[25]

And fourth, there is a generational divide that can only be made worse by insisting that all blacks share an ethnocultural identity. Many of those who came of age during the civil rights era have a different understanding of what it means to be culturally black than those who grew up after Jim Crow was abolished. This is most evident in the intense intergenerational disagreement over the value and positive or negative influence of hip-hop culture.[26] Some of

this disagreement is political. Some blacks contest the political content of rap lyrics and the images seen in music videos and hip-hop-
inspired advertisements. Many feel that hip-hop representations
degrade women, glorify violence, belittle the value of education,
make light of drug abuse, reproduce pathological behavior, and reinforce negative stereotypes about blacks. Those who identify with
the culture believe that it affirms women's sexual freedom, accu-
rately depicts the grim realities of ghetto life, critiques a failing
school system, highlights the hypocrisy of the war on drugs, provides a soul-preserving source of comfort in impoverished conditions, and furnishes black youth with an identity that is not beholden to the politics of respectability. Such debate is healthy and,
in any case, unavoidable if black political solidarity is to be sustained in the post–civil rights era. Some of the generational conflict surrounding hip-hop culture is simply aesthetic: blacks have
sharply divergent views about whether the culture contains beauty
and genuine artistry. Debate over such questions can also be
healthy—and fun. Yet consensus on the aesthetic worth of hip hop
is not on the horizon.

However, all blacks have a vested interest in racial equality, regardless of their cultural identification, class position, gender, or
age (though the urgency with which one pursues racial justice will
likely depend on, among other things, whether one also suffers under class subordination, male domination, both, or neither). And
given their common classification as thinly black, blacks can identify with each other across these differences, for they share the susceptibility to antiblack racism that this classification makes possible. As Du Bois often emphasized, recognition of this common
interest and mutual identification can lend much-needed motivational strength to a morally based, joint commitment to ending racism, especially when it is accompanied by the special concern, loyalty, and trust that are characteristic of solidarity. Moreover, as
Orlando Patterson has argued, though both blacks and whites have

an interest in overcoming racism and racial antagonism, blacks must play a larger part in bringing this about, not only because they stand to gain more from it, but because whites have much less to lose from the status quo.[27]

It is doubtful that blacks will ever come to consensus on the meaning of "blackness." Though the quest for collective self-definition may not be an entirely futile one, blacks cannot afford to rest their hopes for racial justice on its success. And they certainly should not postpone the collective effort to bring about such justice until they secure this elusive common identity. Blacks can and should agree, in the present, to collectively resist racial injustice, not only because it is the morally responsible thing to do but also because it negatively affects them all, albeit to varying degrees and in different ways. Mobilizing and coordinating this effort will be difficult enough without adding the unnecessary and divisive requirement that blacks embrace and preserve a distinctive ethnocultural identity.

One final reason to doubt that a common identity would contribute to black solidarity and thus to the elimination of racial injustice is that if blacks were to push for a thicker collective identity, this would strain their already delicate bonds of unity. For although most blacks believe in the struggle for racial equality and the value of black communal relations, they also value the freedom to choose their cultural affiliations and to decide on their own conception of human flourishing.[28] If there is group pressure to conform to some prototype of blackness, which collective identity theory would seem to require, this would likely create "core" and "fringe" subgroups, thus alienating those on the fringe and providing them with an incentive to defect from the collective effort. Those who only marginally fit the black prototype may feel that accepting a conventional black identity is unduly burdensome and consequently may only halfheartedly participate, if at all, in the black fight against racism, especially if by acting alone they can manage, perhaps through their superior class position, to escape some of the more severe forms of racial injustice. Thus, a prescribed black identity could have the unintended consequence of inviting blacks who do not identify with the prevailing conception of blackness to protest against black intolerance, to form alternative alliances, to become egoistic, or to be simply complacent.

At this point, a critic might ask: But what about the assimilated black who has rejected his black identity in favor of a white persona and cultural lifestyle; can other blacks in the collective struggle really trust him when he shows no loyalty to black culture? The answer depends on how he conducts himself in other contexts, especially those that bear directly on the struggle for racial justice. Granted, sometimes when a black person chooses not to identify with black culture, this is accompanied by a lack of identification with the struggle against racial injustice. And cultural identification has long been a test of group loyalty and critical consciousness among blacks, as many realize that some among them will inevitably attempt to escape the stigma of blackness by taking on cultural attributes associated with "respectable" whites. Though this sometimes happens, especially among elites, it would be unjustified to presume that every time a black person adopts a "white" cultural identity, he or she is effectively lost to the struggle.

Sometimes nonblack modes of self-presentation are taken up so that the person can gain entry into institutions and social environments dominated by whites. Sometimes such a person was not socialized into black culture to begin with, and so is not presenting a persona at all. Sometimes she may simply find an alternative cultural identity more intrinsically appealing. And sometimes she may be operating with an unconventional though no less valid interpretation of blackness. As I argued earlier, we cannot simply infer a lack of loyalty and trustworthiness from the fact that a person does not define herself in terms of black culture. Many so-called assimilated blacks have played important roles in the struggle against racism, and it would be unreasonable and insulting to doubt their commitment to black solidarity simply because they did not embrace what some define as an appropriate black ethnocultural identity. As Bernard Boxill wisely reminds us (though his black trope is now somewhat dated), "it is false and vicious to infer that every assimilated black, or every black-skinned writer or poet who does not display 'soul,' is imitative and servile."[29] In short, the cultural test of group loyalty often produces false negatives.

The fact is, a person can show loyalty to the cause of black liberation and thus her trustworthiness as an ally in black resistance to racism through ways other than cultural identification. She can, for example, work to help ensure that the next generation of blacks has a lighter burden of racial oppression than the present one. Such work and protest against racism and its legacy should be sufficient to eliminate any suspicion that might arise due to the person's lack of black cultural identification. If the person were truly self-hating and servile, then she would be unlikely to openly struggle and sacrifice to advance the interests of the very group whose abject status is the source of her self-contempt. Blacks should be careful not to reject potential allies on the ground that these persons do not share their ethnocultural identity. It is much more important, indeed critical, that race-conscious blacks seek solidarity with others who share their antiracist values, along with their commitment to eliminating racial oppression and the social problems it causes.

Virtues of Pluralism and Inclusiveness

One response to these considerations is to insist that there already exists an inclusive and widely shared black identity and thus that blacks need only preserve it. Yet this claim is simply implausible. Blacks, taken in the thin sense, are an ethnically and culturally diverse group. This diversity includes differences in physical appearance, language, customs, religion, political outlook, moral values, aesthetic tastes, cuisine, fashion, traditions, national origin, and more.[30] The cultural and ethnic diversity of blacks should be especially obvious once we consider the various cultural traits embraced by recent black immigrants from Africa, Latin America, Europe, and the Caribbean. These other communities of African descent are themselves subject to antiblack prejudice in the United States and beyond. One could of course mean to include under "black identity" *all* of the cultural traits that are embraced and reproduced by blacks. This, however, would have the effect of rendering collective identity theory vacuous, because blacks cannot help taking on cultural traits of one sort or another, and therefore the imperative to "conserve blackness" would have no prescriptive force—it would not require blacks to do anything but literally "be themselves." If we view everything that black people do as "black," then blackness becomes a matter of ontology, sinking us right back into the quicksand of essentialism from which we should be actively trying to escape.

Alternatively, one might argue that it is possible to construct a pluralistic and nuanced conception of black identity, rather than a monolithic and unduly restrictive one. Again, this may be true. Yet no matter where one sets the boundaries of thick blackness, if it is meaningful enough to have normative, and not merely descriptive, force, some blacks will be left out or forced into submission. The collective identity theorist might not be troubled by this result, because he may insist that not all blacks are needed in the struggle against antiblack racism and some, if not most, will be indifferent to the fight for racial justice anyway. However, as was discussed in Chapter 2, we cannot determine on the basis of cultural identification alone who will or won't be willing to make such a solidaristic commitment. Thus it is more reasonable to be as inclusive as is consistent with the basic goals of such unity, as there is power in numbers. Indeed, it may turn out that the least "black" among us are among those most dedicated to the cause of racial justice, despite the widespread assumption to the contrary.[31] In any case, insisting on a specific conception of black identity, regardless of how pluralistic it is taken to be, is still vulnerable to the criticisms raised earlier against an essentialist discourse of black authenticity: blacks will find themselves in an unnecessary, contentious, distracting, and interminable debate over what counts as "black" and who will decide.

But let us suppose that cultivating a collective black identity were a realistic possibility for the near future. It might nevertheless be too dangerous to try to bring this about, for it is possible to go too far in creating group cohesiveness. The attempt to forge a collective black identity could unwittingly produce a groupthink mentality. The symptoms of groupthink include such things as collective efforts to rationalize the group's subordinate condition; social pressure on fellow members who reject in-group or out-group stereotypes; self-censorship of deviations from some presumed group consensus; and allegiance to ideologues who screen the group from information that might threaten its self-image. Striving to create a shared black identity could lead to this uncritical and often unconscious drive for unanimity and positive self-conception. This would have disastrous consequences for the cause of black liberation, by engendering defective collective decision-making, such as assuming that traditional solutions to black oppression must be correct; failing to reconsider initially discarded strategies or programs of action; dismissing criticisms of conventional narratives and goals; and ignoring social-scientific analyses that diverge from black common sense. Blacks must avoid these pitfalls, but unfortunately they have not always done so.[32]

One such pitfall deserves further comment. Many conceptions of black identity include, if only implicitly, an account of the nature of black oppression. In the black nationalist tradition, these narratives generally emphasize the pervasiveness of white supremacy. The legacy of slavery and current racism are treated as the primary obstacles to black flourishing, and shared narratives about racial oppression are reproduced as a part of black cultural heritage. To the extent that this cultural inheritance is embraced as an essential core of black identity itself, it could prove to be a self-imposed obstacle to black emancipation. Thus, for example, when a person accepts a particular analysis of the black condition *as a black person*— as a feature of who he *is* and not just what he believes—this can lead him to be stubbornly resistant to changing his view of the nature and causes of the black condition in the face of overwhelming evidence. To change his mind about such fundamental social matters would be to him (though he may not consciously recognize it as such) not just a shift in opinion based on evidence but a tragic loss of self-identity, which few are willing to consider, let alone seriously countenance. Now when a whole community accepts a particular analysis of their collective condition as a necessary component of who they are *as a people,* this can make it extremely difficult for them to reevaluate their shared standing or to recognize differences in standing between the various subgroups within the community. The point here is that an uncritical attachment to a particular conception of blackness where this includes a common narrative about the social status and material conditions of the group can undermine the group's ability to arrive at an objective assessment of their shared problems and possible solutions. Given the need to distinguish between the impact on blacks' life prospects of current racism, historical racism, and nonracial social dynamics, it is essential that blacks not embrace a collective ethnocultural identity that collapses these distinctions or misconstrues their current significance.

What must be recognized here is that "blackness," as a modality or child of "race," is an ideological construct that African-descended peoples have inherited as a legacy of the transatlantic slave trade. Like many such constructs, including "nation" and "ethnicity," it is extremely malleable and capacious, and so blacks have naturally fought—sometimes with their oppressors, sometimes with each other—to remold it to suit their own purposes. Consequently, blackness can be, and has been, given multiple meanings, which vary with the interpreters, their motives for using the notion, and the social circumstances. Thus, despite the obvious practical significance of the label *black,* agreement on its positive meaning must be limited to the claim that there are a number of loosely associated and variously interpreted *black identities.* The one link that often does exist between these multiple identities, however, is that many of them have been formed in an antiblack social environment, and each, in its own way, will likely bear the marks of race-based ill treatment. Yet the aim of black political solidarity should not be to discover the essential group-affirming core of all modalities of blackness, but to release all of these identities from racial stigma.

Paul Gilroy has advocated a conception of black identity based on a set of loosely related narratives that, according to him, have been produced in response to the experience of transatlantic black oppression. The multiple and globally dispersed practices that reproduce these stories can be viewed as constituting a sort of "tradition," which all blacks may identify with and participate in. Such an account, if adequate, could allow us to speak intelligibly and somewhat concretely of "black identities." However, such a conception of black identity would be of little help to the collective identity theorist, for at least two reasons. First, as Gilroy emphasizes, the Black Atlantic tradition is not rooted in a particular culture or ethnic heritage but is transnational, syncretic, unstable, and always mutating. Part of this lack of "purity" has to do with the inclusion of many European, Anglo-American, and Latin American cultural forms and modes of expression. Thus, although blacks can identify with and lay claim to the Black Atlantic tradition, so can many whites. Second, the Black Atlantic tradition, as Gilroy conceives of it, is nonessentialist. Therefore, there is nothing built into the content or structure of the tradition that determines who can or should identify with it or how any individual should relate to it. A black person who does not identify with it is not thereby inauthentic, and one may appreciate its depth, value, and beauty without necessarily defining one's identity in terms of it. Given the abstract and inclusive nature of the Black Atlantic tradition, there is room for many black identities and no basis for insisting on any one of them as the "real" social identity of blacks.

Although I find the idea of a Black Atlantic cultural tradition appealing, for the reasons given above I would stop short of including it as a necessary component of contemporary black American political engagement. I would urge blacks living in the United States, and by extension those in other parts of the world, to identify with each other on the basis of their experience of racial oppression and commitment to collectively resist it. From the standpoint of black political solidarity, each should be allowed to interpret "blackness" however he or she sees fit, provided the interpretation does not advocate anything immoral and is consistent with the collective struggle for racial justice.[33] In saying this, I am not suggesting, as some have, that individual blacks should give up their various black identities in favor of an American, a cosmopolitan, or simply a "human" identity. Though there should be more mindfulness of the dangers and limitations of "blackness," I see no reason to object to blacks identifying with what they regard as their ethnocultural heritage. What I resist is the tendency to think that blacks must *share* a distinctive black identity if they are to be a unified force against racial injustice.

Is Thin Blackness Too Thin?

The advocate of collective identity theory might object as follows: Surely a black solidarity that focuses on resisting racial oppression must at least require that blacks identify with their *thin* blackness, for without such a common identity they will lack a stable foundation for mutual identification. Yet this objection fails. Consider the following variant of the well-worn but still instructive witch anal-ogy.[34] Historically, for example, in medieval Europe and in Salem, Massachusetts, in the late seventeenth century, the trial and subse-quent punishment of "witches" was ostensibly based on the claim that the accused had communed with the forces of the underworld. Though this accusation was certainly unfounded, these so-called witches nevertheless suffered a common fate. Now let us suppose for a moment that some of the accused really did practice witch-craft—that they engaged in sorcery, sought to conspire with the Devil, surreptitiously corrupted good Christians, and so on. Sup-pose further that, at various points, some of their number, for whatever reason, ceased practicing witchcraft and no longer self-identified as "witches." And finally, suppose that at least some of these practitioners of witchcraft believed that there were some among them who were *frauds*, not "real" witches, according to some commonly accepted criteria for being a witch or according to some more controversial and strict criteria. Despite all this, it seems clear that all of these erstwhile, quasi, pseudo-, and would-be witches could have shared bonds of solidarity with each other, not based on their common affirmation of a "witch identity" (for *ex hypothesi* the existence of a *shared* identity was in doubt), but based on their common persecution. For purposes of collective resistance to unjust persecution, they simply could have put aside the ques-tion of who was and who was not an authentic witch and focused their attention and energy on overcoming their common plight.

Black solidarity could have, and should have, an analogous foun-dation. Just as a common belief in the value of "black magic" is not a necessary foundation for "witch" resistance to their unjust perse-cution, a shared belief in the value of a common "black identity" is not needed to ground "black" solidarity against racial domina-tion. The basis of blacks' group identification is not their attach-ment to their thin black identity but rather their shared experience with antiblack racism and their mutual commitment to ending it.

Blacks need only recognize that part of the reason they often suffer mistreatment is that others see them as thickly black (their
thin blackness being merely a "sign" of a deeper difference), and
this racialized perception leads their oppressors to devalue them.[35]
Identification between members of the racially oppressed group
can therefore be based on their common recognition of this sad
and disturbing fact. It would not undermine black solidarity if the
physical and genealogical characteristics that constitute their thin
blackness, apart from the unjust treatment that they engender, were
to have no intrinsic significance for the members of the united oppressed group. Once a racially just social order is achieved, thin
blackness may in fact lose all social and political significance.

Some might suggest that even this stripped-down common-
oppression theory commits itself to a version of the collective identity view, for despite its pretensions to have transcended identity
politics, it nevertheless endorses the cultivation of a thick collective black identity: it urges blacks to see themselves as racially oppressed. This shared identity is based not on race, ethnicity, nationality, or culture, but on the common experience of antiblack
racism. Thus, those blacks who are united by ties of solidarity will
still have a collective identity, and one that is not reducible to their
political principles. This identity might aptly be described as "victims of antiblack racial oppression."

One response to this objection is to simply concede it; that is, we
could accept that the one "thick" collective black identity that continues to be a realistic possibility is constituted by victim status in
an antiblack social world. This approach to the meaning of blackness is not self-defeating or divisive like the other conceptions considered, because the vast majority of blacks rightly accept that antiblack racism continues to exist (though of course they have no wish
to preserve the conditions under which an oppression-based identity would be advantageous or desirable).[36] Such an identity would

not gratuitously add to individual unfreedom, for it is nonracialist and perfectly consistent with tolerance for ethnocultural diversity. Moreover, blacks should not have to go to great lengths to cultivate this identity, for regrettably there is more than enough antiblack sentiment and discrimination still around to sustain it—though, admittedly, it may be necessary to convince some people of the depth of the problem.[37] But this view of "blackness" would not give the collective identity theorist all that he or she wants, for the search for a collective black identity has generally been a struggle to discover or construct a *positive* social identity, one that could be a basis for pride, dignity, and collective self-affirmation. A common identity based on nothing more than the shared experience of racism cannot provide such an identity, for this would, perversely, treat victimhood as something to be proud of—which is not, of course, to say that it is something blacks ought to be ashamed of (see Chapter 2).

Some might argue that a collective identity constituted by a shared oppressed condition can be seen to be positive and group-affirming if viewed from a black theological perspective, say, Christian or Muslim.[38] On this view, God embraces blacks *because* they are oppressed; and he is concerned to help them liberate themselves from their evil oppressors. However, the positive dimension of this kind of blackness is surely derived, not from the oppression itself, but from the virtue associated with the steadfast pursuit of truth and justice *despite* being oppressed and/or from the promise that, through faith and collective struggle, blacks will ultimately be delivered from that oppression. If God did not love what is good and hate what is evil, or if he could help liberate blacks from undeserved domination but did not, then they could hardly take just pride in being "chosen" by him. Yet even if black theology could find in black oppression something to be proud of, a theological account of this sort will not resonate with all blacks, because not all are religious. At best, then, "victims of antiblack racial oppression" could be a positive identity for some. Thus, blacks clearly need a nonsectarian basis for their political solidarity.

Is Pragmatic Black Solidarity (Still) Too Black?

Some will surely wonder why *black* solidarity is needed at all, especially because racism is not unique to the experience of blacks and, as has been emphasized throughout this book, solidarity between antiracist blacks and nonblacks is both possible and necessary. Should we not just reject black solidarity and embrace interracial, antiracist solidarity instead? Anthony Appiah, for example, raises this kind of objection against Du Bois's conception of racial solidarity.[39]

Although blacks should surely work with antiracist nonblacks against racism and other forms of social injustice, there is no principled reason why blacks must give up their solidaristic commitment to each other to do so. The two forms of solidarity are not mutually exclusive. There is room for nested and overlapping forms of antiracist solidarity, just as there is space for more or less exclusive and inclusive collective struggles at other sites of oppression, such as class, gender, culture, and sexuality. Broader forms of antiracist solidarity and coalition building should be cultivated, but there are several reasons why it is prudent for blacks to hold on to their narrower commitment to each other as well, at least for the time being.

First, antiblack racial injustice—like anti-Semitism, anti-Asian racism, the oppression of American Indians, the denial of equal citizenship to Latino groups, and the more recent profiling and harassment of Arab Americans—has features that make it unique as a form of racial subjection in the United States. The enslavement and brutalization of Africans in the New World, the subsequent exclusion of blacks from the mainstream of American civic, economic, and social life, and the peculiar content of antiblack racist ideology, with its images of blacks as lazy, stupid, incompetent, hypersexual, and disposed to gratuitous acts of violence, have combined to give antiblack race prejudice a distinctive character among American forms of racism. There are also severe social problems—joblessness, alarmingly high rates of incarceration, concentrated poverty, failing schools, a violent drug trade—that plague some black communities and that are partly the result of past and present racial discrimination against black people in particular. Although a joint commitment to fighting racial injustice in all its forms can help create interracial solidarity, it is often the shared experience of *specific* forms of racial injustice that creates the strongest motivation to act and the most enduring bonds among victims of racism.[40] This additional motivational impetus is needed to overcome the moral complacency and conservative resistance that inhibit political reform in the racial arena, a political momentum that cannot be achieved by mere abstract calls for greater social justice.[41]

Second, the black experience with racism in America makes it difficult for many blacks to fully trust nonblacks when it comes to fighting against racism, for they have too often been victimized by the racism of nonblacks, even by some who are racially oppressed themselves. What is more, other ethnoracial minority groups have solidaristic commitments of their own, which have sometimes been used to exploit the economic and political disadvantages of African Americans as a group. And whites in power sometimes favor these other groups over blacks, creating resentment and competition between minority groups. In light of this, it should be clear that many black Americans justifiably feel the need to protect themselves against the dangers that may result from competing group loyalties and group interests. A unilateral laying down of solidaristic arms, as it were, would needlessly increase black vulnerability to marginalization. Thus, on pragmatic grounds, blacks should maintain

their political solidarity with each other while simultaneously cultivating greater bonds of unity with progressive members of other
racial groups.

Finally, the common experience of antiblack racism has for cen-
turies provided a firm and well-recognized basis for mutual identification and special concern among blacks. This shared experience
partially accounts for the bonds that exist today, for blacks understand one another's burdens and empathize with each other on this
basis. In light of this common understanding and identification,
the legacy of collective struggle to remove this burden is a cherished
inheritance for many black Americans. As we seek to establish
stronger interracial forms of solidarity in our fight against social injustice, we should not underestimate or devalue the social bond
among blacks. Historically, it has been a great source of strength
and hope, and a highly effective means for mobilizing the population to work for social justice. I believe that it can, and should, continue to do so. In holding out this hope, however, I am not suggesting that black collective action, founded on pragmatic black
solidarity, would be sufficient to eliminate racism. Indeed, it might
be that nothing blacks do, even with the help of members from
other ethnoracial groups, will end antiblack racism.[42] Perhaps the
most that can be realistically hoped for, at least in the foreseeable
future, is that black solidarity affords blacks a limited form of collective self-defense against some of the more burdensome kinds of
racial injustice. But this, I should think, would be sufficient to make
the effort worthwhile.

Conclusion

The Political Morality of Black Solidarity

The conception of solidarity defended in this book is not a radical departure from what many black Americans already accept. Though the basis of black unity is often conflated with classical nationalism, Washingtonian conservatism, Black Power, cultural nationalism, or identity politics, the appropriate foundation is nevertheless implicit in black common sense, a component of those "black strivings" of which Du Bois spoke so eloquently in *The Souls of Black Folk*. Indeed, Du Bois defends, at times, a view very much in line with pragmatic nationalism. In *Dusk of Dawn*, for example, Du Bois reflects on his deep tie to Africa, which he "can feel better than [he] can explain."

> But one thing is sure and that is the fact that since the fifteenth century these ancestors of mine and their other descendants have had a common history; have suffered a common disaster and have one long memory. The actual ties of heritage between the individuals of this group, vary with the ancestors that they have in common and many others: Europeans and Semites, perhaps Mongolians, certainly American Indians. But the physical bond is least and the badge of color relatively unimportant save as a badge; the real essence of this

kinship is its social heritage of slavery; the discrimination and
insult; and this heritage binds together not simply the children of Africa, but extends through yellow Asia and into the
South Seas. It is this unity that draws me to Africa.[1]

Of course Du Bois is describing a Pan-African vision of solidarity, one that includes everyone of African descent, regardless of
where they live or call home, perhaps even extending to all people
of color who have been oppressed by white supremacy and European imperialism. This vision goes beyond what is defended here;
without denying that a broader conception of black unity is possible or desirable, I have focused on the situation of blacks in the
United States. Yet what is important to notice here is that Du Bois
grounds his Pan-African vision, not in a thick collective identity as
he did in "The Conservation of Races," but in the common experience of racial injustice and the stigma of being racialized as
"black." It is the importance of this core idea, drawn from the black
nationalist tradition, that I have wanted to emphasize.

Black Collective Integrity: Political, Not Ethnocultural

In Chapter 6, I argued that the basis of black political unity should
not be a shared black identity, regardless of whether we understand
this identity as a matter of racial essence, ethnicity, culture, or nationality. This is not to deny that there are widely recognized social criteria that enable us to roughly sort people into the familiar "racial" categories of white, black, Asian, Native American, and,
increasingly, Arab. But those who employ this classification system for practical purposes do not necessarily endorse the racialist
beliefs linked to the development of the scheme. In America today, people can publicly self-identify as black, in the thin sense,
without believing that the designation says anything deep about
who they are. Black political solidarity, understood within the normative framework of pragmatic nationalism, uses this classification

scheme, not for positive identity-construction, but to unite those racially designated as black.

The mutual identification among blacks—that familiar sense of "we-ness"—can be rooted, in part, in the shared experience of anti-black racism. This experience enables blacks to empathize with one another and sometimes moves them to provide mutual support in a world that is often hostile to their presence. The common experiences of racial injustice, made possible by their common racial ascription, include such things as carrying the stigma attached to "looking" and "acting" black; having one's life prospects diminished by institutional racism; suffering discrimination on the basis of presumed incompetence; enduring arbitrary exclusion from certain neighborhoods, schools, and social circles; being preemptively regarded as unsuitable for intimate social interaction; navigating the social world with the knowledge that one is often the object of unjustified hatred, contempt, suspicion, or fear; seeking to avoid "confirming" an array of degrading racial stereotypes; serving as the perennial scapegoat for social problems and economic crises; and living with the knowledge that one is vulnerable, at almost any time, to an antiblack attitude, action, social practice, or institutional policy. The common experience of racial oppression can be a valuable source of motivation that blacks should continue to harness in the interest of social justice.

But protracted struggle against oppression can eat away at one's soul, sinking one into the darkness of despair, alienation, self-doubt, or even complacent cynicism. So it is crucial that blacks work together to develop and maintain a vigorous character, since such vigor is necessary for both self-respect and collective self-defense. Recall that Delany called for independence of mind, a willingness to innovate, self-confidence, moderate ambition, courage in the face of opposition, the determination to seek freedom at any cost, and individual and group self-reliance. These qualities of character, to which we should add, following Du Bois, a willingness to sacrifice for group advancement and moral integrity, are especially important among black leadership. A relatively large, vigorous group of black-identified persons is absolutely essential if blacks are to develop a robust solidarity.

However, given the various forms of severe disadvantage to which many blacks are vulnerable, we cannot expect that all, or perhaps even most, blacks will cultivate these traits. Some will inevitably succumb to hopelessness and pessimism. Those living under the burdens of ghetto poverty are perhaps especially susceptible, for they face not only institutional racism but severe economic deprivation as well. Thus it is imperative that more-affluent blacks extend special concern to the least advantaged. This means assisting poor blacks when one can and refraining from self-righteous moralizing about how those in poverty ought to live. Special concern is a constitutive component of any robust solidarity. But such unity is possible only if all with whom blacks seek solidarity feel that they are equally valued members of the community. Those who have been most negatively affected by racial injustice could not feel thus valued if, in the struggle for black freedom and equality, little effort is made to improve their plight. They will naturally feel that they are being sacrificed to improve or maintain the position of more-affluent blacks and may even rebel against the efforts to reform our society. Much-needed assistance from their fellow blacks may, however, inspire in the least advantaged a hope for the future—and a commitment to group solidarity.

Yet black identification and group-based special concern are not sufficient. A robust solidarity must also include a joint commitment to certain values or goals. In addition to racial, ethnic, cultural, and national modes of blackness, there is a specifically *political* mode of blackness. As discussed in Chapter 3, political blackness cannot be a broad political ideology (such as conservatism, comprehensive liberalism, socialism, or classical nationalism). Rather it should be understood as the faithful adherence to certain political principles, including antiracism, equal educational and employment opportunity, and tolerance for group differences and individuality, and to emancipatory goals, such as achieving substantive racial equality—especially in employment, education, and wealth—and ending ghetto poverty.

Indeed, a person's loyalty to the collective struggle should not be measured in terms of the "thickness" of his black identity, but in terms of his commitment to the political principles of pragmatic black nationalism. Group loyalty and mutual trust can be cultivated and reinforced through individual and collective efforts to end racial discrimination, racial inequality, poverty, and intolerance. Those with whom blacks should seek solidarity, then, are not necessarily those who most exhibit a thick black identity, but those who stand firm in resistance to black oppression. Rather than being rooted in race, ethnicity, nationality, or culture, the group's self-conception should be grounded in its antiracist politics and its commitment to racial justice.

Though blacks should be able to agree on basic principles and broad goals, there must be room within pragmatic black solidarity for disagreement over the precise content of political action and policy initiatives. The ideals of racial equality, antipoverty, and tolerance are open to a variety of interpretations, and reasonable people can disagree over the appropriate strategies for overcoming racism and its legacy. Some of these disagreements may run deep, say, between radical democrats and conservatives or between liberals and cultural nationalists. Blacks know, however, that they all want to live in a society where being (regarded as) black is not a disadvantage and where all can live with freedom, dignity, and self-respect regardless of their so-called race. These ideals, principles, and goals can provide black solidarity with a rough normative guide about where to go from here and how to get there. Yet they should debate the practical details of their group action with open minds and without allowing themselves to be sidetracked by the controversy over what it means to be "really" black. The only form of authenticity that has any bearing on pragmatic nationalism is the good-faith effort to remain true to political blackness. Should it happen that social bonds begin to fracture or unravel because of the depth of their political disagreements—and perhaps that time is now—each should be reminded, as Frederick Douglass urged long ago, that the bases of black unity are the mutual recognition of a common subordinate position and the collective commitment to rise above it, not ideological homogeneity.

This commitment includes rooting out race prejudice wherever it exists, even within their own ranks. For though blacks are united by their specific circumstances of oppression, they must stand together against *all* forms of racial oppression if their indignation is not to be merely self-serving. Hence, while being pragmatic does mean being concerned with achieving practical results in light of the sociopolitical context, it does not mean being willing to sacrifice principle for expediency or immediate results. In this way, an oppression-centered black solidarity is not a matter of being anti-white or, for that matter, pro-black, but of abhorring racial injustice. Consequently, extending solidarity to other racially stigmatized groups and even to committed antiracist whites is not precluded. Indeed, blacks can retain their solidarity while participating in multiracial organizations working for social justice more broadly. Thus, progressive antiracists have no reason to oppose black solidarity once its normative basis, political scope, and emancipatory point are properly understood.

The Meaning of Black Self-Determination

This interpretation of black nationalism would be incomplete without an account of the meaning of black self-determination. At least since the nineteenth century, nationalist-oriented African Americans have fought for freedom and equality under the banner "self-determination."[2] Some have used this militant-sounding phrase to call for an independent nation-state with territorial sovereignty or, failing that, some measure of institutional autonomy and political independence within a larger multinational state. Others voiced the phrase in their demands for ethnocultural solidarity and the need to resist pressures of assimilation. It has also functioned simply as a rallying cry to mobilize blacks for collective action against oppression and racial inequality.

In my defense of pragmatic black nationalism, I suggested that the ideal of black self-determination, at least with respect to blacks in America, entails a sharply delimited, trans-institutional, and decentralized form of black political solidarity. This group solidarity would be understood, not as an end in itself, but as a collective strategy for bringing about a social order in which individuals can autonomously define and pursue their conception of the good life without their "blackness" posing any limitation or burden. In the remainder of this section, I want to draw together the strands of the book's argument by highlighting its significance for the debate over the meaning of black self-determination.

As we've seen, the content of "black self-determination" is open to a variety of interpretations, and the meaning of the phrase, as with all such broad ideals, is thoroughly contested. Nevertheless, there are at least two clear parameters for any plausible conception. First, the ideal expresses the claim of a people—black Americans— to pursue their ends without being unjustly constrained or interfered with by outside forces. This demand for freedom from unjust constraint, or so-called negative liberty, may include the realms of politics, economics, culture, interpersonal relations, or all of these. Second, the political thinkers who endorse the ideal regard self-determination as necessary for the members of the group to flourish in the modern world. A political program that includes the goal of self-determination is therefore a demand for the conditions necessary for self-realization, or so-called positive liberty. These rough ideas offer some guidance in interpreting the precise content of black self-determination.

My interpretation is built on three further assumptions. First, the ideal must be defended without reifying the idea of race or relying on romantic racialist narratives about the primordial origins of the African race. I have argued throughout that a black politics founded on racial essentialism is untenable, and that black political action must be conceived without invoking or assuming such organicist notions. Second, the ideal of self-determination must be compatible with respect for intragroup differences, such as gender, sexuality, ethnicity, nationality, and religion. Black Americans have vital interests in common, but they are not a homogeneous group and must respect individual freedom. Third, any plausible defense of black self-determination must not be utopian—applicable only in an ideal but unrealizable world—but must be politically viable given the sociohistorical circumstances of contemporary black Americans. It is clear that the material, political, and social conditions of blacks in the United States have changed significantly—both for better and for worse—since the gains of the civil rights movement. In making these assumptions we narrow the possible conceptions of black self-determination to those that are relevant for a post-racialist, post-essentialist, and post–civil rights, pragmatic black politics.

A philosophical reconstruction of the long-standing ideal of black self-determination requires us to address four distinct but related sets of issues, questions that are both conceptual and normative. First, as the call is for *self*-determination, we must specify what kind of entity the "self" in question is. Must it be, as most nationalists assume, the *collective* self of a cohesive and interdependent community? Or, against the mainstream of nationalist thought, can the relevant "self" be simply a *moral person*, an individual agent capable of developing a sense of justice and a conception of the good?[3] Pragmatic black nationalism invokes both conceptions of the self but assigns them different functions and moral priorities. The plural self, the black "we," is a racialized group living in America that has politicized its peoplehood for purposes of seeking racial justice. It is not, however, a corporate person with the authority to speak or act on behalf of the black nation. The singular self is an individual who has a determinate sense of what racial justice demands and identifies as politically black. Black individuals are the primary units of moral concern, though some may also seek to preserve the integrity of the group as a component of their conception of the good, provided that in doing so they respect the autonomy of those who opt for an alternative conception.

As our concern is with the status of *black* self-determination, a second set of questions focuses on what constitutes the "blackness" of these freedom-seeking selves. As a "thick" concept, blackness has both descriptive and normative content. Or, to put it another way, its use typically entails claims about both what blackness is and what it ought to be. I have argued that, for purposes of black political solidarity, blackness should not be understood in terms of racialist, ethnic, cultural, or national modes of blackness. Instead, "racial" blackness should be understood in terms of one's vulnerability to antiblack racism, and thus the thin criterion for assigning racial membership is sufficient. There is also a political mode of blackness, constituted by a set of antiracist principles and goals. One signals political solidarity by demonstrating a commitment to these principles and goals and by identifying with, showing special concern for, being loyal to, and trusting other blacks. Identification, special concern, and loyalty are to be extended to all blacks, because it is for the sake of the well-being and freedom of all that blacks constitute themselves as a unified group. But trust can reasonably be extended only to those who exhibit black political consciousness, for blacks could not productively engage in collective action unless they knew they could rely on each other. Thin blackness takes priority over thick blackness in determining who is a full member of the solidarity group, and there is a general commitment to black pluralism and cultural tolerance. Thick blackness is not rejected as such. Rather, political self-determination, on a pragmatic nationalist interpretation, is neutral with respect to these modes of blackness, provided they are compatible with social justice. That is, each politically conscious black individual may legitimately differ with respect to his or her particular shade of ethnocultural or national blackness, and some may refuse such an identity altogether. Black Americans are a people—an intergenerational community of descent that is tied by the stigma of race—but not a cohesive cultural or national unit.

Third, what would it mean for the relevant black self to *determine* itself? That is, what kind of autonomy must the black selves possess to be truly free? Pragmatic nationalism holds that freedom from oppression—domination, exploitation, deprivation, exclusion, discrimination, marginalization, and stigmatization—is certainly required. Black Americans as a group are particularly concerned with removing racial obstacles to free and equal citizenship. Pragmatic nationalism also seeks to bring about the social conditions that would enable self-realization. But it does not aim for the self-realization of blacks *as a people,* for it is silent on the worth of particular conceptions of the good. Rather, recognizing the diversity within the black population, it respects the right of each black individual to determine just what self-realization or human flourishing means for him or her. Pragmatic nationalism aims simply to remove the obstacles to individual autonomy caused by racial injustice. Whether black individuals use this autonomy to work together to realize more communitarian values, such as preserving the cultural traditions of the group, is up to them.

The *collective* dimension of black self-determination—black group action that springs, at least in part, from solidarity—is simply a strategy for resisting, defending against, and overcoming racial oppression. Improving the group's position is one way of improving conditions for those individuals oppressed on account of their "race." The freedom blacks ultimately seek, though, is not group self-rule in a separate nation-state or institutional autonomy within the United States, but freedom from racism, relief from the burdens of racial inequality and ghetto poverty, and greater political participation in our multiracial polity. What is "collective," then, is not the fundamental ends but the struggle to achieve them: blacks reserve the right to act independently and to define their own political agenda in order to defend themselves against unjust treatment and to help bring about a racially just society.

Yet, in insisting on the legitimacy of black political solidarity, the pragmatic nationalist recognizes that the actions of the "black nation" cannot, and should not, be modeled on the structure of the modern nation-state. In particular, black political solidarity must be noncorporatist. No black party, association, or institution can legitimately claim to speak for black people as a whole. Instead, there should be multiple and independent black organizations and advocacy groups that take up particular issues that affect black interests. Blacks must also resist political centralization. Institutional infrastructure is certainly needed to put power behind black demands. But black self-organization should be voluntary and rooted in particular communities, where those who will be most significantly affected are able to interpret and articulate their own interests and concrete goals and where they have mechanisms for making their representatives responsive to their concerns. To garner consensus, blacks require broad participation in a multi-sited public sphere, a forum that encourages open and free dialogue about matters of common concern. Here, the broad range of mass media can be utilized—print, television, radio, and digital technology. This is one way to realize democratic participation and collective will-formation without relying exclusively on elected officials to voice black concerns. Thus, black self-determination does not mean black collective self-governance.

Finally, what kind of *ideal* is black self-determination? In accordance with our earlier distinctions, this social ideal can be interpreted and defended within either a classical or a pragmatic nationalist framework. Recall that the classical nationalist holds that black solidarity and voluntary separation under conditions of equality and self-rule is a worthwhile end in itself, and an essential component of the collective self-realization of blacks as a people. Here the collective autonomy of blacks is the fundamental aim, and black self-governance is treated as a necessary element of black flourishing and a core principle. The pragmatic nationalist, on the other hand, maintains that black solidarity and group self-organization is no more than a strategy for creating greater freedom and equality for blacks. Within this framework, black political solidarity need not be regarded as intrinsically valuable; it simply functions as a means to ameliorate the unfair disadvantages of blacks. The freedom and well-being of blacks is still sought, but black group autonomy, to the extent that it is favored, is viewed as only contingently related to black flourishing. Accordingly, if black interests can be adequately advanced through multiracial associations or within a multiracial polity, then this too would be perfectly acceptable.

From Nationalism to Post-Nationalism

Pragmatic nationalism is a form of black solidarity that aims, ultimately, to transcend itself. Its objective, indeed its *raison d'être*, is to bring about a racially just social order. Once this has been achieved, black political solidarity as such would be no longer necessary, and perhaps even counterproductive. Yet this conception of black politics is not an attack on the idea of black peoplehood. I favor politicizing black peoplehood—thinking of black Americans as a nation within a nation—because this is a legitimate and effective way to bring about a society where it is no longer necessary for those who are dark to think of themselves as an independent political unit. Even if these political goals were ultimately achieved, this would not mean that blacks should no longer regard themselves as sharing a meaningful common past and collective future. True, blacks would no longer constitute a "nation" in that politicized sense of the term that has been a central feature of black nationalism since its inception. However, political cohesiveness is not a necessary condition for peoplehood. In fact, once racial justice is achieved through blacks' determined efforts, future generations could take pride in being the descendants of a people who achieved black freedom, and this may inspire them to continue to work for social justice, both in the United States and in the broader world. Many blacks may also more eagerly embrace their various cultural, ethnic, and national identities, for these would then no longer be stigmatized by their association with a subordinate "race." Thus black people and black identities would endure, and even flourish, despite the depoliticization of blackness.

Nothing I have said in this book should be regarded as expressing a sanguine view of black political solidarity. I have sought only to lay down conditions of possibility for such unity. Mine is a philosophical task: I aim to describe not what already is but what, with work, could be. In particular, my defense of pragmatic nationalism does not assume that most blacks already possess a pragmatic black consciousness. Black political culture is still weighted with outmoded and reactionary strands of black nationalism, and too many progressives regard this tradition as inherently problematic. Yes, pragmatic nationalism faces challenges, both within the black population and from the outside. Yet black political solidarity can survive the now well-known critique of ethnoracial essentialism. It can be sustained despite the loss of race as a viable concept in the biological sciences and anthropology. It can be maintained despite the cultural, ethnic, and national diversity within the black population in the United States. It is perfectly compatible with a progressive stance on issues of gender and sexuality. It need not unduly constrain individuality or the freedom to construct a pluralistic identity or to form interracial intimacies. And it can still be a valuable political resource in spite of the class differentiation that exists within the black population. However, this reconstructed black nationalism must be sustained without the demand for a thick collective identity or ideological cohesiveness, for these austere and unrealistic requirements can only impede the collective struggle that lies ahead.

Notes

Introduction

1. See, for example, Robin D. G. Kelley, *Freedom Dreams: The Black Radical Imagination* (Boston: Beacon Press, 2002); Lani Guinier and Gerald Torres, *The Miner's Canary: Enlisting Race, Resisting Power, Transforming Democracy* (Cambridge, Mass.: Harvard University Press, 2002); Paul Gilroy, *Against Race: Imagining Political Culture beyond the Color Line* (Cambridge, Mass.: Harvard University Press, 2000); Rod Bush, *We Are Not What We Seem: Black Nationalism and Class Struggle in the American Century* (New York: New York University Press, 1999); Adolph Reed Jr., *Stirrings in the Jug: Black Politics in the Post-Segregation Era* (Minneapolis: University of Minnesota Press, 1999); Clarence Lusane, *Race in the Global Era: African Americans at the Millennium* (Boston: South End Press, 1997); Joy James, *Transcending the Talented Tenth: Black Leaders and American Intellectuals* (New York: Routledge, 1997); Glenn C. Loury, *One by One from the Inside Out: Essays and Reviews on Race and Responsibility in America* (New York: Free Press, 1995); Manning Marable, *Beyond Black and White: Transforming African-American Politics* (London: Verso, 1995); Cornel West, *Race Matters* (New York: Vintage, 1994); Derrick Bell, *Faces at the Bottom of the Well: The Permanence of Racism* (New York: Basic Books, 1992); and bell hooks, *Yearning: Race, Gender, and Cultural Politics* (Boston: South End Press, 1990).

2. For a devastating critique of conservative treatments of racial justice, see Bernard R. Boxill, *Blacks and Social Justice*, rev. ed. (Lanham, Md.: Rowman and Littlefield, 1992), chaps. 2, 11.

3. But for a compelling defense of the compatibility of nationalism and liberalism, see Yael Tamir, *Liberal Nationalism* (Princeton: Princeton University Press, 1993).

4. For important exceptions, see Boxill, *Blacks and Social Justice;* Kwame Anthony Appiah, *In My Father's House: Africa in the Philosophy of Culture* (New York: Oxford University Press, 1992); and Howard McGary, *Race and Social Justice* (Malden, Mass.: Blackwell, 1999).

5. See John Rawls, *Political Liberalism* (New York: Columbia University Press, 1996) and *Justice as Fairness: A Restatement,* ed. Erin Kelly (Cambridge, Mass.: Harvard University Press, 2001).

6. John Rawls, *A Theory of Justice,* rev. ed. (Cambridge, Mass.: Harvard University Press, 1999), pp. 6–8.

7. The Eastern Division of the American Philosophical Association (APA), the largest professional organization of philosophers in the United States, recognizes "Africana Philosophy" (of which African American philosophy is a part) as a subfield in the discipline, and the APA Committee on Blacks in Philosophy regularly sponsors symposia and special sessions devoted to topics in the area at APA annual divisional meetings. Contemporary representative texts within African American philosophy include Cornel West, *Prophesy Deliverance! An Afro-American Revolutionary Christianity* (Philadelphia: Westminster Press, 1982); Leonard Harris, ed., *Philosophy Born of Struggle: Anthology of Afro-American Philosophy from 1917* (Dubuque, Iowa: Kendall/Hunt, 1983); Boxill, *Blacks and Social Justice;* Howard McGary and Bill E. Lawson, *Between Slavery and Freedom: Philosophy and American Slavery* (Bloomington: Indiana University Press, 1992); Adrian Piper, "Passing for White, Passing for Black," *Transition* 58 (1992): 4–32; Bill E. Lawson, ed., *The Underclass Question* (Philadelphia: Temple University Press, 1992); Appiah, *In My Father's House;* Naomi Zack, *Race and Mixed Race* (Philadelphia: Temple University Press, 1993); Laurence Mordekhai Thomas, *Vessels of Evil: American Slavery and the Holocaust* (Philadelphia: Temple University Press, 1993); Lucius T. Outlaw Jr., *On*

Race and Philosophy (New York: Routledge, 1996); J. L. A. Garcia, "The Heart of Racism," *Journal of Social Philosophy* 27 (1996): 5–45; John P. Pittman, ed., *African-American Perspectives and Philosophical Traditions* (New York: Routledge, 1997); Lewis R. Gordon, ed., *Existence in Black: An Anthology of Black Existential Philosophy* (New York: Routledge, 1997); Greg Moses, *Revolution of Conscience: Martin Luther King, Jr., and the Philosophy of Nonviolence* (New York: Guilford Press, 1997); Robert Gooding-Williams, "Race, Multiculturalism and Democracy," *Constellations* 5 (1998): 18–41; Charles W. Mills, *Blackness Visible: Essays on Race and Philosophy* (Ithaca: Cornell University Press, 1998); McGary, *Race and Social Justice*; Tommy L. Lott, *The Invention of Race: Black Culture and the Politics of Representation* (Malden, Mass.: Blackwell, 1999); Lewis R. Gordon, *Existentia Africana: Understanding Africana Existential Thought* (New York: Routledge, 2000); Robert E. Birt, ed., *The Quest for Community and Identity: Critical Essays in Africana Social Philosophy* (Lanham, Md.: Rowman and Littlefield, 2002); and Tommy L. Lott and John P. Pittman, eds., *A Companion to African-American Philosophy* (Malden, Mass.: Blackwell, 2003).

8. For critical discussions of the racial bias or normative "whiteness" of academic philosophy, see Outlaw, *On Race and Philosophy*; Lewis R. Gordon, *Her Majesty's Other Children: Sketches of Racism from a Neocolonial Age* (Lanham, Md.: Rowman and Littlefield, 1997), chap. 2; and Charles W. Mills, *The Racial Contract* (Ithaca: Cornell University Press, 1997).

9. For a discussion of the importance of historical studies to the development of African American philosophy, see West, *Prophesy Deliverance*, pp. 15–24.

10. In a particularly revealing set of interviews with several leading contemporary African American philosophers, George Yancy explores the many ways in which the black experience can usefully inform and advance philosophical inquiry. See George Yancy, *African-American Philosophers: 17 Conversations* (New York: Routledge, 1998).

11. Mills, *Blackness Visible*, pp. 120–126.

12. See, for example, Emmanuel Chukwudi Eze, ed., *Race and the*

Enlightenment: A Reader (Oxford: Blackwell, 1997); and Robert Bernasconi and Tommy Lott, eds., *The Idea of Race* (Indianapolis: Hackett, 2000).

13. See, for example, Fred Lee Hord (Mzee Lasana Okpara) and Jonathan Scott Lee, eds., *I Am Because We Are: Readings in Black Philosophy* (Amherst: University of Massachusetts Press, 1995); Bernard W. Bell, Emily R. Grosholz, and James B. Stewart, eds., *W. E. B. Du Bois on Race and Culture* (New York: Routledge, 1996); Bill E. Lawson and Frank M. Kirkland, eds., *Frederick Douglass: A Critical Reader* (Malden, Mass.: Blackwell, 1999).

14. W. E. B. Du Bois, *The Autobiography of W. E. B. Du Bois: A Soliloquy on Viewing My Life from the Last Decade of Its First Century* (New York: International Publishers, 1968), p. 148.

1. Two Conceptions of Black Nationalism

1. In a comprehensive empirical analysis of contemporary black political ideologies, Michael Dawson has shown that among African Americans there is broad support for (and very little hard opposition to) several core nationalist ideas, including the creation and control of separate institutions within the black community, black economic and political self-determination, and a belief that African Americans constitute an "internal black nation" within the United States. See Michael C. Dawson, *Black Visions: The Roots of Contemporary African-American Political Ideologies* (Chicago: University of Chicago Press, 2001), esp. chap. 3. Also see Robert A. Brown and Todd C. Shaw, "Separate Nations: Two Attitudinal Dimensions of Black Nationalism," *Journal of Politics* 64 (2002): 22–44; Dean E. Robinson, *Black Nationalism in American Politics and Thought* (Cambridge: Cambridge University Press, 2001), chap. 7; and Jennifer L. Hochschild, *Facing Up to the American Dream: Race, Class, and the Soul of the Nation* (Princeton: Princeton University Press, 1995), chaps. 4–6.

2. See Kwame Anthony Appiah, *In My Father's House: Africa in the Philosophy of Culture* (New York: Oxford University Press, 1992); Adolph Reed Jr., *Stirrings in the Jug: Black Politics in the Post-Segregation Era* (Minneapolis: University of Minnesota Press, 1999); and Paul

Gilroy, *Against Race: Imagining Political Culture Beyond the Color Line* (Cambridge, Mass.: Harvard University Press, 2000). See also Clarence E. Walker, *We Can't Go Home Again: An Argument about Afrocentrism* (New York: Oxford University Press, 2001). It is worth pointing out that, in recent years, Appiah has softened his critical stance toward certain black nationalist ideas. See, for example, his "Race, Culture, Identity: Misunderstood Connections," in K. Anthony Appiah and Amy Gutmann, *Color Conscious: The Political Morality of Race* (Princeton: Princeton University Press, 1996), pp. 30–105; and his "The State and the Shaping of Identity," in *The Tanner Lectures on Human Values*, vol. 23, ed. Grethe B. Peterson (Salt Lake City: University of Utah Press, 2002), pp. 234–299.

3. This more constructive approach to black nationalism—intensely critical yet sympathetic engagement—is exemplified by many of the essays in *Is It Nation Time? Contemporary Essays on Black Power and Black Nationalism*, ed. Eddie Glaude Jr. (Chicago: University of Chicago Press, 2002). Also see Angela Y. Davis, "Black Nationalism: The Sixties and the Nineties," in *The Angela Y. Davis Reader*, ed. Joy James (Malden, Mass.: Blackwell, 1998), pp. 289–293.

4. In his influential discussion of the "nationalist" and "integrationist" strains within black political thought, Harold Cruse famously traces the nationalist strain back to the writings of Delany. See Harold Cruse, *The Crisis of the Negro Intellectual* (New York: Quill, 1984), pp. 4–6, 129, 558. For more on the significance of Delany to the black nationalist tradition, see Floyd John Miller, "The Search for a Black Nationality: Martin R. Delany and the Emigrationist Alternative" (Ph.D. diss., University of Minnesota, 1970); Theodore Draper, *The Rediscovery of Black Nationalism* (New York: Viking, 1970), pp. 21–47; Victor Ullman, *Martin R. Delany: The Beginnings of Black Nationalism* (Boston: Beacon Press, 1971); Dorothy Sterling, *The Making of an Afro-American: Martin Robison Delany* (New York: Da Capo Press, 1971); and Alphonso Pinkney, *Red, Black, and Green: Black Nationalism in the United States* (Cambridge: Cambridge University Press, 1976), pp. 23–27.

5. Martin R. Delany, *The Condition, Elevation, Emigration, and*

Destiny of the Colored People of the United States, Politically Considered (Baltimore: Black Classic Press, 1993).

6. Ibid., pp. 11–13.

7. See Will Kymlicka, *Multicultural Citizenship: A Liberal Theory of Minority Rights* (Oxford: Clarendon, 1995), pp. 10–26. For discussions of how American blacks fit into recent debates over multiculturalism, see Iris Marion Young, *Justice and the Politics of Difference* (Princeton: Princeton University Press, 1990), chap. 6; Kwame Anthony Appiah, "Identity, Authenticity, Survival: Multicultural Societies and Social Reproduction," in *Multiculturalism: Examining the Politics of Recognition,* ed. Amy Gutmann (Princeton: Princeton University Press, 1994), pp. 149–163; Manning Marable, *Beyond Black and White: Transforming African-American Politics* (London: Verso, 1995), chap. 9; Robert Gooding-Williams, "Race, Multiculturalism and Democracy," *Constellations* 5 (1998): 18–41; Will Kymlicka, *Politics in the Vernacular: Nationalism, Multiculturalism, and Citizenship* (Oxford: Oxford University Press, 2001), chap. 9; Brian Barry, *Culture and Equality: An Egalitarian Critique of Multiculturalism* (Cambridge, Mass.: Harvard University Press, 2001), chap. 8; and Amy Gutmann, *Identity and Democracy* (Princeton: Princeton University Press, 2003), chap. 3.

8. See E. U. Essien-Udom, *Black Nationalism: A Search for an Identity in America* (Chicago: University of Chicago Press, 1962), p. 6. For similar conceptions of nationalism, see Benedict Anderson, *Imagined Communities: Reflections on the Origin and Spread of Nationalism,* rev. ed. (London: Verso, 1991), pp. 6–7; E. J. Hobsbawm, *Nations and Nationalism since 1780: Programme, Myth, Reality* (Cambridge: Cambridge University Press, 1990), pp. 9–13; and Ernest Gellner, *Nations and Nationalism* (Ithaca: Cornell University Press, 1983), pp. 1–7.

9. On this definition, prominent contemporary classical black nationalists in the United States would include Maulana Karenga (founder of the cultural nationalist group US and creator of Kwanzaa), Molefi Kete Asante (central theorist and spokesperson for the Afrocentric approach to the study of history and culture), and Minister Louis Farrakhan (leader of the Nation of Islam and principal organizer of the Million Man March, the largest assemblage of blacks in U.S. his-

tory). See, for example, Maulana Karenga, *Introduction to Black Studies* (Los Angeles: University of Sankore Press, 1982); Molefi Kete Asante, *The Afrocentric Idea,* rev. ed. (Philadelphia: Temple University Press, 1998); and Louis Farrakhan, *Back Where We Belong: Selected Speeches by Minister Louis Farrakhan,* ed. Joseph D. Eure and Richard M. Jerome (Philadelphia: PC International Press, 1989).

10. Bernard Boxill makes a similar set of distinctions within the traditional integrationist/separatist framework. See his "Two Traditions in African American Political Philosophy," *Philosophical Forum* 24 (1992–1993): 119–135; see also Howard McGary, *Race and Social Justice* (Oxford: Blackwell, 1999), chap. 3.

11. See Wilson J. Moses, *The Golden Age of Black Nationalism, 1850–1925* (New York: Oxford University Press, 1978). See also John T. McCartney, *Black Power Ideologies: An Essay in African-American Political Thought* (Philadelphia: Temple University Press, 1992); and Robinson, *Black Nationalism.*

12. In a more recent discussion, Moses says the following about "classical" black nationalism: "In its strictest form, classical black nationalism must be defined as the effort by African Americans to create a modern nation-state with distinct geographical boundaries. In a broader sense, it may indicate a spirit of Pan-African unity and an emotional sense of solidarity with the political and economic struggles of African peoples throughout the world. In a very loose sense, it may refer simply to any feelings of pride in a distinct ethnic heritage." See his introduction to *Classical Black Nationalism: From the American Revolution to Marcus Garvey* (New York: New York University Press, 1996), p. 20.

13. August Meier, *Negro Thought in America, 1880–1915: Racial Ideologies in the Age of Booker T. Washington* (Ann Arbor: University of Michigan Press, 1988), p. ix.

14. See the editors' introduction in John H. Bracey Jr., August Meier, and Elliott Rudwick, eds., *Black Nationalism in America* (Indianapolis: Bobbs-Merrill, 1970).

15. I have adapted this conception of how intellectual traditions are constructed from Henry Louis Gates Jr., *The Signifying Monkey: A The-*

ory of African-American Literary Criticism (New York: Oxford University Press, 1988).

16. Think here of other intellectual traditions, such as pragmatism, existentialism, and liberalism. Most philosophers can agree on who belongs in their respective canons. For pragmatism, this would include Peirce, James, Dewey, and Rorty; for existentialism, Kierkegaard, Nietzsche, Heidegger, and Sartre; and for liberalism, Locke, Kant, Mill, and Rawls. But despite this agreement, there is of course endless controversy over the core elements of these traditions. Black nationalism is no different.

17. For a compelling defense of the view that nationalism should not be understood as necessarily tied to claims of political sovereignty, see Rogers Brubaker, "Myths and Misconceptions in the Study of Nationalism," in *The State of the Nation: Ernest Gellner and the Theory of Nationalism,* ed. John A. Hall (Cambridge: Cambridge University Press, 1998), pp. 272–306; see also Yael Tamir, *Liberal Nationalism* (Princeton: Princeton University Press, 1993), chap. 3.

18. I should say, however, that Glaude chooses to speak of the pragmatic conception of the black "race" instead of the pragmatic conception of black "nationalism." See Eddie S. Glaude Jr., *Exodus! Religion, Race, and Nation in Early Nineteenth-Century Black America* (Chicago: University of Chicago Press, 2000); see also Paul C. Taylor, "Pragmatism and Race," in *Pragmatism and the Problem of Race,* ed. Bill E. Lawson and Donald F. Koch (Bloomington: Indiana University Press, 2004), pp. 162–176. For a comprehensive critical discussion of competing conceptions of "nation" and theories of nationalism, see Anthony D. Smith, *Nationalism and Modernism: A Critical Survey of Recent Theories of Nations and Nationalism* (London: Routledge, 1998).

19. Delany, *Condition,* pp. 14–15.

20. Ibid., pp. 41–43.

21. Martin R. Delany, "The Political Destiny of the Colored Race," in *The Ideological Origins of Black Nationalism,* ed. Sterling Stuckey (Boston: Beacon Press, 1972), pp. 196–197.

22. Ibid., pp. 197–198; original emphasis.

23. Paul Gilroy, *The Black Atlantic: Modernity and Double Consciousness* (Cambridge, Mass.: Harvard University Press, 1993), p. 26.

24. Robert S. Levine, *Martin Delany, Frederick Douglass, and the Politics of Representative Identity* (Chapel Hill: University of North Carolina Press, 1997), p. 14. Also see Tolagbe Ogunleye, "Dr. Martin Robison Delany, 19th-Century Africana Womanist: Reflections on His Avant-Garde Politics concerning Gender, Colorism, and Nation Building," *Journal of Black Studies* 28 (1998): 628–649.

25. For useful discussions of pre-emancipation conceptions of black masculinity, see Darlene Clark Hine and Earnestine Jenkins, eds., *A Question of Manhood: A Reader in U.S. Black Men's History and Masculinity*, vol. 1 (Bloomington: University of Indiana Press, 1999). Some have argued that patriarchal conceptions of gender identity are a (near) constitutive component of black nationalist discourses. See, for example, E. Francis White, *Dark Continent of Our Bodies: Black Feminism and the Politics of Respectability* (Philadelphia: Temple University Press, 2001), chap. 3; Hazel V, Carby, *Race Men* (Cambridge, Mass.: Harvard University Press, 1998); and Wahneema Lubiano, "Black Nationalism and Black Common Sense: Policing Ourselves and Others," in *The House That Race Built*, ed. Wahneema Lubiano (New York: Vintage, 1998), pp. 232–252.

26. Delany, *Condition*, pp. 10, 25–30, 170–171, 190–191.

27. Ibid., pp. 39–40.

28. Ibid., pp. 62, 182–183.

29. Ibid., pp. 45–46.

30. Martin R. Delany, *Blake; or, The Huts of America* (Boston: Beacon Press, 1970).

31. See Werner Sollors, *Beyond Ethnicity: Consent and Descent in American Culture* (New York: Oxford University Press, 1986), p. 51. For a rich and insightful discussion of Delany's place in the development of the American literary tradition, see Eric J. Sundquist, *To Wake the Nations: Race in the Making of American Literature* (Cambridge, Mass.: Harvard University Press, 1993), chap. 2. Also see Levine, *Martin Delany*, chap. 5; and Moses, *Golden Age*, chap. 7.

32. Delany, *Blake*, p. 252.

33. See Delany, "Political Destiny," p. 197. Compare Robert M. Kahn, "The Political Ideology of Martin Delany," *Journal of Black Studies* 14 (1984): 415–440.

34. Delany, "Political Destiny," p. 201.

35. We get a hint of this doctrine in *The Condition* as well, as when he approves of the Jewish people "maintaining their national characteristics, and looking forward in high hopes of seeing the day when they may return to their former national position of self-government and independence." Delany, *Condition*, p. 12.

36. Delany, "Political Destiny," p. 201.

37. Appiah, *In My Father's House*, p. 13. There has been much recent philosophical debate about whether we should think of races as real. In addition to Appiah's important work, see, for example, Naomi Zack, *Race and Mixed Race* (Philadelphia: Temple University Press, 1993); Lucius T. Outlaw (Jr.), *On Race and Philosophy* (New York: Routledge, 1996); Charles W. Mills, "'But What Are You *Really?*': The Metaphysics of Race," in Charles W. Mills, *Blackness Visible: Essays on Philosophy and Race* (Ithaca: Cornell University Press, 1998); Philip Kitcher, "Race, Ethnicity, Biology, Culture," in *Racism*, ed. Leonard Harris (Amherst, NY: Humanity Books, 1999), pp. 87–117; Sally Haslanger, "Gender and Race: (What) Are They? (What) Do We Want Them to Be?" *Noûs* 34 (2000): 31–55; Bernard R. Boxill, "Introduction," in *Race and Racism*, ed. Bernard R. Boxill (Oxford: Oxford University Press, 2001), pp. 1–42; Ronald R. Sundstrom, "Race as a Human Kind," *Philosophy and Social Criticism* 28 (2002): 91–115; Lawrence Blum, *"I'm Not a Racist, But . . .": The Moral Quandary of Race* (Ithaca: Cornell University Press, 2002), chaps. 5–9; Michael Hardimon, "The Ordinary Concept of Race," *Journal of Philosophy* 100 (2003): 437–455; and Joshua M. Glasgow, "On the New Biology of Race," *Journal of Philosophy* 100 (2003): 456–474. My sympathies are largely with the antirealists, but I do not rely on racial antirealism as a premise here. I only assume that racialism, as defined above, is false, which few philosophers or political theorists, I take it, would want to deny. This is not to rule out, then, the possibility of defensible nonessentialist ways of conceptualizing race.

38. Delany, "Political Destiny," p. 203.

39. Delany, *Condition*, pp. 62–66, 214.

40. Martin R. Delany, *Principia of Ethnology: The Origin of Races and Color, with an Archeological Compendium of Ethiopian and Egyptian Civilization* (Baltimore: Black Classic Press, 1991).

41. Ibid., pp. 14–15.

42. Ibid., pp. 18, 27.

43. Ibid., pp. 38, 42–59.

44. Ibid., pp. 62, 69–71, 86–89.

45. Delany, "Political Destiny," p. 203.

46. Delany, *Principia*, pp. 81–82.

47. M. R. Delany, "Official Report of the Niger Valley Exploring Party," in *Search for a Place: Black Separatism and Africa, 1860,* by M. R. Delany and Robert Campbell (Ann Arbor: University of Michigan Press, 1969).

48. Ibid., pp. 110–111. See also the appendix in Delany, *Condition,* pp. 210–213.

49. Delany, "Official Report," p. 112. The claim is also repeated in Delany, *Blake,* p. 262.

50. Delany, "Official Report," p. 121; original emphasis.

51. Delany, *Condition*, pp. 209–210.

52. Delany, *Principia*, pp. 15 (the "natural" origins of racial distinctions), 22–24 (independent thought and paternalism), 35 (source of quote, with original emphasis except for the last sentence, which has my emphasis).

53. Delany, *Condition,* p. 8.

54. Delany, *Principia,* pp. 60–61

55. Sterling Stuckey, *Slave Culture: Nationalist Theory and the Foundations of Black America* (New York: Oxford University Press, 1987), p. 229.

56. Delany, *Principia,* pp. 91–94.

57. Sterling, *Making of an Afro-American,* pp. 79–80; and Ullman, *Martin R. Delany,* p. 45.

58. See, for example, Levine, *Martin Delany,* pp. 6–7, 13.

59. Delany, *Condition,* pp. 91–92.

60. Ibid., p. 87.

61. "Placido" is the pen name of the famous Cuban poet Gabriel de la Concepcion Valdes (1809–1844), who was, according to Delany, a mulatto "gentleman, scholar, poet, and intended Chief Engineer of the Army of Liberty and Freedom in Cuba," and who was executed on the charge of high treason and inciting slave insurrections. Delany, *Condition*, p. 203. Also see Floyd J. Miller's note to text in *Blake*, 319. Delany also named one of his sons after the Cuban revolutionary and poet. See Sterling, *Making of an Afro-American*, p. 86.

62. Delany, *Blake*, p. 261.

63. Delany, *Condition*, pp. 12–21.

64. Delany, "Political Destiny," p. 199.

65. See Alexis de Tocqueville, *Democracy in America*, trans. George Lawrence, ed. J. P. Mayer (New York: HarperPerennial, 1988), p. 341; and Delany, "Political Destiny," pp. 198–199.

66. Nell Irvin Painter, "Martin Delany: Elitism and Black Nationalism," in *Black Leaders of the Nineteenth Century*, ed. Leon Litwack and August Meier (Urbana: University of Illinois Press, 1988), pp. 149–171.

67. Delany, *Condition*, pp. 187–188, 197–199, 200–201.

68. Ibid., pp. 147–159.

69. Delany, "Political Destiny," pp. 102–103. In the history of black political thought, there is a recurring debate over whether white racism will ultimately yield to persistent moral criticism, and it is one of the issues that has divided the more militant nationalists (such as Delany, Marcus Garvey, and Malcolm X) from those in the black protest tradition (including Frederick Douglass, W. E. B. Du Bois, and Martin Luther King Jr.). For an illuminating discussion of Delany's views on the ineffectiveness of moral suasion, see Boxill, "Two Traditions," pp. 120–121; also see his "Douglass against the Emigrationists," in *Frederick Douglass: A Critical Reader*, ed. Bill E. Lawson and Frank M. Kirkland (Malden, Mass.: Blackwell, 1999), pp. 21–49.

70. Delany, "Political Destiny," pp. 103–104.

71. Ibid., p. 94; and Delany, *Condition*, p. 205.

72. Delany, *Condition*, pp. 206–208.

73. Ibid., p. 191.

74. Ibid., pp. 48–49, 168, 171, 178; and Delany, *Blake*, p. 287.

75. Quoted in Sterling, *Making of an Afro-American*, pp. 149–150; original emphasis.

76. Delany, *Condition*, pp. 184, 186–187, 192.

77. Ibid., pp. 178–188.

78. Ibid., pp. 62, 173, 181, 179–181, 36–37, 182–183; and Delany, "Political Destiny," pp. 96–97.

79. Cyril E. Griffith, *The African Dream: Martin R. Delany and the Emergence of Pan-African Thought* (University Park: Pennsylvania State University Press, 1975), p. 21. Also see Stuckey, *Slave Culture*, pp. 226–231.

80. Delany, *Condition*, pp. 178n, 189; and Delany, *Blake*, pp. 257–258. For an interesting and provocative discussion of Delany's commitment to cultural syncretism, see Gilroy, *Black Atlantic*, pp. 27–29.

81. Delany, *Blake*, p. 182.

82. This vision is not unlike what David Hollinger has called "civic nationalism," which he usefully contrasts with "ethnic nationalism." See his *Postethnic America: Beyond Multiculturalism*, rev. ed. (New York: Basic Books, 2000), pp. 133–135. It is also compatible with the forms of nonracialist Pan-Africanism (from both the continent and the diaspora) that Appiah would find morally and politically acceptable. See *In My Father's House*, pp. 179–180.

83. Delany, *Condition*, pp. 160–162; Delany, *Blake*, pp. 260–262; and Delany, *Principia*, p. 81. Compare Gilroy, *Black Atlantic*, p. 23.

84. Delany, *Condition*, p. 172.

85. Delany, *Principia*, p. 83; Delany, "Official Report," pp. 108–110; and Delany, *Blake*, p. 262.

86. See, for example, Painter, "Martin Delany," p. 155; Kahn, "Political Ideology," pp. 434–436; and Boxill, "Douglass," pp. 26–29.

87. "Constitution of the African Civilization Society," in *Negro Social and Political Thought, 1850–1920*, ed. Howard Brotz (New York: Basic Books, 1966), pp. 191–196, quote from 194. Also see "Official Report," pp. 77–80, 110–111.

88. Delany, *Principia*, pp. 81–82.

89. Quoted in Painter, "Martin Delany," p. 168.

90. See W. E. B. Du Bois, *Black Reconstruction in America, 1860–1880* (Cleveland: Meridian Books, 1964); C. Vann Woodard, *The Strange Career of Jim Crow*, 3rd rev. ed. (New York: Oxford University Press, 1974); and Eric Foner, *Reconstruction: America's Unfinished Revolution, 1863–1877* (New York: Perennial Library, 1989).

91. For a discussion of the conservative and "elitist" dimensions of Delany's thought and political activism, see Painter, "Martin Delany."

92. Ullman, *Martin R. Delany*, pp. 336–340.

93. Quoted in ibid., p. 486.

94. Douglass argued that by claiming Africa as the national homeland of all blacks, American-born black nationalists were giving comfort and ideological support to white supremacists who would deny blacks U.S. citizenship on classical nationalist grounds. See Frederick Douglass, "African Colonization Society," in *Classical Black Nationalism*, ed. Wilson Jeremiah Moses (New York: New York University Press, 1996), pp. 135–141. Also see Draper, *Rediscovery of Black Nationalism*; Robinson, *Black Nationalism*; and Wilson Jeremiah Moses, *Black Messiahs and Uncle Toms: Social and Literary Manipulations of a Religious Myth*, rev. ed. (University Park: Pennsylvania State University, 1992).

95. Tocqueville, *Democracy in America*, p. 235.

96. See Gilroy, *The Black Atlantic*, pp. 19–29.

97. For a defense of this kind of post-structuralist progressive politics, see Ernesto Laclau and Chantal Mouffe, *Hegemony and Socialist Strategy: Towards a Radical Democratic Politics*, 2nd ed. (London: Verso, 2001); and Gayatri Spivak, *In Other Worlds: Essays in Cultural Politics* (New York: Routledge, 1989), pp. 205–211. For a trenchant and thorough critique of the theoretical underpinnings of strategic essentialism, see Norman Geras, *Discourses of Extremity: Radical Ethics and Post-Marxist Extravagances* (London: Verso, 1990). And for a discussion of the limitations of strategic essentialism with respect to politicized social identities, see Linda Martín Alcoff, "Who's Afraid of Identity Politics," in *Reclaiming Identity: Realist Theory and the Predicament of Postmodernism*, ed. Paula M. L. Moya and Michael R. Hames-García (Berkeley: University of California Press, 2000), pp. 322–325.

2. Class, Poverty, and Shame

1. W. E. B. Du Bois, *The Souls of Black Folk,* ed. David W. Blight and Robert Gooding-Williams (Boston: Bedford Books, 1997).

2. For a particularly insightful discussion of Du Bois's double-consciousness trope, see Shamoon Zamir, *Dark Voices: W. E. B. Du Bois and American Thought, 1888–1903* (Chicago: University of Chicago Press, 1995), chap. 4. Also see Frank M. Kirkland, "Modernity and Intellectual Life in Black," *Philosophical Forum* 24 (1992–1993): 136–165; and Dickson D. Bruce Jr., "W. E. B. Du Bois and the Idea of Double Consciousness," *American Literature* 64 (1992): 299–309. For contemporary reflections on the "dilemma" of double consciousness, see Gerald Early, ed., *Lure and Loathing: Essays on Race, Identity, and the Ambivalence of Assimilation* (New York: Penguin, 1993). For a philosophical discussion and critique of the familiar view that blacks suffer from alienation, see Howard McGary, *Race and Social Justice* (Malden, Mass.: Blackwell, 1999), chap. 1.

3. Du Bois, *Souls of Black Folk,* chap. 6.

4. Ibid., 41.

5. See, for example, Manning Marable, *W. E. B. Du Bois: Black Radical Democrat* (Boston: Twayne, 1986), pp. 31–40; Sterling Stuckey, *Slave Culture: Nationalist Theory and the Foundations of Black America* (New York: Oxford University Press, 1987), chap. 5; and Bernard R. Boxill, "Du Bois on Cultural Pluralism," in *W. E. B. Du Bois on Race and Culture,* ed. Bernard W. Bell, Emily R. Grosholz, and James B. Stewart (New York: Routledge, 1996), pp. 57–85.

6. W. E. B. Du Bois, "The Conservation of Races," in *Negro Social and Political Thought, 1850–1920: Representative Texts,* ed. Howard Brotz (New York: Basic Books, 1966), pp. 487–488; emphasis added.

7. Du Bois, *Souls of Black Folk,* p. 39.

8. W. E. B. Du Bois, "The Talented Tenth: Memorial Address," in Henry Louis Gates Jr. and Cornel West, *The Future of the Race* (New York: Vintage, 1997), p. 165, emphasis added (hereafter cited as "Memorial Address"). Previously published in *Boulé Journal* 15 (October 1948): 3–13.

9. Du Bois, "Memorial Address," p. 163.

10. W. E. B. Du Bois, *Darkwater: Voices from within the Veil* (Mineola, N.Y.: Dover, 1999), chap. 6.

11. For a helpful discussion of the shifts in Du Bois's views on economic justice, see Arnold Rampersad, *The Art and Imagination of W. E. B. Du Bois* (New York: Schocken, 1976), pp. 158–169. Also see Adolph L. Reed Jr., *W. E. B. Du Bois and American Political Thought: Fabianism and the Color Line* (Oxford: Oxford University Press, 1997), pp. 83–89.

12. For an important discussion of the prophetic tradition in black political thought, see Cornel West, *Prophesy Deliverance! An Afro-American Revolutionary Christianity* (Philadelphia: Westminster Press, 1982). See also Wilson Jeremiah Moses, *Black Messiahs and Uncle Toms: Social and Literary Manipulations of a Religious Myth,* rev. ed. (University Park: Pennsylvania State University Press, 1992).

13. See, for example, John C. Turner, *Rediscovering the Social Group: A Self-Categorization Theory* (Oxford: Basil Blackwell, 1987); Michael A. Hogg and Dominic Abrams, *Social Identifications: A Social Psychology of Intergroup Relations and Group Processes* (London: Routledge, 1988); Michael A. Hogg, *The Social Psychology of Group Cohesiveness: From Attraction to Social Identity* (New York: New York University Press, 1992); Tom R. Tyler, Roderick M. Kramer, and Oliver P. John, eds., *The Psychology of the Social Self* (Mahwah, N.J.: Erlbaum, 1999); and Thierry Davos and Mahzarin R. Banaji, "Implicit Self and Identity," in *Handbook of Self and Identity,* ed. Mark R. Leary and June Price Tangney (New York: Guilford Press, 2002), pp. 153–175.

14. J. L. A. Garcia, "The Heart of Racism," *Journal of Social Philosophy* 27 (1996): 14.

15. Booker T. Washington, "Democracy and Education," in Brotz, *Negro Social and Political Thought,* pp. 362–371.

16. Booker T. Washington, "The Educational Outlook in the South," in Brotz, *Negro Social and Political Thought,* p. 353.

17. Booker T. Washington, "Atlanta Exposition Address," in Brotz, *Negro Social and Political Thought,* p. 358.

18. Marcus Garvey, *The Philosophy and Opinions of Marcus Garvey: Or, Africa for the Africans,* ed. Amy Jacques Garvey (Dover, Mass.: Majority Press, 1986).

19. For an analysis comparing Washington's "racial uplift" philosophy to Du Bois's, see Reed, *W. E. B. Du Bois,* pp. 59–63. See also August Meier, *Negro Thought in America, 1880–1915: Racial Ideologies in the Age of Booker T. Washington* (Ann Arbor: University of Michigan Press, 1988). For a comparative take on Du Bois and Garvey, see Moses, *Black Messiahs and Uncle Toms,* chap. 8. For a comprehensive discussion of the personal and political conflicts between Du Bois and Washington, see David Levering Lewis, *W. E. B. Du Bois: Biography of a Race, 1868–1919* (New York: Henry Holt, 1993), chap. 12; and for an account of the conflict between Du Bois and Garvey, see David Levering Lewis, *W. E. B. Du Bois: The Fight for Equality and the American Century, 1919–1963* (New York: Henry Holt, 2000), chap. 2. For helpful analyses of the class and gender dimensions of uplift ideology, see Evelyn Brooks Higginbotham, *Righteous Discontent: The Women's Movement in the Black Baptist Church, 1880–1920* (Cambridge, Mass.: Harvard University Press, 1993); and Kevin K. Gaines, *Uplifting the Race: Black Leadership, Politics, and Culture in the Twentieth Century* (Chapel Hill: University of North Carolina Press, 1996).

20. Du Bois, "Conservation of Races," pp. 489–492; Du Bois, *Souls of Black Folk,* pp. 39, 69–70; and Du Bois, "Memorial Address," pp. 163–166.

21. Du Bois, *Souls of Black Folk,* pp. 71–72.

22. W. E. B. Du Bois, "The Parting of the Ways," in *W. E. B. Du Bois: A Reader,* ed. David Levering Lewis (New York: Henry Holt, 1995), p. 331. Previously published in *World Today* 6 (April 1904): 521–523.

23. W. E. B. Du Bois, "The Talented Tenth," in Gates and West, *Future of the Race,* pp. 133–157 (hereafter cited as "Talented Tenth"). Previously published in *The Negro Problem: A Series of Articles by Representative American Negroes of Today* (New York: James Pott and Co., 1903), pp. 33–75.

24. Du Bois, *Souls of Black Folk,* chap. 3.

25. Du Bois, "Talented Tenth," p. 145–146.

26. Du Bois, "Memorial Address," pp. 165–166. See also Du Bois, "Conservation of Races," 489–492.

27. W. E. B. Du Bois, "The Present Leadership of American Negroes," in Lewis, *W. E. B. Du Bois: A Reader*, p. 356. Previously published in the *National Guardian* (May 20, 1957).

28. W. E. B. Du Bois, "Criteria of Negro Art," *The Crisis* (October 1926). Reprinted in *The Seventh Son: The Thought and Writings of W. E. B. Du Bois*, vol. 2, ed. Julius Lester (New York: Vintage, 1971), pp. 312–321.

29. Du Bois, "Talented Tenth," p. 145; and W. E. B. Du Bois, *Dusk of Dawn: An Essay toward an Autobiography of a Race Concept* (New Brunswick, N.J.: Transaction, 1984), 211–220.

30. Du Bois, *Souls of Black Folk*, p. 94. See also Du Bois, "Talented Tenth," pp. 133, 145–146.

31. Du Bois, *Souls of Black Folk*, p. 95.

32. Du Bois, "Talented Tenth," pp. 149–150.

33. Ibid., pp. 133, 157. Actually, to be precise, the last line of the essay reads: "The Negro race, like all *other* races, is going to be saved by its exceptional men" (emphasis added).

34. Ibid., pp. 133–135; Du Bois, "Memorial Address," pp. 173–174.

35. Du Bois, "Memorial Address," pp. 161–163, 173.

36. Du Bois, *Souls of Black Folk*, p. 70. See also Du Bois, "Present Leadership," pp. 354–357.

37. Du Bois, *Souls of Black Folk*, p. 70.

38. Du Bois, *Dusk of Dawn*, p. 209.

39. W. E. B. Du Bois, "The Class Struggle," *The Crisis* (June 1921). Reprinted in Lewis, *W. E. B. Du Bois: A Reader*, pp. 555–556.

40. W. E. B. Du Bois, "The Negro and Communism," *The Crisis* (September 1931). Reprinted in Lewis, *W. E. B. Du Bois: A Reader*, pp. 583–593.

41. W. E. B. Du Bois, "Marxism and the Negro Problem," *The Crisis* (May 1933). Reprinted in Lewis, *W. E. B. Du Bois: A Reader*, pp. 538–544.

42. Du Bois, *Souls of Black Folk*, p. 66.

43. W. E. B. Du Bois, "On Being Ashamed of Oneself: An Essay on Race Pride," in Lewis, *W. E. B. Du Bois: A Reader*, pp. 76–80. Previously published in *The Crisis* (September 1933).

44. Du Bois, *Souls of Black Folk*, pp. 146–147. I owe this observation about Du Bois to Robert Gooding-Williams.

45. Du Bois, "On Being Ashamed," p. 80.

46. William Julius Wilson, *The Declining Significance of Race* (Chicago: University of Chicago Press, 1978).

47. See, for example, Joy James, *Transcending the Talented Tenth: Black Leaders and American Intellectuals* (New York: Routledge, 1997), pp. 18–27; Hazel V. Carby, *Race Men* (Cambridge, Mass.: Harvard University Press, 1998), pp. 30–41; Reed, *W. E. B. Du Bois*, chap. 5; Cornel West, "Black Strivings in a Twilight Civilization," in Gates and West, *Future of the Race*, pp. 58–71; and Robert Gooding-Williams, *Contributions to the Critique of White Supremacy: Du Bois, Douglass, and Political Philosophy* (Cambridge, Mass.: Harvard University Press, forthcoming). For more sympathetic treatments of Du Bois's conception of leadership, see Howard McGary, *Race and Social Justice* (Malden, Mass.: Blackwell, 1999), chap. 11; and Boxill, "Du Bois on Cultural Pluralism."

48. Du Bois, *Souls of Black Folk*, pp. 64–65.

49. See Du Bois, *Darkwater*, chap. 6. For more on Du Bois's commitment to democratic ideals, see Marable, *W. E. B. Du Bois*.

50. Du Bois, "Memorial Address," p. 174. Compare Henry Louis Gates Jr., "W. E. B. Du Bois and 'The Talented Tenth,'" in Gates and West, *Future of the Race*, pp. 128–132.

51. Du Bois, *Dusk of Dawn*, p. 213.

52. Du Bois, *Souls of Black Folk*, pp. 99–101.

53. Du Bois acknowledges that there will be such exceptions, as when he praises the leadership of Frederick Douglass, the famous self-taught ex-slave whom Du Bois recognizes as "the greatest of American Negro leaders." See Du Bois, *Souls of Black Folk*, p. 66. See also Du Bois, "Talented Tenth," p. 138.

54. Du Bois, *Souls of Black Folk*, p. 101.

55. See Boxill, "Du Bois on Cultural Pluralism," pp. 76–82.

56. I believe the term *Black Marxist* comes from Cedric J. Robinson. For his discussion of Du Bois's engagement with Marxist social theory, see Robinson, *Black Marxism: The Making of the Black Radical Tradition* (Chapel Hill: University of North Carolina Press, 2000), pp. 185–240. I accept Robinson's contention that Du Bois brought together many of the best elements from Marxism and black nationalism—though I would add liberalism as well—to create a new synthesis, a distinctive brand of black radicalism. But I reject his view that Du Bois came, in due course, to reject elite vanguardism in favor of the "spontaneous" radicalism of the masses. In this way I side with those, such as West, Reed, and Gooding-Williams, who contend that Du Bois remained committed to the view that the black intellectual elite should lead the black liberation movement.

57. Du Bois, "Memorial Address," p. 166–169.

58. Du Bois, "Present Leadership," pp. 354–357.

59. Du Bois, "Memorial Address," p. 167.

60. Du Bois chronicles the history of black achievement in several works, including his books *The Negro* (Philadelphia: University of Pennsylvania Press, 2001) and *The World and Africa: An Inquiry into the Part Which Africa Has Played in World History* (New York: International Publishers, 1996).

61. For insightful discussions of the meaning of racial pride, see Bernard R. Boxill, *Blacks and Social Justice,* rev. ed. (Lanham, Md.: Rowman and Littlefield, 1992), pp. 176–179; and Yalonda Howze and David Weberman, "On Racial Kinship," *Social Theory and Practice* 27 (2001): 419–436.

62. For an insightful discussion and critique of this brand of "bourgeois black nationalism," see Robert L. Allen, *Black Awakening in Capitalist America* (Trenton, N.J.: Africa World Press, 1990), pp. 128–192.

3. Black Power Nationalism

1. Michael C. Dawson, *Black Visions: The Roots of Contemporary African-American Ideologies* (Chicago: University of Chicago Press, 2001), chap. 3.

2. Jennifer L. Hochschild, *Facing Up to the American Dream: Race,*

Class, and the Soul of the Nation (Princeton: Princeton University Press, 1995); see also Dawson, *Black Visions,* pp. 273–280.

3. Robert A. Brown and Todd C. Shaw, "Separate Nations: Two Attitudinal Dimensions of Black Nationalism," *Journal of Politics* 64 (February 2002): 22–44.

4. See, for example, Dawson, *Black Visions,* pp. 100–102; and Brown and Shaw, "Separate Nations."

5. See, for example, Adolph Reed Jr., ed., *Without Justice for All: The New Liberalism and Our Retreat from Racial Equality* (Boulder, Co.: Westview Press, 1999); Marcellus Andrews, *The Political Economy of Hope and Fear: Capitalism and the Black Condition in America* (New York: New York University Press, 1999); Martin Gilens, *Why Americans Hate Welfare: Race, Media, and the Politics of Antipoverty Policy* (Chicago: University of Chicago Press, 1999); Tali Mendelberg, *The Race Card: Campaign Strategy, Implicit Messages, and the Norm of Equality* (Princeton: Princeton University Press, 2001); Earl Black and Merle Black, *The Rise of Southern Republicans* (Cambridge, Mass.: Harvard University Press, 2002); and Ronald W. Walters, *White Nationalism, Black Interests: Conservative Public Policy and the Black Community* (Detroit: Wayne State University Press, 2003).

6. For empirical support for this opinion widely held among blacks, see Jim Sidanius, Felicia Pratto, and Lawrence Bobo, "Racism, Conservatism, Affirmative Action, and Intellectual Sophistication: A Matter of Principled Conservatism or Group Dominance?" *Journal of Personality and Social Psychology* 70 (1996): 476–490. For a contrary view, see Paul M. Sniderman and Edward G. Carmines, *Reaching Beyond Race* (Cambridge, Mass.: Harvard University Press, 1997).

7. See Errol A. Henderson, "Black Nationalism and Rap Music," *Journal of Black Studies* 26 (1996): 308–339.

8. Chuck D with Jusuf Jah, *Fight the Power: Rap, Race, and Reality* (New York: Delta, 1997); KRS-One, *Ruminations* (New York: Welcome Rain, 2003).

9. For more on the impact of Malcolm X's ideas on the post–civil rights generation and on black youth culture, with its resulting iconography, see the essays in *Malcolm X: In Our Own Image,* ed. Joe Wood

(New York: St. Martin's Press, 1992); see also Michael Eric Dyson, *Making Malcolm: The Myth and Meaning of Malcolm X* (New York: Oxford University Press, 1995).

10. Elijah Muhammad, *Message to the Blackman in America* (Atlanta: Messenger Elijah Muhammad Propagation Society, 1997); Malcolm X, "A Declaration of Independence," in *Malcolm X Speaks: Selected Speeches and Statements,* ed. George Breitman (New York: Grove Widenfeld, 1965), pp. 18–22; and Malcolm X, "The Ballot or the Bullet," in Breitman, *Malcolm X Speaks,* pp. 38–43.

11. See these three speeches by Malcolm X in Breitman, *Malcolm X Speaks*: "Message to the Grassroots," pp. 4–6; "The Ballot or the Bullet," pp. 23–44; and "The Black Revolution," pp. 45–57.

12. Malcolm X, "Message to the Grassroots," pp. 9–17; and Malcolm X, "The Old Negro and the New Negro," in *The End of White World Supremacy: Four Speeches by Malcolm X,* ed. Imam Benjamin Karim (New York: Arcade, 1971), pp. 81–120.

13. Malcolm X, "The Ballot or the Bullet," pp. 26–31.

14. Malcolm X, "Message to the Grassroots," p. 6.

15. Malcolm X, "A Declaration of Independence," p. 21.

16. Manning Marable, *Race, Reform, and Rebellion: The Second Reconstruction in Black America, 1945–1990,* 2nd ed. (Jackson: University Press of Mississippi, 1991), p. 92.

17. For discussions of the historical context within which the Black Power movement emerged, see Clayborne Carson, *In Struggle: SNCC and the Black Awakening of the 1960s* (Cambridge, Mass.: Harvard University Press, 1981); and Charles M. Payne, *I've Got the Light of Freedom: The Organizing Tradition and the Mississippi Freedom Struggle* (Berkeley: University of California Press, 1995). For riveting firsthand accounts by two major spokespersons from that transitional period, see Stokely Carmichael with Ekwueme Michael Thelwell, *Ready for Revolution: The Life and Struggles of Stokely Carmichael (Kwame Ture)* (New York: Scribner, 2003), pp. 501–551; and Martin Luther King Jr., *Where Do We Go from Here: Chaos or Community?* (Boston: Beacon Press, 1967), chap. 2.

18. Kwame Ture [Stokely Carmichael] and Charles V. Hamilton,

Black Power: The Politics of Liberation (New York: Vintage, 1992), p. 3. For a review of black and white attitudes toward the phrase *Black Power* in the early days of the Black Power movement, see John D. Aberbach and Jack L. Walker, "The Meanings of Black Power: A Comparison of White and Black Interpretations of a Political Slogan," *American Political Science Review* 64 (June 1970): 367–388.

19. Ture and Hamilton, *Black Power,* p. 3.

20. Ibid., pp. 4–10.

21. Ibid., p. 44.

22. Ibid., pp. 83–84.

23. See David M. Cutler, Edward L. Glaeser, and Jacob L. Vigdor, "The Rise and Decline of the American Ghetto," *Journal of Political Economy* 107 (1999): 455–506; and Mary J. Fischer, "The Relative Importance of Income and Race in Determining Residential Outcomes in U.S. Urban Areas, 1970–2000," *Urban Affairs Review* 38 (2003): 669–696.

24. See William Julius Wilson, *The Truly Disadvantaged: The Inner City, the Underclass, and Public Policy* (Chicago: University of Chicago Press, 1987); *When Work Disappears: The World of the New Urban Poor* (New York: Knopf, 1999); and Douglass S. Massey and Nancy A. Denton, *American Apartheid: Segregation and the Making of the Underclass* (Cambridge, Mass.: Harvard University Press, 1993).

25. See Mary Pattillo-McCoy, *Black Picket Fences: Privilege and Peril among the Black Middle Class* (Chicago: University of Chicago Press, 1999).

26. See, for example, Glenn C. Loury, "The Moral Quandary of the Black Community," in *One by One from the Inside Out: Essays and Reviews on Race and Responsibility in America* (New York: Free Press, 1995), pp. 33–49; and Eugene F. Rivers III, "Beyond the Nationalism of Fools: Toward an Agenda for Black Intellectuals," *Boston Review* 20 (Summer 1995): 16–18.

27. For a helpful philosophical discussion of this contentious issue, see Bill E. Lawson, "Uplifting the Race: Middle-Class Blacks and the Truly Disadvantaged," in *The Underclass Question,* ed. Bill E. Lawson (Philadelphia: Temple University Press, 1992), pp. 90–113.

28. The exceptions to this general rule are those cases where the situation of a group is so dire that desperate action seems the only alternative, or where these self-sacrificing individuals are under the spell of religious zealotry. The first is not the situation of the black elite or middle class; the second, I take it, would, even if possible, be undesirable.

29. See Pattillo-McCoy, *Black Picket Fences;* and Massey and Denton, *American Apartheid.*

30. Although it must be said that without residential proximity, the ability of black citizens to elect leaders who are responsive to their local interests will be seriously hampered, especially if there is only weak public or judicial support for the types of redistricting that would create single-member, majority-black voting districts. See Lani Guinier, *The Tyranny of the Majority: Fundamental Fairness in Representative Democracy* (New York: Free Press, 1994), chaps. 3, 5.

31. See Katherine Tate, *From Protest to Politics: The New Black Voters in American Elections,* enlarged ed. (Cambridge, Mass.: Harvard University Press and Russell Sage Foundation, 1994), chap. 4; and Cathy J. Cohen and Michael C. Dawson, "Neighborhood Poverty and African American Politics," *American Political Science Review* 87 (1993): 286–302.

32. Adolph L. Reed Jr., *The Jesse Jackson Phenomenon: The Crisis of Purpose in Afro-American Politics* (New Haven: Yale University Press, 1986), p. 9. Also see Robert L. Allen, *Black Awakening in Capitalist America* (Trenton, N.J.: Africa World Press, 1990), pp. 17–20; and Guinier, *Tyranny of the Majority,* chap. 3.

33. Ture and Hamilton, *Black Power,* p. 14.

34. See Tate, *From Protest to Politics,* chap. 2; and Ellis Cose, *The Rage of a Privileged Class* (New York: HarperPerennial, 1995).

35. Adolph Reed Jr., *Stirrings in the Jug: Black Politics in the Post-Segregation Era* (Minneapolis: University of Minnesota Press, 1999), chap. 4; and Adolph Reed Jr., *Class Notes: Posing as Politics and Other Thoughts on the American Scene* (New York: New Press, 2000), pp. 10–13. Also see Leonard Harris, "Community: What Type of Entity and What Type of Moral Commitment?" in *The Quest for Community and*

Identity: Critical Essays in Africana Social Philosophy, ed. Robert E. Birt (Lanham, Md.: Rowman and Littlefield, 2002), pp. 243–255.

36. Lerone Bennett Jr., *The Challenge of Blackness* (Chicago: Johnson, 1972), p. 45.

37. Harold Cruse, *Plural but Equal: A Critical Study of Blacks and Minorities and America's Plural Society* (New York: William Morrow, 1987), pp. 371–391. Also see the National Black Political Convention (1972), "The Gary Declaration," in *Modern Black Nationalism: From Marcus Garvey to Louis Farrakhan,* ed. William L. Van Deburg (New York: New York University Press, 1997), pp. 138–143.

38. Wilson Jeremiah Moses, *The Golden Age of Black Nationalism, 1850–1925* (Oxford: Oxford University Press, 1978), p. 11.

39. Cathy J. Cohen, *The Boundaries of Blackness: AIDS and the Breakdown of Black Politics* (Chicago: University of Chicago Press, 1999), p. 13; emphasis in the original.

40. See, for example, bell hooks, *Ain't I a Woman: Black Women and Feminism* (Boston: South End Press, 1981); Patricia Hill Collins, *Black Feminist Thought: Knowledge, Consciousness, and the Politics of Empowerment* (New York: Routledge, 1990); Kimberlé W. Crenshaw, "Mapping the Margins: Intersectionality, Identity Politics, and Violence against Women of Color," in *Critical Race Theory,* ed. Kimberlé Crenshaw, Neil Gotanda, Gary Peller, and Kendall Thomas (New York: New Press, 1995); Hazel V. Carby, *Race Men* (Cambridge, Mass.: Harvard University Press, 1998); Joy James, *Transcending the Talented Tenth: Black Leaders and American Intellectuals* (New York: Routledge, 1997); and E. Frances White, *Dark Continent of Our Bodies: Black Feminism and the Politics of Respectability* (Philadelphia: Temple University Press, 2001).

41. See Reed, *Jesse Jackson Phenomenon,* chap. 4. For a contrary view, see Cornel West, *Prophesy Deliverance! An Afro-American Revolutionary Christianity* (Philadelphia: Westminster Press, 1982), chap. 4.

42. Evelyn Brooks Higginbotham, *Righteous Discontent: The Women's Movement in the Black Baptist Church, 1880–1920* (Cambridge, Mass.: Harvard University Press, 1993).

43. Cohen, *Boundaries of Blackness*. Also see Cornel West, *Race Matters* (New York: Vintage, 1994), pp. 119–131.

44. See Naomi Zack, *Race and Mixed Race* (Philadelphia: Temple University Press, 1993); Lisa Jones, "Is Biracial Enough? Or, What's This about a Multiracial Category on the Census? A Conversation," in *Bulletproof Diva: Tales of Race, Sex, and Hair* (New York: Anchor, 1994); Naomi Zack, ed., *American Mixed Race: The Culture of Microdiversity* (Lanham, Md.: Rowman and Littlefield, 1995); Ronald R. Sundstrom, "Being and Being Mixed-Race," *Social Theory and Practice* 27 (2001): 285–307; Werner Sollors, ed., *Interracialism: Black–White Intermarriage in American History, Literature, and Law* (Oxford: Oxford University Press, 2000); and Randall Kennedy, *Interracial Intimacies: Sex, Marriage, Identity, and Adoption* (New York: Pantheon, 2003).

45. Melvin L. Oliver and Thomas M. Shapiro, *Black Wealth/White Wealth: A New Perspective on Racial Inequality* (New York: Routledge, 1995), p. 85.

46. Dawson, *Black Visions*.

47. William Julius Wilson, *The Declining Significance of Race: Blacks and Changing American Institutions*, 2nd ed. (Chicago: University of Chicago Press, 1980).

48. West, *Prophesy Deliverance*, chap. 4.

49. See bell hooks, *Feminist Theory: From Margin to Center* (Cambridge, Mass.: South End Press, 1984).

50. The term *microdiversity*, according to Naomi Zack, "points to the reality that many individuals are racially diverse within themselves and not merely diverse as members of groups that are believed, in often erroneous ways, to be racially different from other groups." See her "Mixed Black and White Race and Public Policy," *Hypatia* 10 (1995): 120–132, p. 130.

51. Anthony W. Marx, *Making Race and Nation: A Comparison of the United States, South Africa, and Brazil* (Cambridge: Cambridge University Press, 1998); and Carol M. Swain, *The New White Nationalism in America: Its Challenge to Integration* (Cambridge: Cambridge University Press, 2002).

52. Lani Guinier and Gerald Torres, *The Miner's Canary: Enlisting Race, Resisting Power, Transforming Democracy* (Cambridge, Mass.: Harvard University Press, 2002), chap. 4. This is not, of course, to deny the obvious fact that there is often fierce competition over scarce resources and valued positions between different racial groups, even among racial minorities. For more on this point, see Cruse, *Plural but Equal;* and Richard Delgado, "Linking Arms: Recent Books on Interracial Coalition as an Avenue of Social Reform," *Cornell Law Review* 88 (March 2003): 855–884.

53. Bayard Rustin and Martin Luther King Jr. powerfully developed these criticisms and others in the early days of the Black Power movement. See Bayard Rustin, "From Protest to Politics: The Future of the Civil Rights Movement" and "The Failure of Black Separatism," both in *Time on Two Crosses: The Collected Writings of Bayard Rustin,* ed. Devon W. Carbado and Donald Weise (San Francisco: Cleis Press, 2003), pp. 116–129, 217–236; and King, *Where Do We Go from Here,* chap. 2.

54. William Julius Wilson, *The Bridge over the Racial Divide: Rising Inequality and Coalition Politics* (Berkeley: University of California Press, 1999).

55. See Guinier and Torres, *Miner's Canary.*

56. Following Rawls, I treat "reasonableness" here as a kind of moral sensibility, a sense of reciprocity or fairness. He says, "Persons are reasonable in one basic aspect when, among equals say, they are ready to propose principles and standards as fair terms of cooperation and to abide by them willingly, given the assurance that others will likewise do so. Those norms they view as reasonable for everyone to accept and therefore as justifiable to them; and they are ready to discuss the fair terms that others propose." See John Rawls, *Political Liberalism* (New York: Columbia University Press, 1996), p. 49.

57. See Glenn C. Loury, *The Anatomy of Racial Inequality* (Cambridge, Mass.: Harvard University Press, 2002); Adrian M. S. Piper, "Two Kinds of Discrimination," in *Race and Racism,* ed. Bernard R. Boxill (Oxford: Oxford University Press, 2001), pp. 193–237; and Kimberlé W. Crenshaw, "Race, Reform, and Retrenchment: Transfor-

mation and Legitimation in Antidiscrimination Law," in Crenshaw et al., *Critical Race Theory,* pp. 103–122.

58. See Swain, *New White Nationalism.* For my earlier discussion of Du Bois's critique of Washington's views, see Chapter 2.

59. For more on this point, see Bernard R. Boxill, *Blacks and Social Justice,* rev. ed. (Lanham, Md.: Rowman and Littlefield, 1992), chaps. 9, 11.

60. For more on this point, see Michael Walzer, "The Obligations of Oppressed Minorities," in *Obligations: Essays on Disobedience, War, and Citizenship* (Cambridge, Mass.: Harvard University Press, 1970), pp. 46–70.

4. Black Solidarity after Black Power

1. See Raphael J. Sonenshein, *Politics in Black and White: Race and Power in Los Angeles* (Princeton: Princeton University Press, 1993); and Manning Marable, *Beyond Black and White: Transforming African-American Politics* (London: Verso, 1995).

2. Compare Marcellus Andrews, *The Political Economy of Hope and Fear: Capitalism and the Black Condition in America* (New York: New York University Press, 1999).

3. For a defense of this conception of racism, see my "Ideology, Racism, and Critical Social Theory," *Philosophical Forum* 34 (Summer 2003): 153–188; and my "Is Racism in the 'Heart'?" *Journal of Social Philosophy* 33 (Fall 2002): 411–420. Also see Robert Miles, *Racism* (London: Routledge, 1989); Barbara J. Fields, "Slavery, Race and Ideology in the United States of America," *New Left Review* 181 (1990): 95–118; Colette Guillaumin, *Racism, Sexism, Power, and Ideology* (London: Routledge, 1995); and George M. Fredrickson, *Racism: A Short History* (Princeton: Princeton University Press, 2002).

4. See Edna Bonacich, "Advanced Capitalism and Black/White Race Relations in the United States: A Split Labor Market Interpretation," *American Sociological Review* 41 (1976): 34–51. Also see David R. Roediger, *The Wages of Whiteness: Race and the Making of the American Working Class* (London: Verso, 1991).

5. For empirical evidence for this claim, see Lawrence Bobo, James

R. Klugel, and Ryan A. Smith, "Laissez-Faire Racism: The Crystalliza-tion of a Kinder, Gentler, Antiblack Ideology," in *Racial Attitudes in the 1990s,* ed. Steven A. Tuch and Jack K. Martin (Westport, Conn.: Praeger, 1997), pp. 15–41; Martin Gilens, *Why Americans Hate Welfare: Race, Media, and the Politics of Antipoverty Policy* (Chicago: Univer-sity of Chicago Press, 1999); Thomas C. Holt, *The Problem of Race in the Twenty-first Century* (Cambridge, Mass.: Harvard University Press, 2000); and Tali Mendelberg, *The Race Card: Campaign Strategy, Im-plicit Messages, and the Norm of Equality* (Princeton: Princeton Univer-sity Press, 2001).

6. Dalton Conley, *Being Black, Living in the Red: Race, Wealth, and Social Policy in America* (Berkeley: University of California Press, 1999); Jim Sidanius and Felicia Pratto, *Social Dominance: An Inter-group Theory of Social Hierarchy and Oppression* (Cambridge: Cam-bridge University Press, 1999), pp. 178–191; and Melvin L. Oliver and Thomas M. Shapiro, *Black Wealth/White Wealth: A New Perspective on Racial Inequality* (New York: Routledge, 1995).

7. Oliver and Shapiro, *Black Wealth/White Wealth,* p. 44.

8. For a helpful philosophical discussion of how to conceptualize "institutional racism," see Lawrence Blum, *"I'm Not a Racist, But . . .": The Moral Quandary of Race* (Ithaca: Cornell University Press, 2002), chap. 1. See also my "Race and Social Justice: Rawlsian Consider-ations," *Fordham Law Review* 72 (2004): 1697–1714.

9. William Julius Wilson, *When Work Disappears: The World of the New Urban Poor* (New York: Vintage, 1996), chap. 3.

10. See Michele M. Moody-Adams, "Race, Class, and the Social Construction of Self-Respect," in *African-American Perspectives and Philosophical Traditions,* ed. John P. Pittman (New York: Routledge, 1997), pp. 251–266.

11. See, for example, Marable, *Beyond Black and White,* chaps. 16–18.

12. William Julius Wilson, *The Bridge over the Racial Divide: Ris-ing Inequality and Coalition Politics* (Berkeley: University of California Press, 1999), chap. 5.

13. Charles Taylor, "The Politics of Recognition," in *Multicultural-*

ism: Examining the Politics of Recognition, ed. Amy Gutmann (Princeton: Princeton University Press, 1994), pp. 25–73. For a helpful discussion of what is and what is not "identity politics," see Iris Marion Young, *Inclusion and Democracy* (Oxford: Oxford University Press, 2000), pp. 102–107; also see Nancy Fraser, *Justice Interruptus: Critical Reflections on the "Postsocialist" Condition* (New York: Routledge, 1997), chap. 1; and Linda Martín Alcoff, "Who's Afraid of Identity Politics," in *Reclaiming Identity: Realist Theory and the Predicament of Postmodernism,* ed. Paula M. L. Moya and Michael R. Hames-García (Berkeley: University of California Press, 2000), pp. 312–344.

14. Adolph Reed Jr., *Stirrings in the Jug: Black Politics in the Post-Segregation Era* (Minneapolis: University of Minnesota Press, 1999), p. 50.

15. For helpful discussions of the problem of environmental racism, see Laura Westra and Bill E. Lawson, eds., *Faces of Environmental Racism: Confronting Issues of Global Justice,* 2nd ed. (Lanham, Md.: Rowman and Littlefield, 2001).

16. There is, however, a weak sense in which the political activity of any group of blacks can be thought of as black politics. Some social scientists, for example, regard black politics as simply the political behavior of black people, whatever its content or aims. On this approach, the "blackness" of politics is defined, not by the political ideology, beliefs, values, or goals of the people concerned, but by their racial identity. For the purposes of social science, there may be nothing wrong with this usage. But our interest is in discovering a defensible normative basis for black political solidarity. Since the black population is quite diverse in its political views, it will always be pertinent to ask what, if anything, makes the political activity of a group of blacks *black.* Or, put another way: what basic principles or objectives bind (or should bind) blacks qua blacks in political unity? The sheer number or concentration of blacks who engage in some political action or take a stance on some public issue cannot answer this question.

17. See Fields, "Slavery, Race and Ideology," p. 98. Also see Barbara J. Fields, "Ideology and Race in American History," in *Region, Race, and Reconstruction: Essays in Honor of C. Vann Woodward,* ed. J. Morgan

Kousser and James M. McPherson (New York: Oxford University Press, 1982), pp. 143–177.

18. The idea of a black *modus vivendi,* along with the account of its limitations, draws upon John Rawls, *Political Liberalism* (New York: Columbia University Press, 1996), pp. 146–150.

19. Indeed, Reed has come pretty close to stating just such a position. See Adolph L. Reed Jr., "Black Particularity Reconsidered," *Telos* 39 (Spring 1979): 71–93. Reprinted in *Is It Nation Time? Contemporary Essays on Black Power and Black Nationalism,* ed. Eddie S. Glaude Jr. (Chicago: University of Chicago Press, 2002), pp. 39–66.

20. For compelling critiques of the family/race metaphor and its invocation in discourses of racial solidarity, see Paul Gilroy, "It's a Family Affair," in *Black Popular Culture,* ed. Gina Dent (New York: New Press, 1990); Kwame Anthony Appiah, "Racisms," in *Anatomy of Racism,* ed. David Theo Goldberg (Minneapolis: University of Minnesota Press, 1990), pp. 13–15; and Patricia Hill Collins, *Fighting Words: African American Women and the Search for Justice* (Minneapolis: University of Minnesota Press, 1998), pp. 167–174.

21. See, for example, Carol M. Swain, *Black Faces, Black Interests: The Representation of African Americans in Congress,* enlarged ed. (Cambridge, Mass: Harvard University Press, 1995), pp. 5–11.

22. For more on this point, see Bernard R. Boxill, *Blacks and Social Justice,* rev. ed. (Lanham, Md.: Rowman and Littlefield, 1992), chaps. 1–3; Gertrude Ezorsky, *Racism and Justice: The Case for Affirmative Action* (Ithaca: Cornell University Press, 1991); T. M. Scanlon, "The Diversity of Objections to Inequality," in *The Difficulty of Tolerance: Essays in Political Philosophy* (Cambridge: Cambridge University Press, 2003), pp. 202–218; and Glenn C. Loury, *The Anatomy of Racial Inequality* (Cambridge, Mass.: Harvard University Press, 2002), chap. 4.

5. Race, Culture, and Politics

1. William L. Van Deburg, *New Day in Babylon: The Black Power Movement and American Culture, 1965–1975* (Chicago: University of Chicago Press, 1992).

2. W. E. B. Du Bois, *The Souls of Black Folk,* ed. David W. Blight

and Robert Gooding-Williams (Boston: Bedford Books, 1997); Alain Locke, "The New Negro," in *The New Negro*, ed. Alain Locke (New York: Atheneum, 1969); Imamu Amiri Baraka [LeRoi Jones], *Blues People: Negro Music in White America* (New York: Morrow, 1963); Harold Cruse, *The Crisis of the Negro Intellectual* (New York: Quill, 1984)); Haki R. Madhubuti, *From Plan to Planet: Life-Studies; The Need for African Minds and Institutions* (Chicago: Third World Press, 1973); Maulana Karenga, "Society, Culture, and the Problem of Self-Consciousness: A Kawaida Analysis," in *Philosophy Born of Struggle: Anthology of Afro-American Philosophy from 1917,* ed. Leonard Harris (Dubuque, Iowa: Kendall/Hunt, 1983); and Molefi Kete Asante, *The Afrocentric Idea,* rev. ed. (Philadelphia: Temple University Press, 1998).

3. See Max Weber, *Economy and Society: An Outline of Interpretive Sociology,* ed. Guenther Roth and Claus Wittich (Berkeley: University of California Press, 1978), pp. 18–22; and Max Weber, *The Methodology of the Social Sciences,* trans. and ed. Edward A. Shils and Henry A. Finch (New York: Free Press, 1949), pp. 89–101.

4. See, for instance, Lawrence W. Levine, *Black Culture and Black Consciousness: Afro-American Folk Thought from Slavery to Freedom* (New York: Oxford University Press, 1977); Sterling Stuckey, *Slave Culture: Nationalist Theory and the Foundations of Black America* (New York: Oxford University Press, 1987); Henry Louis Gates Jr., *The Signifying Monkey: A Theory of African-American Literary Criticism* (Oxford: Oxford University Press, 1998); Wilson Jeremiah Moses, *Black Messiahs and Uncle Toms: Social and Literary Manipulations of a Religious Myth,* rev. ed. (University Park: Pennsylvania State University Press, 1992); and Tricia Rose, *Black Noise: Rap Music and Black Culture in Contemporary America* (Hanover, N.H.: University Press of New England, 1994).

5. See Brian Barry, *Culture and Equality: An Egalitarian Critique of Multiculturalism* (Cambridge, Mass.: Harvard University Press, 2001), chap. 4.

6. Sidney W. Mintz and Richard Price, *The Birth of African-American Culture: An Anthropological Perspective* (Boston: Beacon

Press, 1976); and Paul Gilroy, *The Black Atlantic: Modernity and Double Consciousness* (Cambridge, Mass.: Harvard University Press, 1993).

7. Stuart Hall, "What Is This 'Black' in Black Popular Culture?" in *Black Popular Culture*, ed. Gina Dent (New York: New Press, 1998), p. 22.

8. Ralph Ellison, "What America Would Be Like without Blacks," in *The Collected Essays of Ralph Ellison*, ed. John F. Callahan (New York: Modern Library, 1995), p. 580.

9. Henry Louis Gates Jr., *Loose Canons: Notes on the Culture Wars* (New York: Oxford University Press, 1992), p. 109.

10. See Gates, *The Signifying Monkey*, esp. chap. 2.

11. See Chandran Kukathas, "Are There Any Cultural Rights?" *Political Theory* 20 (1992): 105–139; and Seyla Benhabib, *The Claims of Culture: Equality and Diversity in the Global Era* (Princeton: Princeton University Press, 2002).

12. See Clarence Lusane, *Race in the Global Era: African Americans at the Millennium* (Boston: South End Press, 1997), pp. 85–116.

13. Paul Gilroy, *Against Race: Imagining Political Culture beyond the Color Line* (Cambridge, Mass.: Harvard University Press, 2000), p. 214.

14. David Held, Anthony McGrew, David Goldblatt, and Jonathan Perraton, *Global Transformations* (Stanford: Stanford University Press, 1999).

15. See, for example, Émile Durkheim, *The Division of Labor in Society*, trans. W. D. Halls (New York: Free Press, 1984); Émile Durkheim, *Suicide: A Study in Sociology*, trans. and ed. John A. Spaulding and George Simpson (New York: Free Press, 1951); and Max Weber, "The Social Psychology of the World Religions," in *From Max Weber: Essays in Sociology*, trans. and ed. H. H. Gerth and C. Wright Mills (New York: Oxford University Press), pp. 267–301.

16. Eugene D. Genovese examines how the ideology of paternalism served to rationalize and reproduce the slave system of the South in his *Roll Jordan, Roll: The World the Slaves Made* (New York: Vintage, 1976). Howard McGary provides an insightful philosophical discussion of this ideology in "Paternalism and Slavery," in Howard McGary and Bill

E. Lawson, *Between Slavery and Freedom: Philosophy and American Slavery* (Bloomington: Indiana University Press, 1992).

17. For a useful discussion of the ways supportive black communities have aided blacks in their struggle against this type of alienation, see Howard McGary, "Alienation and the African-American Experience," in his *Race and Social Justice* (Malden, Mass.: Blackwell, 1999), pp. 19–24.

18. Bernard R. Boxill develops this and related points in *Blacks and Social Justice,* rev. ed. (Lanham, Md.: Rowman and Littlefield, 1992), chap. 9. See also Laurence Thomas, "Self-Respect: Theory and Practice," in *Philosophy Born of Struggle,* pp. 174–189.

19. E. Franklin Frazier, *The Negro Church in America* / C. Eric Lincoln, *The Black Church Since Frazier* (New York: Schocken, 1974). See also Cornel West, *Prophesy Deliverance! An Afro-American Revolutionary Christianity* (Philadelphia: Westminster Press, 1982).

20. See, for example, Asante, *The Afrocentric Idea.*

21. Frustrated by the persistence of white racism, black nationalists too often become obsessed with showing that everything about white people is suspect, evil, or rotten to the core. This unfortunate tendency has led some to claim that white culture must be eschewed altogether and that blacks should avoid contact with whites whenever possible. Some even urge blacks to reject the most basic categories of modern Western thought—reason, democracy, equality, individual rights, and autonomy—notwithstanding the irony that this position has striking similarities with certain currents in European Romanticism and postmodernism. Conversely, some black nationalists will go to the wall to defend every element of what they regard as black culture, even to the point of insisting that things that appear to be vices are really virtues, or claiming that what looks like acquiescence to hegemony is actually resistance. My point here is not to encourage a more thorough but clearly invidious comparison of the elements of white and black cultures. Rather, my concern is to highlight the need to transcend this all-or-nothing approach to ethnoracial cultures, as such an approach is neither needed nor productive.

22. For more on this point, see Boxill, *Blacks and Social Justice,* p. 182.

23. See Levine, *Black Culture and Black Consciousness;* West, *Prophesy Deliverance;* Robin D. G. Kelley, *Race Rebels: Culture, Politics, and the Black Working Class* (New York: Free Press, 1994); and Rose, *Black Noise.*

24. Henry Louis Gates Jr. and Cornel West, *The Future of the Race* (New York: Vintage, 1996), p. xvi.

25. See Oliver C. Cox, *Caste, Class, and Race: A Study in Social Dynamics* (New York: Monthly Review, 1959), chaps. 18, 25.

26. Ibid., p. 321.

27. See William A. Cunningham, John B. Neslek, and Mahzarin R. Banaji, "Implicit and Explicit Ethnocentrism: Revisiting the Ideologies of Prejudice," *Personality and Social Psychology Bulletin* 30 (2004): 1332–1346.

28. Cox, *Caste, Class, and Race,* p. 321. Actually, Cox calls this "social" intolerance, but the term *cultural intolerance* is less ambiguous and conforms to his usage.

29. Ibid., pp. 392–393.

30. For more on this point, see my "Ideology, Racism, and Critical Social Theory," *Philosophical Forum* 34 (2003): 153–188.

31. For more on this point, see Kwame Anthony Appiah, "Identity, Authenticity, Survival: Multicultural Societies and Social Reproduction," in *Multiculturalism: Examining the Politics of Recognition,* ed. Amy Gutmann (Princeton: Princeton University Press, 1994), pp. 149–163; and also see Barry, *Culture and Equality,* pp. 305–317.

32. See Robert Gooding-Williams, "Race, Multiculturalism and Democracy," *Constellations* 5 (1998): 18–41.

33. The idea of "cultural capital" is developed in Pierre Bourdieu, *Distinction: A Social Critique of the Judgement of Taste* (Cambridge, Mass.: Harvard University Press, 1984).

34. Baraka, *Blues People,* pp. 147–148.

35. For an attempt to provide a social-theoretic definition of economic exploitation, see my "Parasites, Pimps, and Capitalists: A Nat-

uralistic Conception of Exploitation," *Social Theory and Practice* 28 (2002): 381–418.

36. Baraka, *Blues People*, pp. 98–112. Also see Evelyn Brooks Higginbotham, "Rethinking Vernacular Culture: Black Religion and Race Records in the 1920s and 1930s," in *The House That Race Built*, ed. Wahneema Lubiano (New York: Vintage, 1998), pp. 157–177.

37. See Clifford Geertz, *The Interpretation of Cultures* (New York: Basic Books, 1973).

6. Social Identity and Group Solidarity

1. See, for example, Kwame Anthony Appiah, "Racisms," in *Anatomy of Racism*, ed. David Theo Goldberg (Minneapolis: University of Minnesota Press, 1990); Randall Kennedy, "My Race Problem—And Ours," *Atlantic Monthly* (May 1997): 55–66; and Paul Gilroy, *Against Race: Imagining Political Culture beyond the Color Line* (Cambridge, Mass.: Harvard University Press, 2000).

2. See Martin R. Delany, "The Political Destiny of the Colored Race," in *The Ideological Origins of Black Nationalism*, ed. Sterling Stuckey (Boston: Beacon Press, 1972); Edward W. Blyden, "The Call of Providence to the Descendants of Africa in America," in *Negro Social and Political Thought*, ed. Howard Brotz (New York: Basic Books, 1966), pp. 112–126; Alexander Crummell, "The Relations and Duties of Free Colored Men in America to Africa," in Brotz, *Negro Social and Political Thought*, pp. 171–180; W. E. B. Du Bois, "The Conservation of Races," in Brotz, *Negro Social and Political Thought*, pp. 483–492; Marcus Garvey, *The Philosophy and Opinions of Marcus Garvey: Or, Africa for the Africans*, ed. Amy Jacques Garvey (Dover, Mass.: Majority Press, 1986); Alain Locke, "The New Negro," in *The New Negro*, ed. Alain Locke (New York: Atheneum, 1969), pp. 3–16; Malcolm X, "Black Man's History," in *The End of White World Supremacy: Four Speeches by Malcolm X*, ed. Imam Benjamin Karim (New York: Arcade, 1971), pp. 23–66; Amiri Baraka, "The Legacy of Malcolm X, and the Coming of the Black Nation," in *The LeRoi Jones/Amiri Baraka Reader*, ed. William J. Harris (New York: Thunder's Mouth Press, 1991), pp. 161–169; Harold Cruse, *The Crisis of the Negro Intellectual* (New

York: Quill, 1984); Kwame Ture (Stokely Carmichael) and Charles V. Hamilton, *Black Power: The Politics of Liberation in America* (New York: Vintage, 1992); Cornel West, *Prophesy Deliverance! An Afro-American Revolutionary Christianity* (Philadelphia: Westminster Press, 1982); Maulana Karenga, "Society, Culture, and the Problem of Self-Consciousness: A Kawaida Analysis," in *Philosophy Born of Struggle: Anthology of Afro-American Philosophy from 1917*, ed. Leonard Harris (Dubuque, Iowa: Kendall/Hunt, 1983), pp. 212–228; Molefi Kete Asante, *The Afrocentric Idea* (Philadelphia: Temple University Press, 1998); and Lucius T. Outlaw Jr., *On Race and Philosophy* (New York: Routledge, 1996), chap. 6. Though not all of these thinkers explicitly defend the collective identity theory, each at least implicitly relies upon it. Moreover, it is arguable that some of them, such as Delany and Du Bois, came to deemphasize the importance of a collective black identity to black solidarity, which is why I say that the view can be found in their "writings and speeches."

3. Du Bois, "Conservation of Races," p. 489; emphasis added.

4. Ibid., p. 491; emphasis added.

5. Ibid., p. 485; emphasis added.

6. See, for example, Kwame Anthony Appiah, *In My Father's House: Africa in the Philosophy of Culture* (New York: Oxford University Press, 1992), pp. 28–46; Frank M. Kirkland, "Modernity and Intellectual Life in Black," *Philosophical Forum* 24 (1992–1993): 136–165; Lucius Outlaw, "On W. E. B. Du Bois's 'The Conservation of Races,'" in *Overcoming Racism and Sexism*, ed. Linda A. Bell and David Blumenfeld (Lanham, Md.: Rowman and Littlefield, 1995), pp. 79–102; Robert Gooding-Williams, "Outlaw, Appiah, and Du Bois's 'The Conservation of Races,'" in *W. E. B. Du Bois on Race and Culture*, ed. Bernard W. Bell, Emily R. Grosholz, and James B. Stewert (New York: Routledge, 1996), pp. 39–56; Bernard R. Boxill, "Du Bois on Cultural Pluralism," in Bell et al., *Du Bois on Race and Culture*, pp. 61–65; Tommy L. Lott, *The Invention of Race: Black Culture and the Politics of Representation* (Malden, Mass.: Blackwell, 1999), pp. 47–66; Paul C. Taylor, "Appiah's Uncompleted Argument: W. E. B. Du Bois and the Reality of Race," *Social Theory and Practice* 26 (2000): 103–128; Patrick Goodin, "Du Bois

and Appiah: The Politics of Race and Racial Identity," in *The Quest for Community and Identity: Critical Essays in Africana Social Philosophy*, ed. Robert E. Birt (Lanham, Md.: Rowman and Littlefield, 2002), pp. 73–83.

7. For an illuminating set of personal and philosophical reflections on racial passing in America, see Adrian Piper, "Passing for White, Passing for Black," *Transition* 58 (1992): 4–32.

8. For a similar conception of blackness, which the above account attempts to build upon, see Bernard R. Boxill, *Blacks and Social Justice*, rev. ed. (Lanham, Md.: Rowman and Littlefield, 1992), p. 178.

9. Those thick conceptions that require something *other*, rather than just something *more*, than the thin criteria for blackness will entail, if only implicitly, a critique and rejection of the thin criteria.

10. Appiah, "Racisms," pp. 4–5.

11. For attempts to make a strong analogy between families and races, see Anna Stubblefield, "Races as Families," *Journal of Social Philosophy* 32 (Spring 2001): 99–112; and Yalonda Howze and David Weberman, "On Racial Kinship," *Social Theory and Practice* 27 (2001): 419–436.

12. For an interpretive reconstruction of the discourse of black kinship that fits the model of thin blackness, see Lionel K. McPherson and Tommie Shelby, "Blackness and Blood: Interpreting African American Identity," *Philosophy and Public Affairs* 32 (2004): 171–192.

13. For illuminating discussions of the relationship between third-person racial ascription and first-person racial self-identification, see Anna Stubblefield, "Racial Identity and Non-Essentialism about Race," *Social Theory and Practice* 21 (1995): 341–368; K. Anthony Appiah, "Race, Culture, Identity: Misunderstood Connections," in K. Anthony Appiah and Amy Gutmann, *Color Conscious: The Political Morality of Race* (Princeton: Princeton University Press, 1996), pp. 76–80; and Robert Gooding-Williams, "Race, Multiculturalism and Democracy," *Constellations* 5 (1998): 18–41.

14. For someone who doubts "the value of the distinction between being authentically black and being inauthentically black," see Gooding-Williams, "Race, Multiculturalism and Democracy," p. 25.

Also see Anthony Appiah, "'But Would That Still Be Me?' Notes on Gender, 'Race,' and Ethnicity, as Sources of 'Identity,'" *Journal of Philosophy* 87 (1990): 493–499. For useful discussions of the different claims of black authenticity, see K. Anthony Appiah, "Identity, Authenticity, and Survival: Multicultural Societies and Social Reproduction," in *Multiculturalism: Examining the Politics of Recognition*, ed. Amy Gutmann (Princeton: Princeton University Press, 1994), pp. 149–163; Lani Guinier, *The Tyranny of the Majority: Fundamental Fairness in Representative Democracy* (New York: Free Press, 1994), pp. 54–58; and Naomi Zack, *Thinking about Race* (Belmont, Calif.: Wadsworth, 1998), pp. 70–72.

15. For an interesting recent discussion of the obligations of subordinate groups in the fight against injustice, see Amy Gutmann, *Identity and Democracy* (Princeton: Princeton University Press, 2003), pp. 138–144.

16. See the statement on "race" by the American Anthropological Association: www.aaanet.org/stmts/racepp.htm (accessed 1/10/05); and the American Association of Physical Anthropologists, "Statement on Biological Aspects of Race," *American Journal of Physical Anthropology* 101 (1996): 569–570.

17. Naomi Zack, *Race and Mixed Race* (Philadelphia: Temple University Press, 1993), p. 75.

18. Cruse, *Crisis of the Negro Intellectual*, p. 556.

19. Gunnar Mydral, *An American Dilemma: The Negro Problem and Modern Democracy* (New York: Harper and Row, 1944), pp. 113–117; and F. James Davis, *Who Is Black? One Nation's Definition* (University Park: Pennsylvania State University Press, 1991).

20. For instructive discussions of the black "no race-mixing" policy, see Charles W. Mills, "Do Black Men Have a Moral Duty to Marry Black Women?" *Journal of Social Philosophy*, 25th Anniversary Special Issue (1994): 131–153; and Anita L. Allen, *Why Privacy Isn't Everything: Feminist Reflections on Personal Accountability* (Lanham, Md.: Rowman and Littlefield, 2003), pp. 97–107.

21. Robert Miles, *Racism* (London: Routledge, 1989), pp. 11–40.

22. See bell hooks, *Feminist Theory: From Margin to Center*, 2nd ed.

(Cambridge, Mass.: South End Press, 1984); and Elizabeth V. Spelman, *Inessential Woman: Problems of Exclusion in Feminist Thought* (Boston: Beacon Press, 1988).

23. See Laurence Mordekhai Thomas, "Group Autonomy and Narrative Identity," in *Color, Class, Identity: The New Politics of Race,* ed. John Arthur and Amy Shapiro (Boulder: Westview Press, 1996), pp. 182–183.

24. For important discussions of this issue, see E. Franklin Frazier, *Black Bourgeoisie* (New York: Free Press, 1957); William Julius Wilson, *The Declining Significance of Race* (Chicago: University of Chicago Press, 1978); Manning Marable, *How Capitalism Underdeveloped Black America* (Boston: South End Press, 1983), chap. 5; Michael C. Dawson, *Behind the Mule: Race and Class in African-American Politics* (Princeton: Princeton University Press, 1994); Kevin K. Gaines, *Uplifting the Race: Black Leadership, Politics, and Culture in the Twentieth Century* (Chapel Hill: University of North Carolina Press, 1996); and Adolph Reed Jr., *Stirrings in the Jug: Black Politics in the Post-Segregation Era* (Minneapolis: University of Minnesota Press, 1999).

25. For important discussions of the relationship between black identity, gender, and politics, see Michele Wallace, *Black Macho and the Myth of the Superwoman* (New York: Dial, 1978); Angela Y. Davis, *Women, Race, and Class* (New York: Random House, 1981); bell hooks, *Ain't I a Woman: Black Women and Feminism* (Boston: South End Press, 1981); Gloria T. Hull, Patricia Bell-Scott, and Barbara Smith, eds., *All the Women Are White, All the Men Are Black, but Some of Us Are Brave: Black Women's Studies* (Old Westbury, N.Y.: Feminist Press, 1982); Paula Giddings, *When and Where I Enter: The Impact of Black Women on Race and Sex in America* (New York: Morrow, 1984); Patricia Hill Collins, *Black Feminist Thought: Knowledge, Consciousness, and the Politics of Empowerment* (New York: Routledge, 1990); Cornel West, *Race Matters* (New York: Vintage, 1994), chap. 2; Evelyn Brooks Higginbotham, *Righteous Discontent: The Women's Movement in the Black Baptist Church, 1880–1920* (Cambridge, Mass.: Harvard University Press, 1993); Hazel V. Carby, *Race Men* (Cambridge, Mass.: Harvard University Press, 1998); Joy James and T. Denean Sharpley-Whit-

ing, eds., *The Black Feminist Reader* (Malden, Mass.: Blackwell, 2000); and E. Frances White, *Dark Continent of Our Bodies: Black Feminism and the Politics of Respectability* (Philadelphia: Temple University Press, 2001).

26. See, for example, Derrick Darby and Tommie Shelby, eds., *Hip Hop and Philosophy: Rhyme to Reason* (Chicago: Open Court, forthcoming); Imani Perry, *Prophets of the Hood: Politics and Poetics in Hip Hop* (Durham: Duke University Press, 2004); Cornel West, *Democracy Matters: Winning the Fight against Imperialism* (New York: Penguin, 2004), chap. 6; Todd Boyd, *The New H.N.I.C.: The Death of Civil Rights and the Reign of Hip Hop* (New York: New York University Press, 2003); Bakari Kitwana, *The Hip Hop Generation: Young Blacks and the Crisis in African American Culture* (New York: Basic Books, 2002); S. Craig Watkins, "'Black Is Back, and It's Bound to Sell!': Nationalist Desire and the Production of Black Popular Culture," in *Is It Nation Time? Contemporary Essays on Black Power and Black Nationalism,* ed. Eddie S. Glaude Jr. (Chicago: University of Chicago Press, 2002), pp. 189–214; Joan Morgan, *When Chickenheads Come Home to Roost: A Hip-Hop Feminist Breaks It Down* (New York: Touchstone, 2000); William Eric Perkins, ed., *Droppin' Science: Critical Essays on Rap Music and Hip Hop Culture* (Philadelphia: Temple University Press, 1996); and Tricia Rose, *Black Noise: Rap Music and Black Culture in Contemporary America* (Hanover, N.H.: University Press of New England, 1994).

27. Orlando Patterson, *The Ordeal of Integration: Progress and Resentment in America's "Racial" Crisis* (Washington, D.C.: Civitas, 1997), p. 202.

28. For helpful discussions of the threat to individual freedom posed by racial identities, see Stubblefield, "Racial Identity and Non-Essentialism about Race"; and Appiah, "Race, Culture, Identity," pp. 97–99.

29. Boxill, *Blacks and Social Justice,* p. 181.

30. Michael Omi and Howard Winant, *Racial Formation in the United States: From the 1960's to the 1990's* (New York: Routledge, 1994), pp. 22–23; and Appiah, "Race, Culture, Identity," pp. 85–90.

31. See Jennifer L. Hochschild, *Facing Up to the American Dream:*

Race, Class, and the Soul of the Nation (Princeton: Princeton University Press, 1995).

32. The symptoms of groupthink are summarized in Michael A. Hogg, *The Social Psychology of Group Cohesiveness: From Attraction to Social Identity* (New York: New York University Press, 1992), pp. 135–137. Hogg bases his summary on I. L. Janis, *Groupthink: Psychological Studies of Policy Decisions and Fiascoes*, 2nd ed. (Boston: Houghton Mifflin, 1982).

33. See Paul Gilroy, *The Black Atlantic: Modernity and Double Consciousness* (Cambridge, Mass.: Harvard University Press, 1993); also see bell hooks, "Postmodern Blackness," in *Yearning: Race, Gender, and Cultural Politics* (Boston: South End Press, 1990); and Linda Martín Alcoff, "Philosophy and Racial Identity," *Philosophy Today* 41 (1997): 67–76.

34. Philosophers often invoke the "witch" as an example of a nonexistent entity, but I think Appiah was the first to use the witch analogy in the context of the metaphysics of race. See, for example, his article on "race" in *Africana: The Encyclopedia of African and African-American Experience*, ed. Kwame Anthony Appiah and Henry Louis Gates Jr. (New York: Basic Books, 1999).

35. For illuminating philosophical reflections on the subtle workings of the "racial gaze," see Jean-Paul Sartre, *Anti-Semite and Jew* (New York: Schocken, 1948); West, *Prophesy Deliverance*, pp. 50–65; Adrian M. S. Piper, "Higher-Order Discrimination," in *Identity, Character, and Morality: Essays in Moral Psychology*, ed. Owen Flanagan and Amelie Rorty (Cambridge, Mass.: MIT Press, 1990); Robert Gooding-Williams, "'Look, a Negro!'" in *Reading Rodney King, Reading Urban Uprising*, ed. Robert Gooding-Williams (New York: Routledge, 1993), pp. 157–177; and Linda Martín Alcoff, "Towards a Phenomenology of Racial Embodiment," *Radical Philosophy* 95 (1999): 15–26.

36. For empirical evidence in support of the claim that blacks overwhelmingly view racism and racial inequality as serious social problems, see Howard Schuman, Charlotte Steeh, Lawrence Bobo, and Maria Krysan, *Racial Attitudes in America: Trends and Interpretations*, rev. ed. (Cambridge, Mass.: Harvard University Press, 1997);

Hochschild, *Facing Up;* and Donald R. Kinder and Lynn M. Sanders, *Divided By Color: Racial Politics and Democratic Ideals* (Chicago: University of Chicago Press, 1996).

37. According to Orlando Patterson, "All things considered, it is reasonable to estimate that about a quarter of the Euro-American population harbors at least mildly racist feelings toward Afro-Americans and that one in five is a hard-core racist. . . . However one may wish to quibble over the meaning of attitude surveys and other data, this is real progress, an enormous change from the fifties and sixties, when the great majority of Euro-Americans were openly racists, measured by whatever means. Nonetheless, when roughly a quarter of all Euro-Americans are racists, it still remains the case that for every two Afro-American persons there are three Euro-American racists. In spite of all the progress among Euro-Americans, this is still an outrageous situation for any Afro-American" (Patterson, *The Ordeal of Integration,* p. 61). Also see Schuman et al., *Racial Attitudes;* David O. Sears, Colette van Laar, Mary Carrillo, and Rick Kosterman, "Is It Really Racism? The Origins of White Americans' Opposition to Race-Targeted Policies," *Public Opinion Quarterly* 61 (1997): 16–53; Lawrence Bobo, James R. Klugel, and Ryan A. Smith, "Laissez-Faire Racism: The Crystallization of a Kinder, Gentler, Antiblack Ideology," in *Racial Attitudes in the 1990s,* ed. Steven A. Tuch and Jack K. Martin (Westport, Conn.: Praeger, 1997), pp. 15–41; David O. Sears, Jim Sidanius, and Lawrence Bobo, eds., *Racialized Politics: The Debate about Racism in America* (Chicago: University of Chicago Press, 2000); and Michael K. Brown, Martin Carnoy, Elliot Currie, Troy Duster, David B. Oppenheimer, Marjorie M. Shultz, and David Wellman, *Whitewashing Race: The Myth of a Color-Blind Society* (Berkeley: University of California Press, 2003).

38. See, for example, Alexander Crummell, "The Progress of Civilization along the West Coast of Africa," in *Classical Black Nationalism: From the American Revolution to Marcus Garvey,* ed. Wilson J. Moses (New York: New York University Press, 1996); James H. Cone, *A Black Theology of Liberation* (Maryknoll, N.Y.: Orbis, 1990); and Elijah Muhammad, *Message to the Blackman in America* (Atlanta: Messenger Elijah Muhammad Propagation Society, 1997).

39. See Appiah, *In My Father's House,* p. 42. Although Appiah's criticism of Du Bois's Pan-Africanism is quite telling, it has little force against the version of black solidarity defended here, for that version, in contrast to Du Bois's, does not rely on the doctrine of racialism, it does not presuppose a common black culture, and it is rooted in the specificity of black oppression in America.

40. For a helpful analysis of the subjective experience of *particular* forms of racism and of the phenomenology of black subordination, see Lewis Gordon, *Existentia Africana: Understanding Africana Thought* (New York: Routledge, 2000), chap. 4.

41. For more on this point, see Lani Guinier and Gerald Torres, *The Miner's Canary: Enlisting Race, Resisting Power, Transforming Democracy* (Cambridge, Mass.: Harvard University Press, 2002).

42. See Derrick Bell, *Faces at the Bottom of the Well: The Permanence of Racism* (New York: Basic Books, 1992).

Conclusion

1. W. E. B. Du Bois, *Dusk of Dawn: An Essay toward an Autobiography of a Race Concept* (New Brunswick, N.J.: Transaction, 1984), p. 117.

2. See Vincent Harding, *There Is a River: The Black Struggle for Freedom in America* (San Diego: Harcourt Brace, 1981); and V. P. Franklin, *Black Self-Determination: A Cultural History of the Faith of the Fathers* (Westport, Conn.: Lawrence Hill, 1984).

3. John Rawls, *A Theory of Justice,* rev. ed. (Cambridge, Mass.: Harvard University Press, 1999), pp. 17, 442; and *Political Liberalism* (New York: Columbia University Press, 1996), pp. 18–22.

Index